Meanings of Modernity

Meanings of Modernity

Britain from the Late-Victorian Era to World War II

Edited by
Martin Daunton and Bernhard Rieger

BERG

Oxford • New York

First published in 2001 by
Berg
Editorial offices:
150 Cowley Road, Oxford, OX4 1JJ, UK
838 Broadway, Third Floor, New York, NY 10003-4812, USA

Berg is an imprint of Oxford International Publishers Ltd.

Library of Congress Cataloging-in-Publication Data
A catalogue record for this book is available from the Library of Congress.

British Library Cataloguing-in-Publication Data
A catalogue record for this book is available from the British Library.

ISBN 1 85973 496 0 (Cloth)
1 85973 402 2 (Paper)

Typeset by JS Typesetting, Wellingborough, Northants.
Printed in the United Kingdom by Biddles Ltd, Guildford and King's Lynn.

Contents

Contents

Acknowledgements

This collection of essays arises from the Neale Colloquium in British History held at University College London in 1998. The Neale Lecture in British History has been an annual event since 1970, sponsored by Jonathan Cape to mark the eightieth birthday of Sir John Neale. We remain grateful to Jonathan Cape for their continued support of the lecture, which now provides the focus for a colloquium. In 1998, we were fortunate to have a lecture by Peter Mandler, which is printed in this volume. It marks the appearance of Sir John Neale in a new guise, not as the historian of the reign of Elizabeth I who is celebrated in many of the previous lectures, but as a historical figure of the twentieth century commenting on English character. We are grateful to the Graduate School of University College London for providing financial support to allow research students to attend the colloquium, and to the British Academy for assistance in bringing speakers from the United States. Chris Beauchamp corrected the disks and Isobel Mclean compiled the index with speed and efficiency. We are also grateful to Axel Körner and Geoff Eley for their comments at the colloquium. As always, Nazneen Razwi of the Department of History at University College London provided the administrative support that has made the Neale colloquium such a successful academic and social event. Both editors have now moved from University College London to new positions; they are confident that the colloquium will continue to flourish in the future.

Martin Daunton and Bernhard Rieger

Notes on Contributors

Elizabeth Buettner is lecturer in British history at the University of York. She has published articles in *Women's History Review* and in *Childhood in Question: Children, Parents and the State* (ed. Anthony Fletcher and Stephen Hussey, Manchester University Press, 1999). She is currently completing a book with the working title *Empire Families: Britons and India, 1857–1947*.

Martin Daunton is currently Professor of Economic History at the University of Cambridge. He has edited the third volume of the *Cambridge Urban History of England, 1840–1950*, and has completed two volumes on the politics of taxation in Britain since 1799 to be published by Cambridge University Press.

Michael Dintenfass teaches history and modern studies at the University of Wisconsin–Milwaukee. The author of several studies of modern British economic and business history, his work on the theory and practice of historical inquiry has recently appeared in the *Journal of Modern History* and *History and Theory*.

Peter Hansen teaches British history and international studies at Worcester Polytechnic Institute, Massachusetts. He is working on a cultural history of mountains and mountaineering since the eighteenth century.

Matthew Hilton is lecturer in social history at the University of Birmingham. He is the author of *Smoking in British Popular Culture, 1800–2000* (Manchester University Press, 2000). He is currently working on a history of politics and consumer society in Britain.

Peter Mandler is Professor of Modern History at London Guildhall University. His most recent book, *The Fall and Rise of the Stately Home*, was published by Yale University Press in 1997 and reissued in paperback in 1999. He is currently writing a book under the working title of *The English National Character: The History of an Idea from Burke to Blair*.

Alex Owen is Professor of History and Gender Studies at Northwestern University. She is completing a book entitled *Magic and Modernity: Occultism and the Culture of Enchantment in Fin-de-Siècle Britain*.

Notes on Contributors

Susan Pedersen is Professor of History at Harvard University. She is the author of *Family, Dependence and the Origins of the Welfare State: Britain and France, 1914–1945* (Cambridge, 1993) and the editor, with Peter Mandler, of *After the Victorians: Private Conscience and Public Duty in Modern Britain* (Routledge, 1994). She is currently completing a biography of Eleanor Rathbone.

Erika Rappaport teaches British history at the University of California, Santa Barbara. She has published *Shopping for Pleasure: Women in the Making of London's West End* (Princeton, 2000). She is now working on a study of consumerism and family life in Victorian England.

Bernhard Rieger received his Ph.D. from University College London and then took a position as assistant professor at Iowa State University, where he teaches European history and the history of technology. He is working on a book about the public meanings of film, flight and passenger liners in Britain and Germany between 1890 and 1940.

Mathew Thomson is a lecturer in the Department of History, University of Warwick. Research for this essay was supported by the Wellcome Trust in the Department of History, University of Sheffield. His publications include *The Problem of Mental Deficiency: Eugenics, Democracy and Social Policy in Britain, 1870–1959* (Oxford University Press, 1998).

Introduction

Bernhard Rieger and *Martin Daunton*

The study of British modernity is in its infancy when compared with the prominence of this field in other national historiographies. Recent years have witnessed a proliferation of historical inquiries into the nature of modernity in nineteenth- and twentieth-century Western Europe. Whether scholars have focused on Italy, France or Germany, they have employed the category of the 'modern' to examine social, political, economic and cultural changes, as well as a pervasive sense of crisis during the period between the 1870s and the 1930s.[1] A host of studies start from the same premise: that European history entered a new phase in this period, and that these fundamental transformations can be analytically captured through the study of modernity. However, these investigations have resorted to varying and sometimes mutually exclusive definitions of modernity in order to find answers to nationally specific questions. For instance, amongst the wide range of approaches found in studies of the history of modernity in Western Europe are to be seen considerations of the complex intermingling of tradition and innovation in early twentieth-century Italy and Germany. Historians have identified the selective and partial embraces of phenomena that anti-democratic movements associated with the 'modern age', thereby helping us to rethink Fascism and National Socialism as part and parcel of 'modernity' rather than to conceive of illiberal and militaristic projects as atavistic and backward-looking.[2] Meanwhile, in the fields of French and Austrian history the concept of modernity has furthered an understanding of the ways contemporaries considered the *fin-de-siècle* as a temporal watershed signalling the advent of a new historical epoch at the turn of the twentieth century.[3] In British history, however, scholars have been far more cautious about adopting modernity as 'a useful category for historical analysis'.[4]

Invoking modernity and British culture between the 1870s and the 1930s in one breath might well strike some readers as a contradiction in terms. A cluster of recent investigations into British social and economic history have been informed by a narrative of national decline that depicts nineteenth-century Britain as an unrivalled leader that became unable to defend its pre-eminent international position in the face of competition from abroad in the late Victorian period. Several scholars like Martin Wiener and Correlli Barnett have forcefully argued that Britain lacked the economic, political and cultural dynamism that would have allowed a more energetic response to the international challenges mounted by Germany and the United States. Crucially, investigations of British decline have frequently taken a cultural turn by attributing the nation's loss of status to dominant values in public life. Britain's political, economic and social elites, it has been held, subscribed to beliefs setting supposedly 'traditional' and 'aristocratic' values over 'innovative' and 'middle-class' notions. An 'anti-modern' mindset thus allegedly lay at the root of the nation's steady 'decline' between the 1870s and the present, with a brief and tentative interlude during the interwar years interpreted as a stay of execution.[5] While this line of reasoning has been widely criticized, few scholars have examined the cultural premises of 'declinism'.[6]

This fixation by many scholars on Britain's supposed decline comes as a surprise when considered alongside the plethora of innovative political, social and cultural developments that reshaped the country after the 1870s, and makes a convenient starting-point for this collection. Of course, Britons grappled with the implications of living in a period of progress or improvement before 1870, and it might be wondered whether this date marked a new phase of debate over the meaning of modernity. In part, the essays themselves provide a justification, showing that the category of the 'modern' was central to British debates about the historical present. The contributions testify to the importance of the category for contemporaries, and indicate that public discussion about the characteristics of the 'modern' present diversified in the late nineteenth century.

Before the 1870s, British investigations of the 'modern' tended to be cast in terms that focused on the direct consequences of industrial development. Topics such as labour conditions, urban growth and housing dominated debates about the social effects of 'modern' industry during the first two-thirds of the nineteenth century. At the same time, prominent Victorian 'sages' like Thomas Carlyle, A. W. N. Pugin, John Ruskin and Thomas Arnold – to name but the best-known – alerted contemporaries to the cultural repercussions of industrialization. Although the participants in these early debates approached and evaluated Britain in different ways, most of them concentrated on questions that considered the recent economic transformations as the most striking feature of British 'modernity'. From the 1870s, however, debates about the characteristics defining Britain as 'modern' came to include a host of topics that appeared to bear no direct relationship to the process of industrialization. After all, industrialization now seemed to be inescapable rather than a choice; and the fear that economic growth would reach an upper limit with the onset of a 'stationary state' no longer seemed so plausible as more people started to share in the benefits of continued growth. The broadening of public discussions about the modern from 1870 corresponds to the country's recent transition from an industrializing to an industrial society, and to the realization that economic growth was not constrained.[7] Social, political, cultural and economic change came to be registered in an ever-expanding range of contexts.

The many prominent changes during this period include a fundamental 'shift in authority and prestige' from religious to scientific elites, thus precipitating a breakthrough of predominantly secular modes of inquiry and analysis.[8] In politics, the extension of the franchise after the Reform Act of 1867 contributed to the transformation of British political culture, ushering in the age of mass politics and transforming the organization of political parties. Moreover, a reconfiguration of international conditions coincided with a new phase in the history of empire that fuelled a more widespread and aggressive popular imperialism in the metropole.[9] At the same time, increases in middle- and working-class affluence underpinned the rise of novel and highly visible forms of popular entertainment, leisure, and consumption.[10] As women claimed and gained access to various public realms, widespread and contentious debates took place concerning the 'problem' of unstable gender hierarchies.[11] These developments mark only several examples of the wide range of innovative phenomena experienced in Britain between 1870 and 1940.

This collection considers how Britons made sense of pervasive change by addressing their society as 'modern' between 1870 and 1940. In this introduction, we situate British negotiations of modernity within a broader European context by adopting a comparative perspective. Like other European observers, some British commentators undoubtedly criticized and turned against the perceived traits and trends of the 'modern age', but denunciations of modernity's symptoms represented only one reaction to encounters with transformation and innovation. The contributors to this volume identify shifting and frequently contradictory meanings of modernity by examining discourses produced in a variety of British cultural arenas between the late nineteenth century and the Second World War. As the articles in this book demonstrate, when Britons talked and thought about themes as distinct as occultism, psychology, exhibitions, smoking, coal-mining, national character, female shoppers, mountaineering, or imperialism, they repeatedly resorted to the term 'modern' to describe their society. Of course, many other arenas could be chosen to indicate the contested meanings of modernity, especially new technologies such as electricity, the motor car, cinema, recorded music and the aeroplane. However, the point of this collection is not to be all-encompassing; it is to suggest methodologies that can be applied to a wide range of specific commodities and processes in order to understand the varied and complex construction of narratives by which change was given meaning. Modernity was understood by contemporaries, and should be understood by historians, through close readings within specific locales and venues.

Given the variety of topics covered by debates about the modern, the authors of the chapters in this book had to employ different methodologies to enhance our understanding of the historical meanings of modernity. While some pieces can be located in the established field of intellectual history, others are more strongly informed by approaches developed in the 'new cultural history' and in cultural studies. These varying methodologies not only illustrate the diverse ways modernity has come to be investigated, but also provide an indication of its complexity. Just as Britons used the term 'modern' to describe a broad range of phenomena between 1870 and 1940, so have scholars had to produce flexible methodological tools to retrieve the meanings of modernity. In other words, there is not one predominant approach to a topic as multifaceted as the study of the semantics of modernity. At the same time, methodological breadth should not be confused with arbitrariness or unreflective eclecticism. All the authors emphasize that close readings of historical texts must constitute the focus of explorations that illuminate historically specific meanings of modernity.

Reflecting more widespread historical practice, the contributions to this book may be placed on a continuum between two poles. At the one end are located those who organize their analyses around the narrative constructions of the modern to highlight the term's multifarious and often inconsistent meanings in the sources. At the other pole we find historians whose work is explicitly informed by theories of modernity, and who test these theories in historically specific contexts, thereby challenging and modifying existing conceptual frameworks. These varied approaches to the study of the semantics of modernity derive from the fact that at present there is no generally accepted theoretical definition of modernity among scholars. In part, rival interpretations have arisen because current conceptualizations of modernity are rarely founded on the teleological notions prevalent in earlier 'modernization theory'.[12] Recent approaches have abandoned prescriptive models determining the extent to which individual societies could be considered thoroughly 'modern' at different times. Instead, authors have stressed that political, economic, social, and cultural transformations have resulted in different forms of 'modern' societies whose features varied both over time and between nations. Thus, scholars are abandoning the study of a monolithic modernity in favour of investigating 'modernities'. Novices to the field sometimes find studies of modernities inconsistent and confusing because their theoretical premises can be incompatible. However, a detailed critique of historical and sociological theories devoted to modernity lies beyond the scope of this book. Our aim here is to explore and comprehend how contemporaries perceived and expressed Britain as a distinctly modern country between the 1870s and the 1930s. In short, what was considered modern in Britain, and why?

In this context, we concern ourselves only marginally with artistic modernism, a term that describes the anti-academic, innovative, initially iconoclastic and stylistically heterogeneous aesthetic movements that came into existence during the last third of the nineteenth century.[13] It is easy to assume that Britain was only marginally affected by these movements. The arts and craft movement in architecture, or pastoralism in music, may be contrasted with the Bauhaus or second

Viennese school in order to suggest that British culture was somehow anti-modern, sunk in nostalgia for a world that was lost. But it would be misleading to suggest a simple identity between attitudes to modernism in art and wider attitudes to modernity. Histories of artistic modernism may themselves be read as narratives of change created by one social group as one interpretation of the emergence of a modern world. However, the cultural forms of modernism adopted by an artistic elite should not be confused with the ways in which different groups in society negotiated various meanings of modernity. This book emphasizes contemporaries' conviction of living in and through an era of profound, man-made changes as the defining hallmark that observers associated with modernity. As in other European countries, British observers employed the language of the modern to address the present as a period of both transformation and transition. Conceiving of the present as a time of change had major implications for definitions of temporality that informed debates about the modern. Faced with fundamental transformations in society, politics, economic enterprise and culture, many contemporaries encountered difficulties in locating the present within a coherent temporal order. In a social world in which the present appeared as a temporal stage whose defining features were merely transitory, establishing meaningful links between the past, the present and the future presented a difficult task. After all, phenomena providing connections to the past could disappear at any time. In numerous contexts, the language of the modern provided a highly flexible tool to describe the temporal status of the present as problematic.[14]

Debates about modernity conceived relations between past, present and future in varying ways. Many scholars of modernity have stressed that a sense of rupture in the historical continuum and a loss of coherence underlay characteristic experiences of modernity.[15] In this view, a deep discontinuity separated the past from a present that appeared as radically distinct from former times. These contemporary accounts considered a return to past times as impossible, and history appeared as 'a lost domain'.[16] Even so, these accounts were far from being unhistorical, for these interpretations of modernity emphasized the features separating past from present through creating narratives of historical rupture. At the same time, these accounts of rupture should not obscure the fact that casting the present as uniquely distinct from the past was by no means the only mode of interpreting temporal relations in debates about modernity. Some contemporaries redoubled their efforts to preserve or recapture aspects of the past in order to anchor the present in history. 'Invention of traditions' often served a compensatory purpose by creating continuities between the past and the 'modern' present. The folk-song revival, idealizations of village life and the cult of the monarchy were at least in part motivated by a desire to forge connections between the present and imagined pasts. Alternatively, observers invoked traditions of modernity, arguing that seemingly exceptional traits of the present possessed precursors in the past. As repeated innovations appeared to follow discernible patterns, interpretations managed to locate the 'modern' present in models of intelligible development. Economic and technological innovations as well as parliamentary reforms between 1870 and 1940 were frequently narrated in terms of British traditions of modernity in earlier periods. Thus, conceptions of the 'modern' present as a time of change and transition bore a deep historical imprint that contemporaries formulated by stressing either discontinuities or continuities between the past and the present. As we will argue at greater length below, a specific interaction between tales of continuity and temporal rupture characterized British debates about modernity between 1870 and the outbreak of the Second World War.[17]

Many individuals were convinced that they had entered a new and unique historical era: 'modern times'. This book explores these sentiments with particular reference to two phenomena. First, Erika Rappaport and Matthew Hilton examine how transformations in the realm of material culture interacted with changing regimes of consumption to give rise to new conceptions of the individual in British society. Rappaport addresses the relationship between conceptions of gender and modernity in urban environments and demonstrates how, in the late nineteenth century, consumerism furthered women's attempts to gain legitimate access to public spaces that had previously been considered almost exclusively male realms. Hilton analyses advertising campaigns for cigarette smoking that cast a predominantly male individual consumer as part of a larger 'mass' through modernist aesthetics. Both contributions highlight how gender, consumption and representations of Britain as a 'modern' society were interlinked. Second, Alex Owen and Mathew Thomson respectively address the cultures of occultism and the spread of popular psychology, which gave rise to, and disseminated, new understandings of individual subjectivity. Both chapters reveal how systematic investigations of the 'irrational' aspects of the human psyche were seen as characteristically modern enterprises that marked departures for contemporary ideas about the individual and society. These initiatives were conceived of as truly modern ventures because they aimed to account for aspects of human psychology that had previously remained beyond systematic study. In addition, Owen's and Thomson's contributions directly address the tensions between concepts of rationality and irrationality in negotiations of modernity. Owen, for instance, shows that spiritual journeys into the self – or explorations of the irrational – required much discipline and training. Thomson reminds us that popular psychology appeared as peculiarly modern because it alerted contemporaries to the fact that the irrational or unconscious could be the subject of systematic, or rational, investigation. Thus, master narratives casting modernity's history as a process of rationalization that purportedly marginalized and repressed the irrational have failed to address a prominent feature of contemporary debates between 1870 and 1940.[18] As a result of widespread convictions that the worlds of spirituality and the human psyche lent themselves to rational investigation, debates about irrationality commanded a prominent place in British negotiations of modernity in our period. At the same time, contemporary acknowledgements of the non-rational elements of human nature added to the unease many felt about the 'modern' world in which they lived. For instance, opponents of electoral reform frequently argued that extensions of the franchise would create a highly volatile modern polity because of the inclusion of voters whose intellectual credentials appeared doubtful.[19]

Sentiments of ambivalence often featured prominently in negotiations of modernity. Since the present was repeatedly described as an era of fundamental and multifarious innovation, experiences of change often led to a disorientating sense of transitoriness that the language of the 'modern' was particularly suited to capture. The sense of the instability of modern times hinged on conceptualizations of change, with those who emphasized the creative and positive dimensions of innovation being equally conscious of its destructive aspects. In order to create the new, the old or traditional had to be displaced or destroyed. Since change thus incorporated both creative and destructive dimensions, contemporaries who embraced or rejected modernity frequently did so only partially and selectively. This ability to formulate ambiguous evaluations of the present distinguished languages of the modern from earlier rhetorics of 'improvement' and 'progress'. The rhetoric of the 'modern' captured the sense that the present was transitory and open more effectively than the older language of 'improvement', which was suitable for descriptions of specific and discrete reforms embedded in a static social model. In contrast to the word 'modern', the term 'improvement' did not stress the dynamism that contemporaries found so characteristic of their times between 1870 and 1940. While concepts of the 'modern' and of 'progress' conceived the historical process as a succession of fundamental changes, they differed with respect to their assessment of the effects of transformations. Debates about 'progress' examined public claims about whether, after allowing for occasional setbacks, historical developments followed linear trajectories towards a positive end. They tended to encourage a moral standard that forced contemporaries to either praise or condemn the present. Less burdened with teleological notions, the language of the 'modern' cast history in terms of dynamic change and granted space to a wide range of moral judgements about the present as the outcome of transformations. The rhetoric of the 'modern' provided the means of examining the results of historical change, allowing observers to identify the ambivalence of negative and positive traits in the 'modern' present.

Peter Hansen's article on mountaineering provides a case in point. He shows that, while British mountaineers criticized urban life as alienating and mundane, this rather conventional assessment did not lead them to condemn the modern age in its entirety. Instead, mountaineers cast their achievements in stories that combined motifs of flight from the stifling effects of metropolitan life with accounts of a search for a novel, uncorrupted selfhood in seemingly untarnished natural environments. While depicting their achievements as specifically modern, British mountaineers took great care to highlight differences between themselves and indigenous inhabitants of mountainous regions by characterizing the latter as 'pre-modern'. Simultaneously, climbers insisted that they could only enact their modern selfhood in remote areas that were secluded from the influences of contemporary Western society. Thus, denunciations of and praise for the 'modern' went hand in hand, and the line separating emphatically pro-modern and anti-modern sentiments was not necessarily clear-cut. Elizabeth Buettner's chapter points in a similar direction. When members of the colonial elite returned from India to retire in Britain, they considered the 'depleted supply' of domestic servants a deplorable social development. Discontent with this aspect of contemporary social life led these middle-class Britons to adopt a decidedly modern solution during the interwar years. Equipping their households with electrical appliances, they opted for a 'conservative' embrace of modernity that placed innovative technological artefacts in a domestic environment organized along the lines of conventional gender hierarchies. British life-reform movements during the interwar period exhibit similar traits of partial rejection and adoption of modernity when hiking groups left the city for the weekend in search of alternative lifestyles in the countryside.[20] The rhetoric of the 'modern' thus provided a language to appropriate certain aspects of the age while selectively rejecting others. These ambivalences not only illustrate how difficult contemporaries found it to navigate an age that they repeatedly called 'modern'; they also render it impossible in retrospect to pin down neatly one authoritative meaning of modernity.

Ambivalence in the face of change characterized understandings of modernity, and British evaluations of the present did not generate as deep and pronounced a sense of recurrent crisis as that informing debate in other European countries. By comparison with those of other nations, British negotiations of modernity took place in a climate of *relative* political, economic and social stability. While incorporating notions of ambiguity, many British accounts phrased change and innovation in a rhetoric that emphasized continuous development. Attempts to construct histories of modernity without deep discontinuities were often successful in Britain. This prominence of conceptions of the modern underpinned by notions of historical continuity distinguishes British assessments from similar Continental European discussions between 1870 and 1940. Bernhard Rieger's contribution shows that no matter whether British upper-middle-class commentators considered displays of modernity at the Great Exhibition in Paris in 1900 in favourable or denunciatory terms, they nonetheless incorporated the exhibition into a continuous series of progressive World's Fairs. In contrast, some German observers resorted to languages of historical rupture to describe the same event, and proclaimed the end of an era on this particular occasion. Although sentiments of *fin-de-siècle* certainly existed in Britain, as Alex Owen's article on occultism during the closing years of the nineteenth century demonstrates, they less frequently led to a sense of crisis and rupture than in Germany, Austria and France.[21] Several contributions to this volume further bear out the central role that tales of gradual development played in British formulations of the modern, providing insights into reasons for the strength of notions of steady evolution even as Britain underwent fundamental change.

First of all, the relative stability of the constitutional system between 1870 and 1940 facilitated contemporary assessments of Britain's modernity in terms of political continuity. Of course, the Irish question possessed the potential to disrupt the British constitution; but, from a mainland perspective, its impact remained limited once Eire had been granted independence within the Commonwealth. Thus the explosive energy of the national question, which caused revolutionary upheaval elsewhere, was marginalized in Britain. On the whole, the absence of cataclysmic revolutions – such as those that swept France throughout the nineteenth century or the repeated recastings of state systems in Germany and Italy – favoured narratives phrasing political histories of the nation in registers of even development. Peter Mandler's article demonstrates that conceptions of the English 'national character' that intellectuals developed in the second half of the nineteenth century revolved around deeply historical ideas of modernity. Public debate about the English 'national character' habitually invoked the history of English 'liberties', which, it was argued, stretched back uninterruptedly to the Reformation, thereby anchoring modern Britain in a long and uninterrupted tradition reaching back to the sixteenth century. Although competing interpretations of the country's political history were put forward by Conservatives, Liberals and adherents of Labour, the overwhelming majority of national histories were structured around themes of gradual parliamentary reform. Instead of notions of abrupt convulsions, a model of parliamentary evolution informed influential interpretations of Britain's political past, embracing (and reformulating) originally Whiggish and Liberal conceptions of a progressive development towards 'liberty' and 'freedom'.[22]

The history of modern Britain could be told as a steady success story not only from the angle of constitutional reform but also from the perspective of the country's international position. Although embattled and challenged, Britain retained her position as a global political player throughout our period. By contrast, a stigma of unfulfilled potential made accounts of Germany's mission in the world far more problematic. Although political histories of Germany written in the vein of 'Prussianism' (*Borussianismus*) aimed to create a sense of national longevity by charting Prussia's rise from a small principality in the Middle Ages to a world power in the nineteenth century, such historiographical initiatives became increasingly difficult after the 1890s and practically impossible after the First World War.[23] German propagandists repeatedly claimed that Germany was denied its appropriate and deserved international status. By comparison, British history could more easily and convincingly be written as a story in which a long-term and successful rise to global pre-eminence provided a *leitmotif* linking the modern present with the past. Unlike Germany, Britain appeared as a world power whose modernity could be effectively expressed in historical terms of continuity rather than rupture.

Second, the long-drawn-out process of economic change in Britain, which occurred at more steady rates than in some Continental countries such as Germany and Italy, allowed important sections of the British entrepreneurial elites to cast themselves as modernizers in a spirit of evolution rather than rupture. Despite the common assumption that British industrialists occupied culturally and politically marginal positions, the essay by Michael Dintenfass shows that coal entrepreneurs articulated public narratives conceiving of coal-mining as a 'modern' and innovative business activity that nonetheless had a long-established place in the history of the nation as well as in local communities. Research on the ways cotton masters in Manchester and wool entrepreneurs in Bradford represented themselves illustrates how other members of the British economic elite similarly invested their occupations with a tradition of modernity.[24] Other examples of economic modernity also became firmly aligned with history in different contexts. In the late nineteenth century, for instance, politically conservative landed aristocrats like Lord Salisbury promoted the technology of electricity. Moreover, the 'ancient' livery companies in the City of London – most frequently associated with displays of invented 'medieval' pomp and circumstance – sponsored innovative scientific research at the Northampton Institute and Imperial College.[25] On countless occasions, therefore, an imagery that intermingled tradition and innovation informed prominent concepts of British economic modernity.

Third, class tensions in Britain did not reach the degree of antagonism that characterized social relations in other European countries. Of course, the Edwardian and interwar periods witnessed increasingly pronounced class conflict that culminated in the short-lived General Strike of 1926 and the hunger marches of the early 1930s. In Britain, however, social strife did not escalate to the levels of political violence that in Continental Europe created situations resembling temporary civil war. Although the conversion to a peacetime economy presented Britain with formidable challenges after the end of the Great War, social tensions did *not* erupt into violence and chaos. Fiscal arrangements to meet the massive financial obligations resulting from the war effort aimed to preserve a political consensus by distributing the tax burden in ways that were considered 'fair' and simultaneously prevented hyperinflation.[26] Even as social tensions mounted in the early 1930s as a result of the slump, Britain escaped the recurrent street battles between extremists on the Right and Left that accompanied the downfall of the Weimar Republic and accentuated the grave crisis of parliamentarism in France in 1934.[27] To be sure, social stability was coming under considerable strains in interwar Britain, but the social fabric stopped short of collapsing – a factor that facilitated the construction of concepts casting modernity in terms of continuous and stable class traditions.[28] Of course, the functioning of the parliamentary system, which represented antagonistic class interests, was indispensable to making such interpretations of British society persuasive. In contrast, revolutions and disruptions threw Germany and Italy into disarray, poisoning the social and political atmosphere throughout the twenties and thirties and rendering it impossible to consider both nations' histories in terms of even social development.[29]

This was particularly true of influential interpretations of the modern propagated by the upper middle class, with the British developing a less pronounced sense of crisis and loss of influence than did their counterparts in some Continental countries. This resulted in part from the fact that many social networks remained intact among the British upper middle classes throughout the first half of the twentieth century. As late as 1955, Noel Annan described how closely individual members of the 'intellectual aristocracy' remained interconnected through marriage and family relationships.[30] From the perspective of the upper middle class, the relative stability of the British class system not only worked against the development of a fundamental anti-constitutional political opposition before the 1930s, despite sweeping franchise reform, but also favoured interpretations of modernity in terms of continuous development, because the intellectual elites retained their influential position in a changing society.[31]

In states such as Germany and Italy, however, intense social conflicts coincided with the transition to democratic forms of government, which led large sections of the intellectual and economic elites to equate fully-fledged parliamentarism with a loss of political and social influence. Furthermore, the Continental middle classes as a whole faced stronger economic pressures than their British counterparts. In Germany, hyperinflation in the early 1920s wiped out the savings of wide sections of the *bourgeoisie*, thereby fuelling status insecurities. While hostility to modernity in Germany cannot simply be reduced to issues of immediate economic circumstances, the unstable economic and political climate of the interwar period contributed to a widespread sense of social dislocation among the upper middle classes during the Weimar years.[32] German public moralists often translated political and social unease into critiques that held 'modern times' responsible for the novel problems allegedly facing the country.

In sum, in comparison with Continental Western Europe, many prominent British assessments of modernity between 1870 and 1940 successfully incorporated notions of gradual evolution rather than irreversible rupture. Put differently, contemporary observers saw British modernity as solidly grounded on historical foundations rather than adrift, without direction, in the present. This factor does much to explain why British meanings of modernity have, until recently, been studied so infrequently. Since most current theoretical models emphasize that experiences of discontinuity defined the 'modern', a central aspect of contemporary British concepts of modernity has escaped historians' attention: that on many occasions, Britons understood modernity in terms of continuity and *not* exclusively in terms of fundamental rupture. British debates about modernity encompassed two conceptions of 'change', which either described transformations as radical breaks or cast them as relatively smooth forms of transformation. This dual model of change in British evaluations of modernity in turn played an important role in containing the narratives of fundamental crises that permeated so many Continental assessments of the historical present.[33] In Britain, however, depictions of gradual transitions also stood alongside and thus moderated stories about and calls for sudden transformations. Influential conceptions of modernity as being deeply rooted in the nation's history endowed British debates about the historical present with a quality of stability and robustness rarely to be found in Western European debates about modernity between 1870 and 1940. Several contributions to this volume therefore oblige us to consider notions of temporal continuity in European concepts of the modern.

Narratives of continuous change were not the only way of inserting a dimension of stability into British notions of modernity, and so limiting the sense of disjointedness that surrounded evocations of the modern elsewhere. Owing to Britain's role as the world's foremost colonial power, representations of empire informed a large number of British assessments of modernity between 1870 and 1940. From a 'white' British perspective, on which the contributions to this volume concentrate, imperialism provided a powerful discourse legitimizing Britain as a 'modern' country. In contemporaries' eyes, imperial rule demonstrated the nation's superiority over peoples who were assumed not yet to have reached a 'modern' level of development. Contrasts between conditions in colonial arenas and in metropolitan Britain served to underline how much further Britain had supposedly travelled down the roads of 'progress' and 'enlightenment' in comparison with non-Europeans.[34] Moreover, imperial ideologies tended to repress fundamental critiques of metropolitan modernity, because colonial initiatives invested British culture with a sense of purpose as the country pursued its 'civilizing mission' in all corners of the globe. While many contemporaries took pride in colonialism's record of dispensing 'modern' British values, adherents of different political creeds forcefully disagreed about the appropriate means and the desirable ends of empire. Conservative imperialists, for instance, might view empire as a tool for creating a large-scale market on which they believed a 'modern' economy had to be based.[35] Feminists for their part held a different view, promoting empire as a means of protecting 'native' women from the chauvinism that they identified in colonial societies.[36] Socialists also propagated a culture of imperial reform, considering colonialism as a means to launch non-European societies on the road towards more egalitarian and non-exploitative forms of social organization.[37] Despite marked variations between these different legitimations of imperialism, positive assessments of colonial initiatives outweighed radical critiques in the metropole and, in turn, enhanced positive appraisals of Britain as a modern country. Discourses of imperialism also helped defuse criticisms of metropolitan culture. As Peter Hansen's chapter illustrates, mountaineering tours offered an escape from mundane aspects of modern metropolitan life and allowed Britons to search for an 'alternative modernity' in imperial surroundings as they contrasted themselves with purportedly traditional lifestyles. On the whole, imperialism's high prestige furthered the sense of cultural stability that characterized British debates about modernity. Finally, the chapters on imperialism remind us that we cannot conceive of British conceptions of modernity in dichotomous terms that separate the metropole neatly from the periphery, since British identities that struck contemporaries as decidedly modern were frequently forged in colonial arenas.[38]

The imperial project, however, was increasingly called into question during the interwar period, and with it one of the basic cultural foundations of British assessments of modernity. The proliferation of independence movements in the colonies played a major part in challenging imperialism in the metropolis. Nothing bears out this claim better than the warm reception Gandhi received among Labour supporters during his participation in the round table conferences in Britain in 1930 and 1931. At the same time, trends in metropolitan cultural and political life also raised doubts about the supposed advantages of imperialism. Susan Pedersen's chapter documents how members of the political and literary elites began to distance themselves from imperialism's 'civilizing' aims, which, as a result, lost their legitimizing function in wider debates about British modernity. Moreover, the colonial elites themselves were developing increasingly critical attitudes towards metropolitan life, as the contribution by Elizabeth Buettner suggests. When Britons living and working in India returned to the metropole, they frequently voiced feelings of alienation from its supposedly modern features, such as the pace and cost of city life or the difficulties of hiring servants. A direct link existed between more reserved attitudes to colonialism and critical assessments of 'modern' metropolitan life in elite circles in the interwar period. As observers began to argue that contemporary Britain no longer provided a desirable model to which the 'civilizing mission' and colonized societies should appeal and aspire, imperial projects were increasingly left devoid of ideological reference points. Conversely, narratives of British modernity lost one of their long-standing sources of legitimation.

Thus diffuse pressures both built upon and decreased the salience of established British conceptions of the modern between the wars, so that 1940 forms a convenient end-point for this collection of essays. Arguably, the Second World War marks a greater break than the First World War, whose place in any assessment of modernity remains problematical. Recent historical debates have grappled with the question how deep a rupture the Great War constituted in contemporary evaluations of modernity.[39] The experience of carnage followed by political and social revolutions abroad posed a major interpretational challenge to those who attempted to make sense of Britain as a modern society. John Maynard Keynes's assessment of the public mood in 1920 is symptomatic in this context: 'In England the outward aspect of life does not yet teach us to feel in the least that an age is over. We are busy picking up the threads of our life where we dropped them.'[40] Thus the Great War enhanced the problems of locating concepts of British modernity within frameworks of continuity. The violence unleashed on the battlefields powerfully alerted contemporaries to a new and dark side of their 'modern' age. Moreover, the war had demonstrated the fragility of the nation's status as a world power, on which many positive assessments of British modernity rested. In the domestic arena it became clear that the war had challenged established notions of masculinity and femininity, thus precipitating a major renegotiation about the role models deemed appropriate for 'modern' women and men during the twenties and thirties.[41] Simultaneously, a variety of debates on social issues vigorously took public centre-stage, ranging from public health to poverty and unemployment. While these conflicts were relatively mild when compared with the political and social antagonisms in some Continental nations, they signalled the gradual dissolution of long-standing rhetorics of modernity during the 1920s and 1930s.

Still, the major redefinition of British meanings of modernity did not occur until after the Second World War. Although victorious on the battlefield, the nation lost its long-standing status as the leading international player as a result of the rise of the bipolar American–Soviet antagonism. In addition, the demise of Britain as an imperial power contributed to a significant shift in the co-ordinates that determined British modernity. In the domestic context, the Second World War also represented a watershed, setting the stage for large-scale schemes advocating social and economic reconstruction. According to the seminal 1942 Beveridge Report, the war was 'abolishing landmarks of every kind', thereby creating 'a revolutionary moment in the world's history', which, in turn, called for revolutionary measures rather than 'patching'. It was high time, Beveridge continued, that Britain put into place an efficient and co-ordinated social security system that could adequately cope with the pressures generated within a 'modern industrial community'.[42] The postwar period witnessed central and planned state intervention on an unprecedented scale, thereby profoundly changing the relationship between state and society. In other words, the tensions that had already strained various established narratives of British modernity in the interwar years erupted fully after 1945 and led to significant re-negotiations of the semantics of the modern in the United Kingdom. In the transformed postwar world, the established stories of

British modernity emphasizing historical continuity lost their earlier persuasiveness. Viewed from this perspective, the Second World War rather than the Great War proved the more prominent watershed in bringing about a recasting of the meanings of British modernity.[43]

Between 1870 and 1940, Britons repeatedly resorted to the semantics of modernity to make sense of changes in their society, embracing a dual model to conceive of these transformations. Alongside interpretations that employed languages of modernity to consider changes as symptoms of fundamental ruptures in the temporal continuum, another influential intellectual strand addressed the modern in terms of even and gradual development. As a result, British evaluations of modernity appear historically grounded to a larger extent than discourses in other Western European countries. The prominence of historical narratives of continuous evolution in conceptions of the modern should not be mistaken for an underdeveloped awareness of modernity in Britain. This feature of British debate about the modern, however, encourages us to reconsider the categories that have dominated studies of European modernity for some time. Since Britons conceived of their times as 'modern' in languages of gradual development between 1870 and 1940, future forays into this topic need to acknowledge that many con-temporaries did not understand modernity as synonymous with notions of fundamental break and rupture. New approaches to modernity might therefore examine how historical narratives of continuity and discontinuity interacted not only in negotiations of the modern in Britain but elsewhere in Western Europe. At the same time, scholars can no longer restrict their attention to the metropole if they wish to arrive at a comprehensive understanding of British modernity. As we have seen, imperial dimensions exerted a deep influence on contemporary understandings of Britain as a modern nation. In conjunction with recent work on imperial and comparative history, several contributions in this volume can be read as a plea for a further integration of transnational approaches into the study of the British past.

Notes

We would like to thank Liz Buettner, Rebecca Spang, Michael Dintenfass, Axel Körner and Frank Trentmann for discussing issues that are raised in this chapter.

1 For an examination of this period as the 'first crisis of modernity', see Martin Wagner, *A Sociology of Modernity: Liberty and Discipline* (London and New York: Routledge, 1994), pp. 55–69.
2 The literature on Germany continues to grow. Important studies include Jeffrey Herf, *Reactionary Modernism: Technology, Culture and Politics in Weimar and the Third Reich* (Cambridge: Cambridge University Press, 1984); Rainer

Zitelmann, 'Die totalitäre Seite der Moderne', in *Nationalsozialismus und Modernisierung*, ed. Michael Prinz and Rainer Ziltemann (Darmstadt: Wissenschaftliche Buchgesellschaft, 1991), pp. 1–20; Mark Roseman, 'National Socialism and Modernisation', in *Fascist Italy and Nazi Germany: Comparisons and Contrasts*, ed. Richard Bessel (Cambridge: Cambridge University Press, 1996), pp. 197–229; Robert N. Proctor, *The Nazi War on Cancer* (Princeton, NJ: Princeton University Press, 1998). On Italy, see Carl Levy, 'From Fascism to "Post-Fascists": Italian Roads to Modernity', in *Fascist Italy and Nazi Germany: Comparisons and Contrasts*, ed. Richard Bessel (Cambridge: Cambridge University Press, 1996), pp. 165–96. For an excellent analysis of the modernity of Fascism and National Socialism in contrast with other anti-liberal movements in the interwar period, see Eric Hobsbawm, *The Age of Extremes: The Short Twentieth Century, 1914–1991* (London: Abacus, 1995), pp. 109–24.

3 On France, see Eugen Weber, *France: Fin-de-Siècle* (Cambridge, MA: Belknap Press, 1986). On Austria, see Helmut Konrad, 'Zeitgeschichte und Moderne', in *Nach Kakanien: Annäherungen an die Moderne*, ed. Rudolf Haber (Vienna: Böhlau, 1996), pp. 23–57.

4 This phrase borrows from Joan Scott, 'Gender: A Useful Category of Historical Analysis', in *Feminism and History* (Oxford: Oxford University Press, 1996), pp. 152–80. From a cultural studies perspective, see *Modern Times: A Century of English Modernity*, ed. Mica Nava and Alan O'Shea (London: Routledge, 1996).

5 For two influential interventions, see Martin J. Wiener, *English Culture and the Decline of the Industrial Spirit, 1850–1980* (Cambridge: Cambridge University Press, 1981); Corelli Barnett, *The Collapse of British Power* (Gloucester: Allan Sutton, 1984).

6 W. D. Rubinstein, *Capitalism, Culture and Decline in Britain, 1750–1990* (London: Routledge, 1994); David Edgerton, *Science, Technology and British Industrial 'Decline'* (Cambridge: Cambridge University Press, 1996); Martin J. Daunton, 'Gentlemanly Capitalism and British Industry, 1820–1914', *Past and Present* 122 (1989): 118–58. For a critique of 'declinism' from a cultural perspective, see Peter Mandler, 'Against Englishness: English Culture and the Limits of Rural Nostalgia, 1850–1940', *Transactions of the Royal Historical Society*, 6th s., 7 (1997): 155–75.

7 On the change in the nature of British industrialization, and the breaking of constraints on growth, see E. A. Wrigley, *Continuity, Chance and Change: The Character of the Industrial Revolution in England* (Cambridge: Cambridge University Press, 1988).

8 See Frank M. Turner, 'The Victorian Conflict Between Science and Religion: A Professional Dimension', in *Contesting Cultural Authority: Essays in Victorian*

Intellectual Life (Cambridge: Cambridge University Press, 1993), pp. 171–200, esp. 175.

9 See the contributions in *Imperialism and Popular Culture*, ed. John MacKenzie (Manchester: Manchester University Press, 1986).

10 For an introductory overview, see Thomas Richards, *The Commodity Culture of Victorian England: Advertising and Spectacle, 1851–1914* (Stanford, CA: Stanford University Press, 1990). In addition, see the extensive literature quoted in the contribution by Erika Rappaport.

11 For some examples, see Judith Walkowitz, *City of Dreadful Delight: Narratives of Sexual Danger in Late-Victorian London* (Chicago: University of Chicago Press, 1992); Barbara Caine, *English Feminism, 1780–1980* (Oxford: Oxford University Press, 1997), pp. 131–222; Martha Vicinus, *Independent Women: Work and Community for Single Women, 1850–1920* (Chicago: University of Chicago Press, 1985); Susan Kingsley Kent, *Making Peace: The Reconstruction of Gender in Interwar Britain* (Princeton, NJ: Princeton University Press, 1994).

12 Classic formulations of modernization theory can be found in Talcott Parsons, *The System of Modern Societies* (Englewood Cliffs, NJ: Prentice Hall, 1971); Walt W. Rostow, *The Stages of Economic Growth: A Non-Communist Manifesto* (Cambridge: Cambridge University Press, 1960).

13 On English modernism, see Stella Tillyard, *The Impact of Modernism, 1900–1920: Early Modernism and the Arts and Crafts Movement in Edwardian England* (London: Routledge, 1988); *Modern Britain, 1929–1939*, ed. James Peto and Donna Loveday (London: Design Museum, 1999).

14 These considerations are based on Reinhart Koselleck, *Futures Past: On the Semantics of Historical Time* (Cambridge, MA: MIT Press, 1985). Koselleck, however, does not consider the possibility of a sense of modernity formulated through narratives of continuity. On the complex sense of temporality in France between 1870 and 1914, see Matt K. Matsuda, *The Memory of the Modern* (New York: Oxford University Press, 1996).

15 Such a conceptualization informs influential works on the topic including Marshall Berman, *All That Is Solid Melts into Air: The Experience of Modernity* (London: Verso, 1983); David Harvey, *The Condition of Postmodernity: An Enquiry into the Origins of Cultural Change* (Oxford: Blackwell, 1989); Anthony Giddens, *The Consequences of Modernity* (Stanford, CA: Stanford University Press, 1990).

16 Jose Harris, *Private Lives, Public Spirit: Britain 1870–1914* (Harmondsworth: Penguin, 1994), p. 36.

17 On the creation of new traditions, see, David Cannadine, 'The Context, Performance and Meaning of Ritual: The British Monarchy and the "Invention of Tradition", *c.*1820–1977', in Eric Hobsbawm and Terence Ranger (eds), *The Invention of Tradition* (Cambridge: Cambridge University Press, 1983),

pp. 101–64. On the use of classics to interpret change, see Frank M. Turner, *Contesting Cultural Authority: Essays in Victorian Intellectual Life* (Cambridge: Cambridge University Press, 1993), especially Chapter 10, 'Ancient Materialism and Modern Science: Lucretius amongst the Victorians', pp. 262–83.

18 Max Weber provided the classic formulation when he spoke of the 'disenchantment' or *Entzauberung* of the world. See Max Weber, 'Science as a Vocation', in *Max Weber: Essays in Sociology*, ed. and trans. H. H. Gerth and C. Wright Mills (Oxford: Oxford University Press, 1959), pp. 129–56, esp. 139. For Weber's characterization of the European state as rational, see Max Weber, *Gemeinschaft und Gesellschaft: Grundriss einer verstehenden Soziologie*, 5th rev. edn. (Tübingen: Mohr, 1980), pp. 815–68. For a study of this aspect of Weber's thought, see Lawrence A. Scaff, *Fleeing the Iron Cage: Culture, Politics, and Modernity in the Thought of Max Weber* (Berkeley, CA: University of California Press, 1989).

19 On such debates, see Colin Matthew, Ross McKibbin and John Kay, 'The Franchise Factor and the Rise of the Labour Party', in Ross McKibbin, *Ideologies of Class: Social Relations in Britain, 1900–1950* (Oxford: Oxford University Press, 1990), pp. 66–100, esp. 90–1, 93.

20 On 'conservative modernity', see Alison Light, *Forever England: Femininity, Literature and Conservatism Between the Wars* (London: Routledge, 1991), pp. 9–10. On the promotion of electrical appliances to British female consumers, see Carrol Pursell, 'Domesticating Modernity: The Electrical Association for Women, 1924–1986', *British Journal for the History of Science* 32 (1999): 47–67. For an excellent investigation of a life reform movement in England, see Frank Trentmann, 'Civilization and its Discontents: English Neo-Romanticism and the Transformation of Anti-Modernism in Twentieth Century Western Culture', *Journal of Contemporary History* 29 (1994): 583–625.

21 Recent work has stressed the importance of a *fin-de-siècle* in Britain. Regrettably, these inquiries have not adopted a comparative perspective. See *Cultural Politics at the* Fin-de-Siècle, ed. Sally Ledger and Scott McCracken (Cambridge: Cambridge University Press, 1995); Sally Ledger, *The New Woman: Fiction and Feminism at the* Fin-de-Siècle (Manchester: Manchester University Press, 1998).

22 John Burrow, *A Liberal Descent: Victorian Historians and the English Past* (Cambridge: Cambridge University Press, 1981). On the Labour view of parliamentary reform as an intrinsic part of British history, see Paul Ward, *Red Flag and Union Jack: England, Patriotism and the British Left, 1881–1924* (Woodbridge: The Boydell Press, 1998), pp. 22–6, 153–4. See also Robert Colls, 'Englishness and the Political Culture', in *Englishness: Politics and Culture, 1880–1920*, ed. Robert Colls and Philip Dodd (London: Croom Helm, 1986), pp. 29–61.

23 The development of interpretations of Prussia's historic role in German history are examined in Wolfgang Hardtwig, 'Von Preußens Aufgabe in Deutschland zu Deutschlands Aufgabe in der Welt: Liberalismus und borussianisches Geschichtsbild zwischen Revolution und Imperialismus', in *Geschichtskultur und Wissenschaft* (Munich: dtv, 1990), pp. 103–60.

24 Malcolm Hardman, *Ruskin and Bradford: An Experiment in Victorian Cultural History* (London: Manchester University Press, 1986). See also Charles Delheim, *The Faces of the Past: The Preservation of the Medieval Inheritance in Modern England* (Cambridge: Cambridge University Press, 1982).

25 On Salisbury and electricity, see Asa Briggs, *Victorian Things* (Harmondsworth: Penguin, 1990), pp. 373–5. On the livery companies, see Peter M. Claus, '"Real Liberals" and Conservation in the City of London, 1848–1886' (Ph.D. thesis, Open University, 1998).

26 Martin J. Daunton, 'How To Pay for the War: State, Society and Taxation in Britain, 1917–1924', *English Historical Review* 111 (1996): 882–919.

27 On German street battles between National Socialists and Communists, see Eve Rosenhaft, 'Links gleich Rechts? Militante Straßengewalt um 1930', in *Physische Gewalt: Studien zur Geschichte der Neuzeit*, ed. Thomas Lindenberger and Alf Lüdtke (Frankfurt: Suhrkamp, 1995), pp. 238–75. On the crisis of French parliamentarism, see Eugen Weber, *The Hollow Years: France in the 1930s* (New York: Norton, 1994), pp. 147–81.

28 On the relative stability of class models in twentieth-century Britain, see David Cannadine, *Class in Britain* (New Haven, CT and London: Yale University Press, 1998), esp. pp. 110–48.

29 On political turmoil in Italy during the twenties, see Adrian Lyttleton, 'Fascism and Violence in Post-War Italy: Political Strategy and Social Conflict', in *Social Protest, Violence and Terror in Nineteenth- and Twentieth-Century Europe*, ed. Wolfgang J. Mommsen and Gerhard Hirschfeld (London: Macmillan, 1982), pp. 257–74. On the German revolution, see Detlev J. K. Peukert, *The Weimar Republic: Crisis of Classical Modernity* (London: Allen Lane, 1991), pp. 21–51.

30 Noel Annan, 'The Intellectual Aristocracy', in *Studies in Social History: A Tribute to G. M. Trevelyan*, ed. J. H. Plumb (London: Longman, Green and Co., 1955), pp. 241–87.

31 Stefan Collini, *Public Moralists: Political Thought and Intellectual Life in Britain, 1830–1930* (Oxford: Clarendon Press, 1993).

32 The classic argument for the German case is put forward in Fritz K. Ringer, *The Decline of the German Mandarins: The German Academic Community, 1890–1933* (Cambridge, MA: Harvard University Press, 1969).

33 For an excellent investigation of the difficulties that German architectural preservationists faced in their attempts to establish a sense of continuity through

the protection and maintenance of urban monuments, see Rudy Koshar, *Germany's Transient Pasts: Preservation and National Memory in the Twentieth Century* (Chapel Hill, NC: The University of North Carolina Press, 1998).

34 Of course, such stereotypical judgements could be found in France as well. See Michael Adas, *Machines as the Measure of Men: Science, Technology, and Ideologies of Western Dominance* (Ithaca, NY: Cornell University Press, 1989).

35 For a detailed examination of such arguments before 1914, see E. H. H. Green, *The Crisis of Conservatism: The Politics, Economics and Ideology of the British Conservative Party, 1880–1914* (London: Routledge, 1995), esp. pp. 59–77, 194–206.

36 Antoinette Burton, *Burdens of History: British Feminists, Indian Women, and Imperial Culture, 1865–1915* (Chapel Hill, NC: University of North Carolina Press, 1994).

37 For a succinct overview of the attitudes to empire across the political spectrum, see P. J. Marshall, '1918 to 1960s: Keeping Afloat', in *The Cambridge Illustrated History of the British Empire* (Cambridge: Cambridge University Press, 1996), pp. 80–107, esp. 84–5.

38 Bernhard Rieger would like to thank Angela Woollacott for stressing this point in a private conversation. Scholarship exploring this theme includes Angela Woollacot, '"All This Is Empire, I Told Myself": Australian Women's Voyages "Home" and the Articulation of Colonial Whiteness', *American Historical Review* 102 (1997): 1003–29, esp. 1009–11; Catherine Hall, 'Histories, Empires and the Post-Colonial Moment', in *The Postcolonial Question: Common Skies, Divided Horizons*, ed. Iain Chambers and Lidia Curti (New York: Routledge, 1998), pp. 65–77; Antoinette Burton, *At the Heart of Empire: Indians and the Colonial Encounter in Late-Victorian Britain* (Berkeley, CA: University of California Press, 1998). Paul Gilroy, *The Black Atlantic: Modernity and Double Consciousness* (Cambridge, MA: Harvard University Press, 1993).

39 Jay Winter has argued against interpreting the Great War as a cultural turning-point in *Sites of Memory, Sites of Mourning: The Great War in European Cultural History* (Cambridge: Cambridge University Press, 1996). He reacted to works such as Modris Eksteins, *The Rites of Spring: The Great War and the Birth of the Modern Age* (Boston: Houghton Mifflin, 1989).

40 John Maynard Keynes, *The Economic Consequences of the Peace* (London: Macmillan, 1920), p. 2.

41 For the best concise introduction to these issues, see Susan Kingsley Kent, *Gender and Power in Britain, 1660–1990* (London: Routledge, 1999), pp. 257–310.

42 *Social Insurance and Allied Services: Report by Sir William Beveridge* (London: HMSO, 1942), pp. 5–8.

43 See the contributions in *Moments of Modernity: Reconstructing Britain, 1945–1964*, ed. Becky Conekin, Frank Mort and Chris Waters (London: Rivers Oram Press, 1999).

Part I
Popular Culture, Selfhood and Modernity

–2–

Travelling in the Lady Guides' London: Consumption, Modernity, and the *Fin-de-Siècle* Metropolis

Erika D. Rappaport

In December of 1888 a meeting was held at the Royal Society of British Artists to discuss a new scheme for middle-class female employment.[1] This gathering launched the Lady Guide Association, an organization dedicated to promoting and profiting from the commercialization of public life in late-Victorian London.[2] The group was formed ostensibly to hire and train unemployed but well-born women as travel agents, tour guides, chaperons, and professional shoppers. These 'ladies' would then 'guide' visitors on sightseeing and shopping trips, while the Association's offices would provide them with a meeting- or resting-place during their hectic day in town. In essence, this association of bourgeois women hoped to remake England's capital city into a comfortable, intelligible, and pleasurable arena for themselves and for others. They facilitated and embodied the transformation of the late-Victorian metropolis into a tourist site and shopping centre, an arena for female work and leisure, and a national symbol.[3]

The Lady Guide Association opens up an avenue for thinking about gender, mass consumption, and metropolitan culture during the *fin-de-siècle* and addresses wider questions concerning the nature of English modernity. Debates about the consciousness or 'psychic formations of modernity' have ranged from considering the impact of new forms of production and consumption, mass communications and travel, and the growing rationalization and bureaucratization of labour, business and the state to the role of technology, and, perhaps most crucially, to the place of the ever-growing metropolis in shaping everyday life, social interactions, and formations of identity. Those interested in the English experience of modernity during the late-nineteenth and early-twentieth centuries have also emphasized national economic decline and a concomitant popularization of imperialism.[4]

Feminist scholars, however, have typically eschewed such questions in favour of debating whether or not such models of modernity are inevitably gendered. Literary critics, art historians, cultural theorists, and historians have questioned whether men and women have experienced modernity in the same way, since most theories focus upon the social and psychological consequences of changes in the public sphere. This feminist debate has become more or less fixated on the gendered nature of the *flâneur*, the urban stroller and chronicler whom many have identified as the quintessential modern subject.[5] Some feminists have maintained that middle-class women's exclusion from metropolitan public spaces meant that the literature and painting of modern life has represented a wholly masculine perspective. The art historian Griselda Pollock, for example, has written that the *flâneur* symbolized 'the privilege or freedom to move about the public arenas of the city observed but never interacting, consuming the sights through a controlling but rarely acknowledged gaze. The *flâneur* embodies the gaze of modernity which is both covetous and erotic.' He is, Pollock writes, 'an exclusively masculine type.'[6] In Susan Buck-Morss's reading of Benjamin, the *flâneur* was also a masculine subject whose counterpart, the prostitute, was 'the embodiment of objectivity, not subjectivity'.[7] For these authors modern urban relations were visual and sexual. Men gaze at women and women transform themselves into objects to be looked at. In this view, the *flâneuse* cannot exist not so much because she is literally barred from public life, but because public women were inevitably relegated to the status of the prostitute, or the object of a male gaze.

In a related vein, some critics have posited that modernist writers conceived of the prostitute as an allegory of modern commodified subjectivity. Walter Benjamin, for example observed, '[i]n the prostitution of the metropolis, the woman herself becomes an article that is mass-produced'.[8] Andreas Huyssen further argued that a feminized vision of mass culture was 'modernism's Other'.[9] In all these approaches there are no female subjects. Instead, women serve as the triggers of male fantasies about industrialization, urbanization, commodification, and modernity. Though these theorists ignore the experiences of 'real' women, gender and sexuality have been central to their conceptualizations of urban modernity.

Recent research, however, has shown that bourgeois women were actively engaged with metropolitan public cultures during the *fin-de-siècle*. More than mere subjects of a male gaze or symbols of the degradation of the modern metropolis, women have achieved the status of urban stroller and voyeur and have had a hand in constructing a vision of the late-Victorian and Edwardian city.[10] In the 1880s and 1890s quite a few middle and upper-class women, including Elizabeth Gaskell, Flora Tristan, and Amy Levy, adopted the persona of writer and urban observer. Their physical freedom and artistic vision was constrained nonetheless, Deborah Nord writes, by their inability 'to make themselves invisible and ignored', and by their consciousness of transgressing acceptable class and gender norms.[11] In this view, the city and new literary forms were crucial constituents of the modern urban woman, yet her experiences were marked by an ever-present awareness of transgression and danger.

These debates about women and modernity have thus focused on the construction of vision and gender relations within a metropolitan context. Though it is now possible to argue that there were some women who adopted the role of the *flâneuse*, we still have little sense of whether this role contributed to the rationalization, commodification, and urbanization of public life or whether bourgeois women conceived of such transformations as in any way 'modern'. The Lady Guide Association's history presents an example of how some women engaged with the problems and possibilities of *fin-de-siècle* urban culture and its increasing emphasis on mass consumption, tourism, and entertainment. This group professionalized the *flâneuse* and interpreted the commodification of London as a means of reasserting England's national dominance. Many Britons construed mass consumption and tourism as among the destructive forces of modern life. However, the Guides, like many businessmen, believed that such changes could serve their own and their nation's economic interests. While rarely describing their activities as modern, they recognized that they were carving out a new social role for themselves and for other bourgeois women. Instead of asking whether the *flâneuse* existed either in reality or in the popular imagination, the Lady Guide Association's history illuminates some of the domestic and international conditions that allowed for her emergence and that she in turn influenced.

By the time that the Guides opened their first office in London's West End in the late 1880s, this neighbourhood had long been known as a centre of commercialized leisure and pleasurable consumption. Regent Street, Oxford Street, Bond Street, the Burlington Arcade and the surrounding area were firmly established as a shopping and entertainment centre. Small boutiques and burgeoning new department stores as well as a vast selection of restaurants, tea shops, theatres, and hotels were clustered together, igniting the desires of an increasingly diverse crowd of pleasure-seekers.[12]

Many urban 'boosters', especially journalists, guidebook writers, and business 'experts', conceived of the West End and its commercial enterprises as modern institutions. For example, the well-known guidebook author, Charles Eyre Pascoe, began his 1885 edition of *London of To-Day* with the assertion that London was 'a new city'.[13] Pascoe elaborated to the effect that the sites and entertainments that tourists so enjoyed had only been built during the preceding half-century. Indeed, much of western London, especially its suburbs and its commercial districts, consisted of nineteenth-century creations. Their newness did not necessarily signify modernity. Yet there were many who did see this neighbourhood and its businesses as modern. For example, *Modern London: The World's Metropolis, an Epitome of Results*, an encyclopaedia of the capital's most 'progressive' enterprises, assumed that London's modernity was derived from her mass commerce, particularly the large-scale and ever-diversifying retail establishments that crowded West End streets. While some of these businesses, such as Fortnum, Mason & Company in Piccadilly, were known for their established reputations, the author emphasized their efficient management and up-to-date methods. So, for example, somewhat older stores such as Marshall and Snelgrove's, which had been founded in 1837, admirably applied '[e]very modern method and appliance, which in any way facilitate the transaction of business'. It was therefore a thoroughly 'systematic organization'.[14]

This language of commercial modernity flourished in the trade press of the era. Journals such as *Modern Business*, *Modern Retailing* or *Progressive Confectioner* offered traders a guide to the most recent business methods while also attempting to capture and ignite that aura of newness that excited many during the *fin-de-siècle*. *Modern Business*, for example, was founded in 1908 to 'promote modern, efficient business methods' among both wholesalers and retailers.[15] This journal deemed businesses 'modern' if they emphasized 'efficiency', indulged in ornate forms of display and advertising, and appealed to a mass, not a class-specific market. The journal's heroes were men such as Joseph Lyons, the famous catering entrepreneur, and Gordon Selfridge, the maverick American department store mogul. Both businessmen were actively promoting new products, new types of commercial enterprises, and new methods of consumption. Both were also central players in the creation of the West End as a site of mass leisure and entertainment.[16]

Like Victorian and Edwardian business experts, mainstream journalists and popular authors also associated commercial institutions such as department stores, large hotels, and restaurants with modernity. The journalist and popular novelist Arnold Bennett epitomized this tendency in a series of Edwardian novels exploring aspects of what he called 'modern times'. At the heart of several of these stories were larger-than-life entrepreneurs who sold entertainment to the masses.[17] While the term 'modernity' had many meanings, Bennett was essentially working with the same assumptions as the editors of the retail and advertising trade journals. Like them, he focused on the overwhelming scale of the enterprises, their emphasis on spectacle and display, and their trade in entertainment as well as goods.

In texts such as *Modern London* or Bennett's *The City of Pleasure: A Fantasia on Modern Times* the male entrepreneur is the author or architect of modernity. He is the purveyor of a new age marked both by new sensual pleasures and rationalized, bureaucratized business techniques and labour practices. Women appear in such stories, to be sure, but in the text and as readers they act as the consumers of this vision of modernity. Mica Nava has insisted in her study of gender and modernity that such female consumers were central to the workings of the consumer economy and culture, and that theirs was a major, if overlooked, narrative of modernity.[18] I would like to suggest here that women writers and entrepreneurs were also the creators of this culture of consumer pleasures, a culture that many viewed as distinctively modern.

The Lady Guide Association did not literally build London's streets, shops and tourist sights, but, like other facets of the tourist industry, it sold access to this city and shaped the way it was perceived.[19] It also helped to invent an 'authentic'

London of churches, royal palaces, and other features of what might be labelled the 'historical' city.[20] Indeed, London was often sold to tourists as an ancient relic rather than a modern invention. If some guidebooks underscored London's newness, others emphasized its age. For example, Herbert Fry began the 1888 edition of his popular guidebook with the assertion that 'This great town with all its ancient associations, its venerable edifices, its varied memories, is a grand Heirloom descended to us from the historical past, of which every Briton should be proud.'[21] Guidebooks thus emphasized different facets of London and different meanings of old and new; but it hardly mattered. The 'historical' and 'modern' cities merged into a single compelling consumer-oriented experience.[22]

The Lady Guides contributed to and profited from the growing complexity of an expanding and increasingly spectacular metropolis. The commodification of London, worries about Britain's status as a world power, and class and gender tensions in the capital justified the formation of this new type of female worker. The group was in part a response to the intense anxiety that Judith Walkowitz has shown characterized urban gender relations during these years. Although the connection was never made explicit, it is perhaps no coincidence that the Guides were formed only weeks after Jack the Ripper claimed his last victim. If the media representation of the Ripper murders cast the city as a dangerous place for women, the LGA challenged this narrative by presenting London as a respectable consumer-oriented pleasure centre. Walkowitz has argued that in the late 1880s 'commercial narratives' were 'overshadowed by representations of urban pathology and decline'.[23] Nevertheless, a large segment of London's business community went to great lengths to present urban life, and women's place within it, in a positive light. This view of the city was partly an outgrowth of a feminist culture that promoted female entrepreneurship; but it also reflected a liberal, commercial, and imperial sensibility.[24]

In public lectures, booklets, and their journal, *Progress: The Organ of the Lady Guide Association*, as well as in guidebooks, newspapers and upper-class women's magazines such as *The Lady* and *Queen*, the Guides and their supporters developed their vision of London and the urban woman. In each of these locations the LGA was said to benefit unemployed middle-class women, London's pleasure-seekers, and the city itself.

When lecturing to an audience of potential supporters, the LGA's founder and president, Miss Edith Davis, repeatedly stressed London's symbolic potential, describing it as 'the chief representative' of England and the 'pride' of its 'countrymen'. She insisted that Englishness resided in the city, not in the country. When a foreigner visits London, she maintained, they feel 'a sense of security, [and] . . . knowledge that they are in the midst of a nation avowedly the most liberal, free, honest and hospitable'. Davis saw it as self-evident that 'the wide-spread fame of the great Metropolis as a city of wonders has filled the heart of strangers with a longing to see and know, to feel themselves at home', and to understand 'the glories under the rule and guardianship of the greatest Sovereign in the world'. By making London more accessible, the LGA would therefore, 'redeem the pledge of our nationality'.[25] The 'city of wonders' thus conveyed what Davis believed were core facets of Englishness: monarchy, liberty, and hospitality.[26] Davis did not merely see London as a context for imperial display. She implied that its streets, shops, and historical sights were the very fabric of such spectacles.

Yet Davis admitted that this reading of the city was not an obvious one. In order to justify a need for the Guides she had to acknowledge that London was difficult to comprehend and that its pleasures were not immediately intelligible. Its size, complexity and diversity, she suggested, often led to unrewarding and expensive visits. However, with a Guide's aid strangers would 'avoid the loss of time and money which occurs through not knowing the right omnibus, the right train, the correct cab fare, and the difference of prices in shopping in Bond Street, Westbourne Grove, or the City, and so on'. They would also 'be introduced to all the buildings, sights, picture galleries, entertainments (instructive and social), shops, &c'.[27] Davis was arguing, then, that if shopping and sightseeing were conducted efficiently, foreigners would know that they were in the world's most 'liberal' and 'honest' nation.

Guidebooks frequently made similar claims: that London's complexity was appealing, but could also be overwhelming. For example, *Ward and Lock's Pictorial Guide to London* warned that 'the deepest impression left on the mind after a first visit to the great metropolis, is generally that produced by immense size, and the apparent difficulty of describing it as enclosed within recognizable limits'. However, 'in due time', and presumably after buying this book, 'the mind becomes familiarized' and 'the details assume just prominence'. The visitor is then able to appreciate London's 'magnificence of architecture' and 'multitudinous objects of interest'.[28] Like this guidebook, the LGA assumed that specialized knowledge made the city intelligible and thus pleasurable for strangers.

On a more practical level, Davis believed that aiding shoppers and sightseers was good for British business. She recognized the growing importance of foreign spenders, and explained to supporters that her 'association will be a means of reviving trade generally'.[29] While many critics denounced tourists and shoppers as frivolous and aimless creatures, Davis proposed that they were economic assets who gained important political lessons while consuming in London.

If Davis recognized that strangers needed to be properly guided to see this spectacular city, she also felt they required a place where they could gratify their bodily needs. She spoke of the Association's Regent Street office, for example, as 'a place of welcome to our foreign country sisters and brothers, their introduction, the passport to their freedom, the open sesame to their enjoyment'.[30] The office included a money exchange, a safe for client's valuables, a lavatory, a small restaurant, and various reading and writing rooms.[31] *Queen* described it as 'a centre in the metropolis where all strangers and visitors shall call upon their arrival, make known their wants, ask advice, receive information upon any and every point, [and] find comfortable reception rooms where they can receive friends, trades-people, and others'.[32] The offices were central to the Guide's vision of hospitality in that they furnished middle-class clients with a home away from home or a private base from which they could enjoy the public sphere.

Until the 1870s, middle-class urban women had often complained that there were no public places that would serve their private needs. There were very few hotels or restaurants acceptable to middle-class families. There were no public lavatories, and institutions such as department stores were only just beginning to introduce such services in the 1870s.[33] However, there was a tremendous expansion of such urban amenities over the next decades. Various types of eateries, women's clubs, and travel agencies such as American Express and the Great Eastern Railway Company's 'American Rendezvous' began to sell urban guidance and domestic comforts to an increasingly mobile international bourgeoisie.[34] The LGA was but a single representative of this broader transformation in metropolitan public life.

The LGA's offices were virtually indistinguishable from those of American Express or the American Rendezvous, but their exclusive use of female guides was a significant departure from their competition's practice. Indeed, some of the services these women performed were definitely not available at American Express. Lady Guides often worked as temporary housekeepers, chaperons, and hostesses. Because they were 'ladies by birth and education', Davis suggested that her employees could act in any capacity where the 'manners of a *lady*' were required. They helped plan and even attended dinner parties,[35] could babysit for a suburban mother so that she could better 'enjoy a day's shopping and revel in the sales undisturbed by thoughts of her babies',[36] or would personally shop for their clients. The Shopping Department was even staffed by, as one of the LGA's brochures explained, a Guide that had been 'Certificated for Shopping'.[37] In addition to domestic help and urban guidance, then, one could hire a well-born but highly-trained 'Lady' with fashion sense.

While other forces were telling women that shopping was a leisure activity, the Lady Guides defined it as an extension of bourgeois women's work. Essentially they were attempting to professionalize, bureaucratize, and rationalize shopping. This idea had been developing at least since the 1870s, when both fashion and feminist journals began to publish letters from women who either wanted to become or to hire a London commission agent. In one such letter a reader of the feminist paper, *The Woman's Gazette* wrote: 'I often wished I knew someone in London to whom I could write and ask to execute my orders' since her relatives and friends resented 'the time that is taken up by executing such requests from country cousins'. Of course, one could write directly to the shops, but this woman explained that 'ladies in the country do not always know what *are* the best shops for their purpose'.[38] Other letters documented the woes of unemployed women, annoyed Londoners and their country cousins.[39] Each resented the way in which an informal women's culture had become central to the nation's distribution system. These writers all recognized shopping as work for which one should be financially compensated. The LGA shared this conviction, hoping to professionalize what was more typically perceived as a female duty or pleasure.

Like many similar groups during this period, the Guides focused on teaching bourgeois women the skills needed for professional employment in England's growing service sector.[40] Davis claimed that she would hire any well-born woman who was properly educated and passed an examination in her particular area of expertise. She responded to critics of middle-class female employment by arguing that guiding gave ladies 'fair remuneration for fair work without usurping man's prerogative'.[41] The *Graphic* likewise defended the Guides against critics who scoffed at 'the idea of women guiding men! As if they were not doing so in thousands of cases, every hour of every day!'[42] Davis also assured sceptics that she 'allows no woman to occupy the place more fitted for a man. Thus, its Departments of Money Exchange, House Agency, Accountant, and so forth have gentlemen for their direction'.[43] While Davis felt women could and should have careers, she was not overturning all gender hierarchies. She did not offer her female employees the higher-paid and higher-status positions in the organization. Davis hoped to expand women's sphere without treading on commonly held assumptions about gender and work.

A fictional tale, 'The Ladies Guide's Valentine', similarly supported the New Woman worker in the city while assuring readers she was not a danger to her class or her sex. Published in the February 1891 issue of the women's magazine, *The Lady*, the story begins when a brother and sister, Hartley and Henrietta Grainger, have realized that although they have travelled to London together they do not wish to visit the same city. Henrietta yearns to go 'sightseeing' and Hartley wants to attend a series of scientific lectures. On the verge of tears, Henrietta finds she must 'smother her girl-like longings "for a good time"' after her brother tells her, 'in somewhat melancholy tones, "I would not disappoint you for the world, but you might just as well ask your spaniel to conduct you over London. I am quite hopeless in these matters. I don't even remember where the Royal Academy is – somewhere in Kensington I suppose."'[44] Henrietta responds to this admission of ignorance by asking if she might hire a guide to help with their visit. Hartley agrees to accompany his sister and the guide anywhere except 'to waxwork shows and – the milliner's'.[45]

However, when he sees that his sister has hired a 'lady' guide, he cries out that such a figure must be 'Monstrous!' and then asks 'Who would wish to place a lady in such a position?' The Lady Guide, Miss Morrison, 'sweetly' answers, 'We cannot choose our work . . . When a woman is left unprovided for, she has to do that for which she is best fitted.'[46] Hartley's scientific bent persuades him to accept this Darwinian explanation of the rise of a new sub-species of female and to agree to be 'guided' by a woman. For several weeks, Dorothea Morrison guides the Grainger siblings through London, and because of her Cambridge education and the fact that she is the niece of a famous professor, even introduces Hartley to London's scientific community.

The story thus constructs London as a sphere for female autonomy and independence while maintaining a clear sense of gender difference. The narrative initially sets up an opposition between a male London of science and rationality and a female London of consumption and, presumably, irrationality. Dorothea's scientific understanding undercuts this dichotomy; yet, by the end of the story, gender difference reasserts itself in the form of heterosexual pleasure as Hartley and Dorothea fall in love. With the marriage that is assumed to conclude the story, we find that Dorothea's work and her sweet character have returned her to her proper class and her proper sphere. Although the tale promoted the LGA and its version of the New Woman worker, it also implied that such work was a temporary means by which appropriate class and gender norms may be preserved. Nonetheless, the story challenged bourgeois gender ideology by showing a respectable solitary woman working in the public spaces of the metropolis.

As this tale suggests, many observers assumed that, although families travelled together, they would not want to see or do the same things while away from home. One article amusingly noted that men are simply terrible guides, for 'even when they are "on duty" husbands have been known to express impatience if they are kept waiting outside or inside of shops, while brothers have a bad reputation for shirking their fraternal duties, reserving their attentions for other fellow's sisters.' Female guides, however, would 'never grumble . . . even assist and encourage that delightfully long shopping, that delicious lingering over bargains, that hesitation between competitive shapes and colours, which so beautifully fill up women's thoughts when let loose in the happy hunting-grounds of Oxford Street, Regent Street and Piccadilly'.[47] The Guides capitalized upon these commonly held beliefs about gender and consumption. For most Victorians urban shopping, whether defined as work or leisure, belonged to the world of women. Its terrain, the 'happy hunting-grounds of Oxford Street, Regent Street and Piccadilly', was not, however, an exclusively female or bourgeois world.

Many areas of London contained both respectable and unsavoury characters and transactions. Even the most elite and aristocratic enterprises involved unregulated liaisons between buyers and sellers. Arthur Munby, notorious for his interest in Victorian working women, was fascinated by the mixture of respectable and unrespectable behaviour in West End shops. He enjoyed flirting with shop-girls who he believed were also part-time prostitutes.[48] This vision of shop-girls delighted male strollers and made all women vulnerable to harassment and charges of soliciting when they walked West End shopping streets.[49] Some observers therefore worried that the Lady Guides would suffer indignities while wandering through London. Others hoped the Guides could make the city safe and respectable for other women. The *Spectator*, for example, admired the Guides because they could 'meet single and unprotected young ladies at the stations, and deposit them in safe, clean, and respectable lodgings'.[50] The *Daily Telegraph* explicitly commented that ladies who know 'several foreign languages and have the topography and curiosities of London at their fingers' ends' will protect 'ignorant and inquisitive strangers' from 'the harpies who walk by day or the adventurers who prowl at night'. She will lead clients

> to fair-dealing merchants, and warn them off from the haunts of rogues. If we think of restaurants alone, there are places in the centre of London associated in minds of men about town with scenes of midnight dissipation. No honest man would like to see a lady enter such places, yet a stranger in London visiting them by daylight might not detect their objectionable character.[51]

The Lady Guides were thus understood as masters of the subtle distinctions between the respectable and the unrespectable, the fashionable and the unfashionable West End of the 1880s and 1890s. Profiting from the complexities of *fin-de-siècle* urban life, they were seen as detectives able to read the 'contested terrain' of the late-Victorian street. The class and gender tensions that plagued the late-Victorian metropolis had opened a space for the LGA. The Guides and their supporters believed that urban knowledge allowed women to maintain their respectability and avoid harassment.

Their appearance at the end of the century also reflected a belief that bourgeois women's independence in city streets was a welcome sign of modernity. During the 1880s, many commentators noted that the time-honoured institution of the chaperon was becoming a bit old-fashioned.[52] Margaret Fletcher, for example, remembered that it was during these years that 'escorts were beginning to be thought unnecessary'. Girls could, as she put it, 'companion one another'.[53] Dorothy Peel similarly recalled that 'nice girls' from the suburbs were going 'about by themselves' and becoming 'independent by the help of the train'.[54] An 1882 article entitled, 'Walking Alone', published in *Queen*, remarked that 'although a generation ago it was not considered proper . . . for young ladies of good style and repute to walk the streets of London . . . at the present day a chaperon is the last thing desired of the modern girl, who loves liberty more than safety'. According to this journalist, the modern girl relied on 'her own courage and cleverness . . . to carry her out of dangers and difficulties of [sic] which her mother, when her age, was not supposed to know even existed'. The modern girl was thus cognizant of the dangers that awaited her, but pretended, according to this author, to be 'unconcerned' on 'her lonely walks through the crowded West-end streets'.[55] A view was developing, then, that knowledge, confidence, and expertise could make the city a safe and pleasurable place for 'modern' middle-class women and girls. This conviction and a lack of consensus on the chaperon issue garnered support for the Guides. For they could be seen as modern chaperons, perfectly suited for guiding modern girls. The *Daily Telegraph* told readers, for example, that 'many a father anxious to allow his daughter freedom, but too old to follow them about and not liking to let them go alone, will welcome an active and judicious Lady Guide as the very thing long wanted'.[56]

If the last decade of the nineteenth century gave birth to new ideas and reactions to women's independence, it was also a moment when a great many strangers – especially Americans – were travelling to and shopping in London. American women were an acknowledged aspect of the West End consumer scene in the 1880s. English retailers had come to believe that, as one trade journal commented, the American woman possessed a 'national love of shopping'.[57] In addition to aiding the freedom of 'modern girls' and helping ignorant female shoppers, the Guides claimed to serve this new contingent of wealthy international shoppers.

The Guides turned their urban knowledge, which was derived from their class and gender position, into skilled work. Like men of their class, they sought to control a rapidly transforming economy and culture; and they received widespread praise for their efforts. Not only did they claim support from the royal family and highly-placed members of English Society, but the media also embraced their efforts. One journalist for *Queen* commented in 1894 'the Lady Guide has come to stay'.[58]

However, the Lady Guides actually disappeared by 1902.[59] A correspondent for *The Englishwoman* believed that, despite the LGA's value:

> the public seems to prefer to lionise itself when it comes to London: to do its own shopping, to take its own tickets for concerts and theatres, to engage its own houses, rooms at hotels, or apartments, to meet itself at the railway stations . . .
>
> Our country cousins will go to the wrong shops in blissful ignorance . . . American cousins will rush unguided through England, missing the best things to be seen . . . Our cousins German, as well as other foreigners, will murder our language, and get cheated for their pains.[60]

Though this journalist blamed the Guides' failure on the ignorance of consumers, it is not clear what led to their demise. The number of urban visitors certainly did not decrease after the turn of the century. Davis may have lost interest in or been unable to raise enough capital to sustain the organization. Her staff may have accepted more stable, higher-paying employment, which was increasingly available.

Her business may simply have failed because the services she provided became so accessible.

Women's magazines and guidebooks published 'shopping guides'; businesses such as American Express, and even professional 'shoppers' became an ever-present aspect of urban commercial culture into the 1920s and 1930s and beyond.[61] Baedeker's and other traditional guidebooks began devoting greater space to London's commercial culture, while cheaper forms of urban guidance also began to target the lower-middle-class and even the working-class consumer. For only a penny, the *A.B.C. Amusement Guide and Record* directed readers to London's museums, dramatic and musical events, shops, and restaurants.[62] Similarly, newspapers such as the *Pall Mall Gazette, Evening News, Daily Chronicle*, and *Daily Mail* also guided readers through the London's commercial culture. In May of 1907, for example, the *Evening News* sponsored a contest for the 'reader who maps out a model course of enjoyment which costs exactly £1'.[63] Around the same time, the *PMG* began a weekly series, 'Shopping and Shopland', which promised to betray the 'secrets of the smart', to teach the masses how the wealthy navigated 'the maze of West End shopping'.[64] The *PMG* also addressed the pleasure-seeking foreign tourist. In 1909 it began a new series 'designed to guide the stranger in the social intricacies of London', to show the visitor 'the London of the Londoner'.[65]

The profusion of all sorts of shopping and tourist guides and institutions may have spelled the end of the Lady Guide Association. The LGA's importance, however, was not its successes or failures, but rather how it fitted within the economic, cultural, and social transformations taking place in the late-Victorian metropolis. The LGA produced London as an attraction by constructing safe havens and exciting sights for shoppers and tourists. In doing so, the Guides aided in the creation of a new consumer-oriented London and invented a new type of female worker. As modern consumer cultures colonized and reconfigured metropolitan landscapes across Europe and America, women have been most frequently understood as passive consumers or objects of exchange. The Guides certainly constructed their female clients as consumers. However, they did not necessarily see this identity as a passive one, nor did they see women as objects to be consumed by male urban strollers. The Lady Guides argued instead that a commodified London symbolized England's liberal achievement and that middle-class women could and should translate this vision of the city to native ramblers and to the rest of world.

The Guides saw what they were doing as new, but they did not self-consciously speak of the city, consumerism, or themselves as specifically 'modern'. Neverthe-less, they represented a way of being in the world that theorists have long identified as modern, if also masculine. In his classic discussion, 'The Metropolis and Mental Life', Georg Simmel, for example, suggested that the 'metropolitan type of man –

which, of course, exists in a thousand variants – develops an organ protecting him against the currents and discrepancies of his external environment which would uproot him. He reacts with his head instead of his heart.'[66] Simmel assumed that the excessive stimulation and rapid transformations of the metropolis as well as its domination by the 'money economy' forced 'man' to become an excessively rational, calculating being. Moreover, Simmel singled out London in this essay by quoting the dictum that 'London has never acted as England's heart but often as England's intellect and always as her moneybag!'[67]

The Lady Guides certainly privileged their rationality over their emotions, delighted in the dominance of the 'money economy', and assumed that specialized knowledge protected them and others from the potentially disintegrating and uprooting aspects of the modern metropolis. Unlike Simmel, the Guides were essentially optimistic about urban life. Yet they shared his emphasis on reason as a means of mastering the urban realm. In one respect, they could simply be seen as one of the many 'variants' of the 'metropolitan type of man'. This should not be taken to mean that models of modernity described by Simmel and others may be applied to women as well as to men, or that they describe the English situation perfectly. It does imply, however, that further reflections on English modernity must pay greater attention to how women and men reacted to and shaped the urban environment and the commercial economy and culture.

As some have already begun to suggest, the advent of mass consumption was perceived as drawing women into the public spaces of the city in wholly new ways. This new urban woman was associated both positively and negatively with 'modernity'. We need a greater understanding of her experiences; but we also need a fuller consideration of how her presence influenced notions of masculinity during the *fin-de-siècle* and in the early twentieth century, when theorists began to speak of modern subjects as 'metropolitan men'.

Notes

1 *Queen*, 5 January 1889: 22.
2 On the many formations of 'the public' in the nineteenth century, see Geoff Eley, 'Nations, Publics and Political Cultures: Placing Habermas in the Nineteenth Century', in *Habermas and the Public Sphere*, ed. Craig Calhoun (Cambridge, MA: MIT Press, 1989), pp. 289–339 and Jürgen Habermas in *The Structural Transformation of the Public Sphere: An Inquiry into a Category of Bourgeois Society* (Cambridge, MA: MIT Press, 1989). On women and the public, see Mary Ryan, *Women in Public: Between Banners and Ballots, 1825–1880* (Baltimore, MD: Johns Hopkins University Press, 1990); Leonore Davidoff, 'Regarding Some "Old Husbands' Tales": Public and Private in Feminist History', in *Worlds Between: Historical Perspectives on Gender and*

Class (New York and London: Routledge, 1995) and Nancy Fraser, 'Rethinking the Public Sphere: A Contribution to the Critique of Actually-Existing Democracy', in *Habermas and the Public Sphere.*

3 For the history of these changes, see Erika Rappaport, *Shopping for Pleasure: Women in the Making of London's West End* (Princeton, NJ: Princeton University Press, 2000).

4 Alan O'Shea and Mica Nava use the phrase 'psychic formations of modernity' in *Modern Times: Reflections on a Century of English Modernity*, ed. Alan O'Shea and Mica Nava (London and New York: Routledge, 1996), p. 2. O'Shea's chapter, 'English Subjects of Modernity', provides an overview of much of the literature on modernity: *ibid.*, pp. 7–37. Also see the related essays in this same volume, which are all influenced by but reconsider the model of modernity conveyed in such works as Marshall Berman's, *All That is Solid Melts into Air: The Experience of Modernity* (New York: Viking Penguin, 1988); David Frisby, *Fragments of Modernity: Georg Simmel, Siegfried Kracauer and Walter Benjamin* (London: Heinemann, 1985); and Susan Buck-Morss, *Walter Benjamin and the Arcades Project* (Cambridge, MA: MIT Press, 1989).

5 Raymond Williams, *The Country and The City* (New York: Oxford University Press, 1973), p. 233; Janet Wolff, 'The Culture of Separate Spheres: The Role of Culture in Public and Private Life', in *The Culture of Capital: Art, Power and the Nineteenth-Century Middle-Class*, ed. John Seed and Janet Wolff (Manchester: Manchester University Press, 1988); Janet Wolff, 'The Invisible Flâneuse: Women and the Literature of Modernity', *Theory, Culture and Society* 2, no. 3 (1985): 37–46 and Griselda Pollock, *Vision and Difference: Femininity, Feminism and Histories of Art* (London & New York: Routledge, 1988), pp. 50–90.

6 Pollock, *Vision and Difference*, p. 67.

7 Susan Buck-Morss, 'The Flâneur, the Sandwichman and the Whore: the Politics of Loitering', *New German Critique* 39 (Fall 1986): 105, 120.

8 Walter Benjamin, 'Central Park', introduction by Lloyd Spencer, *New German Critique* 34 (Winter 1985): 40. For related arguments, see Elizabeth Wilson, *The Sphinx in the City: Urban Life, the Control of Disorder, and Women* (Berkeley, CA and Los Angeles: University of California Press, 1991); Christine Buci-Glucksmann, 'Catastrophic Utopia: The Feminine as Allegory of the Modern', *Representations* 14 (Spring 1986): 220-9; and Laurie Teal, 'The Hollow Woman: Modernism, the Prostitute and Commodity Aesthetics', *Differences: A Journal of Feminist Cultural Studies* 7, no. 3 (1995): 80–108.

9 Andreas Huyssen, 'Mass Culture as Woman, Modernism's Other', in *Studies in Entertainment: Critical Approaches to Mass Culture*, ed. Tania Modleski (Bloomington and Indianapolis, IN: Indiana University Press, 1986).

10 Elizabeth Wilson has criticized Pollock and Wolff for accepting women's absence from the public as fact rather than ideology: Elizabeth Wilson, 'The Invisible Flâneur', *New Left Review* 191 (January–February 1992): 90–110, especially 104–5 and *Adorned in Dreams: Fashion and Modernity* (London: Virago, 1985), pp. 30–1. For a similar point, see Mica Nava, 'Modernity's Disavowal: Women, the City and the Department Store', in *Modern Times*, pp. 38–76; Anne Friedberg, *Window Shopping: Cinema and the Postmodern* (Berkeley, CA, Los Angeles and Oxford: University of California Press, 1993); Deborah Epstein Nord, *Walking the Victorian Streets: Women, Representation and the City* (Ithaca, NY and London: Cornell University Press, 1995); Judith R. Walkowitz, *City of Dreadful Delight: Narratives of Sexual Danger in Late-Victorian London* (Chicago: Chicago University Press, 1992); and Priscilla Parkhurst Ferguson, 'The Flâneur: Urbanization and its Discontents', in *Home and its Dislocations in Nineteenth Century France*, ed. Suzanne Nash (New York: State University of New York Press, 1993).

11 Nord, *Walking the Victorian Streets*, pp. 4, 117.

12 Rappaport, *Shopping for Pleasure*. On the history of English shopping, see Alison Adburgham, *Shops and Shopping: 1800–1914: Where and in What Manner the Well-Dressed Englishwoman Bought Her Clothes*, 2nd edn (London: Barrie & Jenkins, 1989); Dorothy Davis, *Fairs, Shops and Super-markets: A History of English Shopping* (Toronto: The University of Toronto Press, 1966); John Benson, *The Rise of Consumer Society in Britain, 1880–1980* (London: Longman, 1994), pp. 59–81; and Rachel Bowlby, *Just Looking: Consumer Culture in Dreiser, Gissing and Zola* (New York and London: Methuen, 1985). On department stores, see Bill Lancaster, *The Department Store: A Social History* (London and New York: Leicester University Press, 1995); Rudi Laermans, 'Learning to Consume: Early Department Stores and the Shaping of the Modern Consumer Culture (1860–1914)', *Theory, Culture and Society*, 10 (1993): 79–102; Gareth Shaw, 'The Evolution and Impact of Large-Scale Retailing in Britain' (pp. 135–65) and 'The European Scene: Britain and Germany' (pp. 17–34), both in *The Evolution of Retail Systems, c.1800–1914*, ed. John Benson and Gareth Shaw (Leicester: Leicester University Press, 1992); James B. Jefferys, *Retail Trading in Great Britain: 1850–1950* (Cambridge: Cambridge University Press, 1954); John William Ferry, *A History of the Department Store* (New York: Macmillan, 1960); and Hrandt Pasdermadjian, *The Department Store: Its Origins, Evolution, and Economics* (London: Newman Books, 1954). Also see Hamish Fraser, *The Coming of the Mass Market, 1850–1914* (Hamden, CT: Archon, 1981).

13 Charles Eyre Pascoe, *London of To-Day: An Illustrated Handbook for the Season* (Boston: Robert Brothers, 1885), p. 15.

14 *Modern London: The World's Metropolis, An Epitome of Results* (London: Historical Publishing Co., 1890), p. 82.

15 *Modern Business* 1 (February–July 1908): 1.

16 For Gordon Selfridge's promotion of commercial modernity to a mass, female market, see Erika D. Rappaport, '"A New Era of Shopping": The Promotion of Women's Pleasure in London's West End, 1909–1914', in *Cinema and the Invention of Modern Life*, ed. Leo Charney and Vanessa R. Schwartz (Berkeley, CA, Los Angeles and London: University of California Press, 1995): pp. 130–55. Nava also touches on Selfridge's in her essay, 'Modernity's Disavowal'.

17 See, for example, Arnold Bennett, *The Grand Babylon Hotel: A Fantasia on Modern Times* (London: Chatto and Windus, 1902) and *The City of Pleasure: A Fantasia on Modern Times* (London: Chatto and Windus, 1907).

18 Nava, 'Modernity's Disavowal'.

19 For the creation of places as tourist sights, see Dean MacCannel, *The Tourist: A New Theory of the Leisure Class* (New York: Schocken Books, 1976); and his most recent, *Consuming Places* (London and New York: Routledge, 1995); Gerry Kearns and Chris Philo, *Selling Places: The City as Cultural Capital, Past and Present* (Oxford and New York, Pergamon, 1993); *Marketing Tourism Places*, ed. Gregory Ashworth and Brian Goodall (London: Routledge, 1990); and G. H. Ashworth and J. E. Tunbridge, *The Tourist-Historic City* (London: Belhaven Press, 1990). For related studies, see John Urry, *The Tourist Gaze: Leisure and Travel in Contemporary Societies* (London: Sage Publications, 1990); and James Buzard, *The Beaten Track: European Tourism, Literature, and the Ways to Culture, 1800–1918* (Oxford: Clarendon, 1993). Also see P. D. Glennie and N. J. Thrift, 'Modernity, Urbanism and Modern Consumption', *Environment and Planning D: Society and Space* 10 (1992): 423–43.

20 On travel and the search for an authentic experience, see Erik Cohen, 'Authenticity and Commoditization in Tourism', *Annals of Tourism Research* 15 (1988): 371–86 and his 'The Tourist Guide: The Origins, Structure and Dynamics of a Role', *The Annals of Tourism Research* 12 (1985): 5–29 and Elizabeth C. Fine and Jean Haskell Speer, 'Tour Guide Performances as Sight Sacralization', *The Annals of Tourism Research* 12 (1985): 73–95.

21 Herbert Fry, *London*, 8th edn (London: W. H. Allen, 1888), preface.

22 On shopping, sightseeing, modernity and postmodernity, see Friedberg, *Window Shopping*.

23 Walkowitz, *City of Dreadful Delight*, p. 25.

24 Of course, as Antoinette Burton has recently suggested, such positions were not mutually exclusive: Antoinette Burton, *Burdens of History: British Feminists, Indian Women, and Imperial Culture, 1865–1915* (Chapel Hill, NC and London: University of North Carolina Press, 1994).

25 *Progress: The Organ of the Lady Guide Association* (1889–90): 2.

26 Among the many relevant sources on 'Englishness', see Robert Colls and Philip Dodd, *Englishness: Politics and Culture, 1880–1920* (London: Croom Helm, 1986); Brian Doyle, *England and Englishness* (London: Routledge, 1987); Eric Hobsbawm and Terence Ranger (eds), *The Invention of Tradition* (Cambridge: Cambridge University Press, 1983); Raphael Samuel (ed.), *Patriotism: The Making and Unmaking of British National Identity*, 3 vols, (London: Routledge, 1989); and Bill Schwarz (ed.), *The Expansion of England: Race, Ethnicity and Cultural History* (London: Routledge, 1996).

27 *Progress*: 2.

28 *Ward and Lock's Pictorial Guide to London* (London: Ward and Lock and Company, 1879), pp. 2–3.

29 *Progress*: 5.

30 *Progress*: 2.

31 *Progress*: 35.

32 *Queen*, 5 January 1889: 22.

33 See Chapters 1 and 3 of Rappaport, *Shopping for Pleasure*. See also Robert Thorne, 'Places of Refreshment in the Nineteenth Century City', in *Buildings and Society: Essays on the Social Development of the Built Environment*, ed. Anthony D. King (London: Routledge and Kegan Paul, 1980), pp. 228–53.

34 Alden Hatch, *American Express: A Century of Service, 1850–1950* (New York: Doubleday, 1950), pp. 100–1; Peter Grossman, *American Express: The Unofficial History of the People who Built the Great Financial Empire* (New York: Crown Publishers, 1987), p. 113. The American Rendezvous, at 2 Cockspur Street, was run by Charles Alvin Gillig. For a description of the business, see Gillig's annual guidebook, *Charles Alvin Gillig's London Guide*, 14th edn (London: Charles Alvin Gillig, 1900), pp. 53–4.

35 *Progress*: 3.

36 *Queen*, 12 July 1890: 74.

37 *Particulars, &c. of the Lady Guide Association, Ltd., The London and International Reception, Inquiry, Information, and Supply Bureau*, p. 71.

38 *The Woman's Gazette*, 1, no.5 (February 1876): 76.

39 *The Lady*, 5, 12, and 19 November 1885. See similar letters in *Queen* on 15 October 1892: 647; 6 October 1894: 601; 6 September 1896: 461; and 24 October 1896: 792.

40 See George Gissing's characterization of these groups in *The Odd Women* (1893; London: Penguin, 1983); David Rubinstein, *Before the Suffragettes: Women's Emancipation in the 1890s* (New York: St Martin's Press, 1986); and Lee Holcombe, *Victorian Ladies at Work: Working Women in England and Wales* (Hampden, CT: Archon, 1973).

41 *Progress*: 5.

42 *The Graphic*, reprinted in *Progress*: 9.

43 *Progress*: 22.

44 'The Lady Guide's Valentine', *The Lady*, 12 February 1891: 194.

45 *The Lady*, 12 February 1891: 195.

46 *The Lady*, 12 February 1891: 195.

47 *Daily Telegraph*, reprinted in *Progress*: 7–8.

48 Recorded by Arthur J. Munby, *Red Note-Books*, 1860–1, quoted in Francoise Barret-Ducrocq, *Love in the Time of Victoria: Sexuality, Class and Gender in Nineteenth-Century London* (London and New York: Verso, 1991), p. 52.

49 Walkowitz, *City of Dreadful Delight* and her recent essay, 'Going Public: Shopping, Street Harassment, and Streetwalking in Late Victorian London', *Representations*, no. 62 (Spring 1998): 1–30. On the sexual dynamics of the West End, also see Tracy Davis, *Actresses as Working Women: Their Social Identity in Victorian Culture* (London and New York: Routledge, 1991).

50 *The Spectator*, reprinted in *Progress*: 10.

51 *Daily Telegraph*, reprinted in *Progress*: 7–8.

52 In 1889 *The Lady* even blamed 'the American invasion from which Society is suffering' for 'the distinct and steady decline in the time-honoured office of a chaperon': *The Lady* 21 February 1889: 185.

53 Margaret Fletcher, *O, Call Back Yesterday* (Oxford: Basil Blackwell, 1939), pp. 114–15.

54 Dorothy Constance Peel, *Life's Enchanted Cup: An Autobiography (1872–1933)* (London: John Lane and the Bodley Head, 1933), pp. 62, 95.

55 *Queen*, 5 June 1882: 375.

56 *Daily Telegraph*, reprinted in *Progress*: 8.

57 'Shopping in London, Paris and New York', *Drapers' Record*, 16 November 1888: 575.

58 *Queen*, 14 July 1894: 89.

59 'The Lady Guides', *Queen*, 5 April 1902: 595. The exact date the Association closed its doors is unknown. In 1899 it was still in operation, but had moved to a single office at 20 Haymarket.

60 Darley Dale, 'Occupations for Women – The Lady Guide', *The Englishwoman*, 9 April 1899: 317.

61 See, for example, the *Manchester Guardian*'s article 'Shopping by Proxy: An American Idea', 25 October 1927 (Fawcett Library, Newspaper Cuttings, #381.2:331.4). Among the many new 'shopping guides', see *The West End Advertiser* (1891); *Shopping: A Journal of Society for Society* (July 1895); *Shopping: A Literary and Artistic Mirror of the World of Women* (August 1902); *The London & Suburban A.B.C. Shopping Guide* (March 1911); *Shopping Life: The Only Journal Which Makes a Direct Appeal to the Shopping Public* (November 1921–December 1924); *Shopping Notes and News* (December 1924–September 1926); *Olivia's Shopping and How She Does It: A Prejudiced*

Guide to the London Shops (London: Gay and Bird, 1906); Frances Sheafer Waxman, *A Shopping Guide to Paris and London* (New York: McBride, Nast, 1912) and Elizabeth Montizambert, *London Discoveries in Shops and Restaurants* (London: Women Publishers, 1924).

62 Later editions of Baedeker's London guide devote a great deal more space to shopping than earlier editions. By the 1902 edition there is a separate section, for example, on 'Shops, Bazaars, and Markets': Karl Baedeker, *London and Its Environs: Handbook for Travellers* (London: Dulau and Co., 1902).

63 *Evening News*, 17 May 1907: 3.

64 *PMG*, 24 May 1900: 11.

65 *PMG*, 10 May 1900: 10.

66 Georg Simmel, *The Sociology of George Simmel*, trans. and ed. Kurt H. Wolff (London, Collier-MacMillan, 1964), p. 410.

67 Simmel, *Sociology*, p. 412.

3

Advertising, the Modernist Aesthetic of the Marketplace? The Cultural Relationship Between the Tobacco Manufacturer and the 'Mass' of Consumers in Britain, 1870–1940

Matthew Hilton

In 1923, an article appearing in the *Paris Radical Daily* argued that modernity was symbolized through the act of smoking:

> *Priser* – the act of taking a dainty pinch of delicate powder between one's thumb and finger and placing it to one's nose – was a gesture of the *ancien régime*. *Fumer* – that is to say to puff a pipe, a cigar, or a cigarette – was typical of the *nouveau régime*. The snuffbox and the pipe . . . therefore transmit to us the sentiments of two epochs.

According to this passage, snuff-taking was regarded by French revolutionaries as aristocratic, effete and decadent. The pipe, however, was the 'asserter of modern ideas'. A political tract of 1832 encouraged men to light their 'Benjamin Constants' or their 'Lafayettes' to assert typical Enlightenment ideas: 'Smoke comrades; smoke, brothers and companions, in defence of our rights and liberties.' Such democratic ideals were not fully realized in nineteenth-century France, as the 'bourgeois-liberal' cigar triumphed over the pipe as the signifier of the new political order.[1]

One might apply a similar and admittedly flippant analysis to Britain, though with a slightly different categorization of modernity. While snuff-taking was also aristocratic and perhaps definitive of eighteenth-century society, the pipe and the cigar triumphed together in the nineteenth century with the rise and expansion of the middle classes. Just as in France, British 'sentiments' were symbolized by the pipe and the cigar, as a smoking culture emerged firmly rooted in a broader liberal ideal.[2] Smokers stressed the liberal virtues of independence and individuality in their consumption practices, and a highly segmented and specialist industry offered a diverse range of goods to cater for a wide variety of tastes. But the machine-made cigarette of the twentieth century represents yet another distinctive period in British history. Technologically-inspired improvements in large-scale production brought about 'the age of the masses': mass manufacture, mass consumption, the mass market and mass culture. The supposedly democratic and egalitarian twentieth century therefore made prominent the tobacco habit of the 'ordinary' man and woman: the Woodbine, Player's Medium, Craven 'A', Ogden's Tabs and the 'fag'. According to this analysis, then, tobacco's modernity was split into two distinct 'sentiments': the liberal culture of bourgeois individualists in the nineteenth century and the rationalist economic structures of the perceived homogeneous mass of individuals in the twentieth. How does such a historical periodization fit in with other definitions of modernity?

Modernity has been frequently seen as paradoxical, in that it encapsulates on the one hand the ephemeral, the transient, the fleeting and the fragmented and, on the other, the rational, the immutable and the eternal. The modernist project, from the Enlightenment onwards, has been to make sense of this fragmentation, to place order on the world and to direct the ephemeral needs and desires of society according to one particular logical plan.[3] While many of these ideas have appeared idealistic and utopian, seeking to create a new society wholly divorced from the structures of the present, the focus in this chapter is on the possibility of a utopia created from within the existing society. It is an account of the vision and modernity of the mass manufacturer and the extent to which it attempted to create logical order out of a diversified and segmented economy.

The idea of tobacco, or more specifically cigarette, manufacturers as modernists works if one understands the efforts to create a mass demand for their products as a capitalist utopian vision. They regarded the perceived virtues of the mass market as the underlying truth of the modern epoch, an immutable entity around which society should be structured. Observing the fragmented and apparently ephemeral desires of the mass of consumers in the late nineteenth and early twentieth centuries, British companies sought to place order on the act of consumption, to direct as many purchasing decisions as possible to their firms' commodities. The principal medium through which this was attempted was the advertisement, whether on a billboard, in a newspaper or on the actual brand's packaging. The advertisement became the icon of the twentieth century, the most persistent element in the visual culture of the vast majority of the population. It utilized imagery and copy that tried to bring all, or as many consumers as possible, under the umbrella of the commodity. In this sense, the advertisement served as the visible emblem of modernity just as much as did the aesthetic creation or the political ensign.

This is not, of course, to suggest that mass manufacturers were successful in realizing their vision or, more specifically, in controlling the purchasing decisions of the nation's populace. There is an extensive literature debating the effectiveness of advertising in influencing consumer behaviour, and one must remember that 'there are in fact no masses; there are only ways of seeing people as masses'.[4] An assessment of the extent to which consumers actually behaved as a homogeneous mass will therefore not be made in this chapter. What this chapter will show is the importance of the economic in directing the cultural formations of modernity, of how the mass, second stage of modernity owes as much to the manufacturer as it does to the works of aesthetic and intellectual elites. Here, the chapter borrows heavily from an American literature on 'modernist' advertising in the interwar period, a time when many companies deliberately referred to a future consumer utopia realizable through the purchase of the products of commodity capitalism. The literature on British advertising in this period is currently sparse, and this chapter acts as a test of applicability to the British context, in what is admittedly only a single-product case-study. It will do this by first examining tobacco advertising in the nineteenth century, demonstrating its accordance with liberal perceptions of masculinity, and then by detailing the various ways in which manufacturers' advertising attempted to create a mass market for the new machine-produced cigarette from the 1880s onwards.

Although the *Paris Daily Radical* asserted that the 'bourgeois-liberal' cigar eventually triumphed over the radical enlightened pipe, in Britain, by the end of the nineteenth century, the cigar and the pipe were smoked harmoniously together in the London clubs and drawing rooms of a bourgeois elite. In liberal politics and culture, independence and individuality were reified into ideals applicable to all walks of life, from self-help, evangelical Protestantism, and Free Trade, to social reform and economic principles about the rational utility maximizer. A particular smoking culture, propagated through the pages of the Victorian periodical literature, was also very much a part of this wider liberal framework. Individual taste was held to exist beyond any homogenizing influence of mass demand and to be independent of the influence or dictates of fashion. Such diversity was aided by a nineteenth-century economy still segmented by many criteria. Manufacturers had to cater to a market divided by region, class, and individual preference, a reality facilitated through the existence of specialist tobacconists who knew how to respond to local tastes and customs. Individualism was best expressed when a consumer could rely on his local tobacconist to mix his favourite type of tobacco, blended from a number of loose tobaccos supplied by the manufacturer, who had not yet sought to control distribution through branding and pre-packaging, the essential pre-requisites for the development of the mass market.[5]

Of the branding that did occur, manufacturers, rather than hoping for one product to appeal to all, had to recognize a variety of consumption patterns. The very names that they chose for pipe tobaccos had to reflect the different tastes that existed. Brand titles were chosen to stress the sweetness of the smoke (Honeycomb, Sweet as a Rose, Sweet Briar, Sunflower, Wild Geranium), its richness of flavour (Gold Leaf, Golden Iris, Golden Cut, Golden Harvest), or its aristocracy or wealthy urbanism (House of Commons, Mayfair, Piccadilly, Old Nobility).[6] Of crucial importance was the range available. A typical example is found in an 1887 advertisement by John Hunter, by no means a large-scale importer and manufacturer of cigars, which listed the twenty-seven types of Havana cigar he sold, the six Mexican and the nineteen British.[7] The manufacturer had to display all his wares, leaving the customer to select the cigar that met his taste, which clearly he himself knew best. Similarly, most pipe tobacco advertisements featured several brands, with some indicator following each name as to its taste or intended market. For instance, Cope Brothers of Liverpool segmented the pipe tobacco market into Cut Cavendish for 'hardy working men, soldiers and sailors', London Shag for 'metropolitans', Tobacco de Luxe for the upper classes, and for the middle-price range there were a number of different tastes: Golden Magnet ('sweetly soothing'), Faust ('delicately fragrant'), Peerless ('exquisitely mild'), and Yankee Pride ('purifies the breath and annihilates the microbe').[8] The differences in design mapped on to the differences in society, arguably to the extent that 'the entire range of manufactured goods constituted a representation of society'.[9]

Cope's also promoted the idea of the tobacco purchaser as a discerning, individualistic 'connoisseur', as opposed to the supposedly more passive 'consumer'. It actively reinforced that general devotion to 'the weed' prevalent in late-nineteenth-century periodicals, but best summarized in J. M. Barrie's eulogy to *My Lady Nicotine*.[10] In the 1870s, Cope's, through their resident artist 'Pipeshank', produced a range of advertisements that featured caricatures of famous literary, cultural, and political figures of the day. They received much favourable attention in the press, which praised Cope's for introducing art into the world of commerce.[11] A series of golfing pictures were produced that humorously portrayed leading politicians, and pictures such as 'The Pursuit of Diva Nicotina', based on an original painting – Sir Noel Paton's 'The Pursuit of Pleasure' – featured nearly thirty caricatures (Figure 3.1). Cope's published accompanying key plates for these advertisements, so that potential smokers could identify figures such as William Morris, Canon Farrar, Lord Lytton, Lily Langtry, Sir Stafford Northcote, Bismarck, and the Emperor of Austria. Trampled underfoot were the anti-tobacco figures of the Revd John Kirk, Dr C. R. Drysdale and Professor F. W. Newman. Above, in the clouds, flew the 'denouncer of doom' with his umbrella of cant, 'livid with impotent spite and envy, utterly unheeded by the ardent votaries in ecstatic pursuit of our most gracious and glorious DIVA NICOTINA'.[12] Other advertisements featured a similar range of real and fictional caricatures collected together 'for the seaside', 'for the holidays', and 'for the tourists'.

The point is that the smoker is assumed to be a man of leisure and sophistication who not only has the time to pore over these cluttered images, but the wit to understand the amusing references. Cope's took the ideal further, publishing between March 1870 and January 1881 its own journal, *Cope's Tobacco Plant*, which has subsequently been described as a distinctive and peculiar piece of Victorian journalism, since it was both part of the trade press and a 'very respectable

Figure 3.1 The pursuit of Diva Nicotina, 1879.

literary journal'.[13] It devoted itself to 'Tobacco; all about Tobacco, and nothing but Tobacco' and, priced at only twopence, the journal obtained a wide readership and a favourable reception in the press.[14] From 1889 to 1894 many of the articles were reworked and published in fourteen issues of *Cope's Smoke Room Booklets*, which concentrated on such topics as the contributions of James Thomson to the original *Cope's Tobacco Plant*, extracts from the literary figures of Lamb, Carlyle and Ruskin, and various collections of poetry that eulogized tobacco and smoking.[15] All this served to instil in smokers a sense of identity as a particular class or 'cult' of society, a group identity principally constructed in reference to the anti-smokers, that body of Temperance radicals who organized themselves in several anti-tobacco societies from as early as 1854.[16] While eulogizing tobacco on one page, *Cope's Tobacco Plant* would elsewhere exaggerate the influence and crankiness of the Anti-Tobacco Society in order for smokers to defend themselves as a group. A 'them and us' rhetoric was deployed, which then shifted to ridicule to maintain a sense of superiority over the 'humbug' philanthropists.[17]

The smoker, then, as depicted by Cope's promotional material, was a distinct being in society with a set of interests that needed defending. But he was also a cultivated and leisured gentleman who had time to read and reflect on lengthy articles devoted to his habit. The publications were for the pipe-smoker, ideally sitting in an armchair, at home, or in a gentleman's smoking room. Each smoker had his favourite pipe, his special tobacco and his own idiosyncrasies in his smoking habit. It was an image of the smoker that fitted well with the liberal bourgeois's perception of himself and it was an image of tobacco far distant from the quick-to-smoke, homogeneous cigarette that was to be heavily promoted to the masses in the twentieth century.

While the individualistic culture of pipe and cigar smoking would survive well into the twentieth century and, indeed, continues even today, it was the advertising for the cigarette that would come to predominate in the budgets of the tobacco manufacturers. By the end of the First World War, over half the sales of tobacco would be in the form of cigarettes,[18] a rapid rise given that cigarettes only came to be machine-made following the installation of the Bonsack cigarette-making machine by W. D. & H. O. Wills of Bristol in 1884.[19] The introduction of new technology in the manufacture of a product previously only consumed by those who could afford the expensive hand-rolled varieties was typical of the rationalization of production and the application of scientific methods associated with the 'Second Industrial Revolution'.[20] The Bonsack machine enabled Wills not only to sell cigarettes at the remarkably cheap price of five for one penny, but to dominate the market and maintain what appeared an unassailable lead over its principal rivals: Lambert & Butler; Gallaher; Cope's; Ogden's; John Player & Sons; and, later, Carreras. When the Imperial Tobacco Company was formed by thirteen of Britain's leading manufacturers in 1901 in response to American Tobacco's invasion of the British market, Wills dominated the new monopoly organization. Imperial now possessed both the machinery and the financial ability to bring in the mass market.[21]

At a time when explicitly modernist artists began to depict utopian futures emerging out of this mechanical age, mass manufacturers also began to translate the technological rationality that produced the highly standardized white cylindrical cigarette, into a social goal.[22] The profits from the economies of scale generated by the new machinery could only be realized if the firm obtained a sufficiently sized market for its products. The principal means of achieving this was through making the firm's advertisement reach a wider audience, either by entering new regions or creating new consumers. Customers, shopping at local stores, had to be transformed into consumers, ready to purchase the new mass-produced goods available nationally.[23] The public had to be educated by the elite of business leaders to the new mass market environment. The position was bluntly expressed by the American department store owner Edward Filene: 'mass production demands the education of the masses . . . masses must learn to behave like human beings in a mass production world.'[24] Economic modernists had to take their advertising images to the general public in order to enrol them into their social vision of mass consumption.[25] Certainly, the attempt to create a mass demand was deliberate; but whether such economic modernists were aware of the broader implications of their activities is less likely. Belligerent US entrepreneurs have become famous for their 'progressive' philosophical slogans about the future potentialities of the market and the irrelevance of the past; but relatively few explicit statements exist in British commercial history. The aggressive marketing strategies and overt attempts at self-promotion by such US businessmen as Gordon Selfridge (of the Oxford Street store) in 1909 and James Buchanan Duke (of the American Tobacco Company) in 1901 stand more as anomalies than as exemplars of British advertising culture. What follows, then, is an analysis that takes the meaning of a mass advertisement as implicit rather than as a visible signifier of an explicit and vocalized commercial environment.

Of course, advertising was not the only means with which tobacco companies sought to create as wide a demand as possible for their product. Throughout the twentieth century coupons were issued, cigarette cards were used since the 1890s, and competitions and publicity stunts were run that involved the collection of empty carton hulls.[26] In addition, firms operated extensive market research schemes, which involved such practices as regularly listening to travelling salesmen's assessments of local markets, the study of press circulations, and the detailed breakdown of sales statistics. And the tobacco industry in particular, owing to Imperial Tobacco's near monopoly, maintained extensive and complicated distribution and price maintenance agreements with retailers and wholesalers to ensure the supply of Imperial products across the country.[27] But the public face of the manufacturers, the means through which they communicated with the mass of consumers and attempted to direct their purchasing decisions, was advertising, the modernist aesthetic of the marketplace.

Four stages have been identified in the history of marketing. The first was the style appropriate to the fragmented Victorian economy, and the second one of 'unification', or mass marketing. The transitional decade was the 1880s, though many of the advertising styles described above persisted well into the twentieth century.[28] The mass advertising described below, therefore, represents a dominant trend, rather than a definitive assessment. But what this new advertising consisted of was the use of lowest common denominators: that is, images either so uncontroversial that they could not offend any particular segment of the market, or that used references so culturally conservative that the advertisements had the potential to appeal to all. This is an argument expounded at length by both Thomas Richards and Lori Ann Loeb, both of whom point to images related to empire, patriotism, monarchy, and the consumer's own body as means by which mass manufacturers attempted to appeal to the largest potential mass of consumers.[29] Some further periodization is perhaps required in the history of tobacco and cigarette advertising, however, as there was a tendency in the late nineteenth and very early twentieth century to use images that celebrated Britain's romantic past, while by the interwar years there was a discernible embrace of the potential of the future, or at least a borrowing of typical aesthetic modernist iconography.

Many advertisements of the late nineteenth century featured the Queen or celebrated some aspect of the aristocracy, institutions that were central to British national identity. Often figures were depicted in period costume – frequently Georgian or classical – in order to lend a solidity to the product, to root the commodity in a sense of Britain's (and possibly the world's) heritage. Such images were common in pipe tobacco advertising, which relied very much on the iconography of national identity. A survey of 190 tobacco names listed in *Tobacco Trade Review* in 1901 shows the extent to which the past played a significant role, thirteen of the brand names actually using the word 'old' in their title. A further thirteen made specific reference to the military (though most companies had a type of 'Navy Cut') and thirty-six referred to a particular aspect of Britain's heritage or to an old institution, such as the aristocracy or some public monument. Typical brand names here, which frequently appeared alongside an appropriate accompanying image, included Master of Foxhounds Mixture, Big Ben, May Fair, Exmoor Hunt, Nation's Pride and Royal Salute. While thirty took their names from the product's origins in America (for example, Golden Virginia), another thirty-five rooted themselves in the British countryside (Double Daffodil, British Oak, Honey Cut, Sweet as the Rose, Marigold).[30]

Many of these themes would be taken up in the advertising for cigarettes, Woodbine being the most popular brand up until the interwar period. More often, a successful pipe tobacco brand name would be used to sell a new cigarette, Player's Country Life and Roll Call being prominent examples. Cigarette card series were also regularly based upon themes related to empire, the monarchy and the military.[31] The naval image persisted in cigarette branding and advertising, with most companies issuing a Navy Cut cigarette, though Player's was to become the most famous. The naval image served a dual purpose, in that it both denoted a popular cultural smoking tradition and connoted one of national pride. The sailor embodied Britishness, and could therefore appeal to the entire population of the country's (at that time male) smokers. The military theme was particularly emphasized during the war, as it brought British traditions up to date. If the references in tobacco advertising to Britain's glorious military and naval past were becoming out of date by 1914, they could be brought right into the present because of the mass nature of the new 'Total War'. In the First World War, although the Woodbine was held to be 'Tommy's favourite fag',[32] Player's Roll Call made use of the Tommy Atkins metaphor to give the cigarette its broadest possible appeal.[33] The 'Tommy' was the ultimate mass man: his identity and individuality were subsumed under the need for a homogeneous image to which the greatest possible number of people could attach their affections and their patriotism. But the use of Tommy in advertising was indicative of a change in promotional style. For whereas military images rooted in the past enabled the individual consumer to reflect on his own identity and note an affinity with the product, the military Tommy was often portrayed as though his whole existence in the war depended on the supply of a particular brand of cigarette: 'Indeed, all these advertisements have one thing in common: the soldiers sealed off in them are treated as if they no longer matter, as if what happened to them hinged on the brand of tobacco they smoked, as if they were not active human agents but rather passive instruments of the goods they consumed.'[34]

This passivity of Tommy, weighed down under the might of the commodity (Figure 3.2), is typical of a new type of representation in advertising that occurred around the turn of the century and that positioned the product in the present, rather than the past. The older Victorian form of advertising attempted to take the product

Figure 3.2 A lesson in English, Smith's advertisement, *c*.1914.

to the consumer by highlighting those of its properties that would suit an individual's taste; but, increasingly, the product now began to feature on its own, detaching itself from any group of consumers. Frequently, the product would be given its own distinctive personality, so that it now held the individuality towards which the mass of consumers (if the advertisement succeeded) would be attracted. The most vigorously presented image of this kind in tobacco advertising in the first two decades of the twentieth century was Carreras' Black Cat, who promoted cigarettes of that name (Figure 3.3). The style would be copied well into the interwar period, with Wills creating Mr Gold and Mr Flake for their Gold Flake cigarettes and Gallaher introducing Sir Park Drive, C.I.G.[35] The trend was typical for the period: a monkey could be found advertising Monkey Brand Soap; the cleaning agent Vim changed into Vimmy; photography had its Kodak Girl; and, more permanently, tyres were advertised by the Michelin Man.[36] To search for meaning or value in these images is, in a certain sense, to miss the point. They were pure gimmicks, but gimmicks devoid of as much significance as possible. They gave the commodity a character that made it autonomous from the consumer.[37] The cigarette then stood beyond all consumers, as the lack of meaning in the image could not attach it to a particular segment of the market. And precisely because the face value of the image was associated with no class of consumer, it therefore had the potential to appeal to as many smokers and non-smokers as possible.

Often, these commodity animations would be involved in an amusing story, humour frequently being employed as another means to unite consumers behind a product. In the cigarette trade, Ogden's led the way, running a series of cartoons in 1901 at the height of the Anglo-American 'Tobacco War'.[38] But by far the most pervasive style of advertising across all commodities was that which referred to the body. Developments in late-nineteenth-century patent medicine advertising arguably created a culture that gave constant attention to the needs of the body and encouraged anxieties about all aspects of the physical self.[39] The patent medicine style soon pervaded other forms of advertising, leading to a general emphasis on health. Lifebuoy soap was the 'children's friend' because it left them in an 'atmosphere of radiant health'[40] and Oxo threw off 'the ill effects of foggy, chilly weather'.[41] By the 1920s and 1930s health issues dominated advertising. Even cigarettes were included in this trend, despite the continued popular usage of such phrases as 'coffin-nails' and 'smoker's heart'. Most famously, Carreras claimed on every packet of its Craven 'A' that the cork-tipped cigarette was 'made specially to prevent sore throats'. Kensitas made the links with health in a less defensive way. In 1930, and borrowing from the Lucky Strike advertising campaigns in the US, they ran a series of advertisements that warned people against over-eating. In one, they pictured a cricketer with a dark shadow in which he has a large stomach and double chin. The copy ran as follows:

Figure 3.3 Black Cat, Carreras advertisement, *c*.1910s.

Trim! Fit! Active! KENSITAS will help to avoid that future shadow. Men prize the hard firm lines of the figure of fitness. They realise the harm of over-indulgence – eating between meals which causes excess weight. Active men decline to lose the invigorating glow of energy by undergoing harsh dieting and drastic reducing – methods condemned by the medical profession. They accept the guidance of MODERATION which advocates sensible nourishment and no excess, even in smoking. They eat healthfully but not immoderately. When tempted to over-indulge – to eat between meals, they say, **"No thanks, I'll smoke a Kensitas instead."**[42]

More generally, advertising began to promote the healthy lifestyle to the extent that it appeared as a general utopian vision; commodity culture could lead to a new, active healthy world. Various cigarettes came to be associated with leisure, Greys with a series of outdoor activities such as ice hockey (with contestants smoking in action) and Turf with the more democratic spectator sports, especially racing and football.[43] But Player's were the tobacco company that most frequently linked smoking to leisure and the healthy outdoors. As the copy for one advert ran, 'Whatever the pleasure, Players complete it',[44] the images in the others of the same series clearly asserting that a healthy lifestyle was incomplete without a cigarette.

If health could symbolize the bright future that lay ahead through commodity consumption, then other symbols made more explicit reference to a modernist project. Wills's Main Line cigarettes were always featured with a train bursting forward into the modern age, the train in advertising representing 'constant movement, change, the ability to transport the individual from one situation to another'.[45] Other symbols of aesthetic modernism, such as cars and aeroplanes, also featured prominently in interwar advertising. And modernism's standardized plain primary-coloured surfaces found their way into brand packaging, as with Craven 'A', and in the white backgrounds of large advertisements that served to make more prominent the pictured packet of cigarettes. Figure 3.4 contrasts the new style of Craven 'A' with the other design of Woodbine. As Patricia Johnston has argued of American advertising, modernism's attention to sharp contrast and oblique perspective were utilized to stress a commodity's progressive newness, its essential 'modernity' (Figure 3.5).[46]

It has been argued of British design that there was an 'English compromise' in which elements of the past, the present and the future were all brought together in one image. Paul Greenhalgh suggests that consumers and designers of the decorative arts in Britain at the turn of the century began to seek solace from the upheaval of the modern world by turning to the past. By the interwar period, design thus combined both the old and the new so that, for example, traditional national identity might be laid out according to modernist principles of representation.[47] One might expect advertising to have been influenced much less by the past, as the future might have been embraced more emphatically to celebrate the innovatory

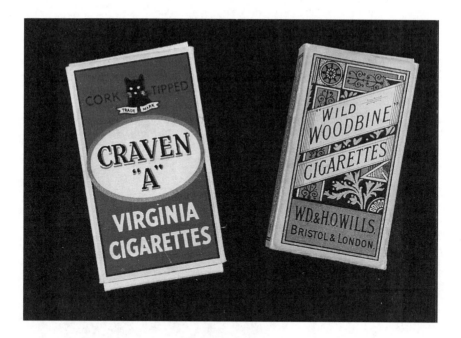

Figure 3.4 Packets of Craven A and Woodbine, *c.*1930s.

nature of products. This has been demonstrated to have been the case in America; but the British context is slightly different. It is not that there was a deliberate compromise in cigarette advertising styles; it is more that British modernity in these images simply was always a combination of the past and the future. Indeed, it is this intrinsic interweaving of the two that had the potential to give British commercial advertising's modernism its strength. Images referring to the future were made safe if rooted in the past, and capitalism's consumerist utopia could be depicted as essentially British as well as as a perfectly natural and normal progressive development from the present.

The most prominent example of this trend in advertising is the Player's Sailor. First used in 1883, the lifebuoy being added in 1888, 'Hero' appeared young and old, bearded and clean-shaven, until his image was standardized in 1927 with a design first used in 1905 (Figure 3.6).[48] His original conception, in referring to the national naval heritage, owed much to that late Victorian practice of drawing on traditional symbols of the British past to solidify the image of a new product. By the interwar period, however, he increasingly appeared in a more modernist setting, his image being fixed against a clean white background or positioned alongside other pictures, such as those of young people enjoying healthy exercise. The old was therefore inseparable from the new, opening up the appeal of Hero to new groups of consumers. Indeed, this seems to have been demonstrably the case,

Figure 3.5 Sales still going up, Gallaher Park Drive advertisement, 1931.

as Player's became something of an androgynous cigarette, unlike the other two leading brands, Craven A and Woodbine, which in practice maintained strongly gendered associations. The modernist elements of Player's advertising opened the product to mass consumption, while the sailor epitomized a dominant notion of British masculinity, yet one that had sufficient maturity to represent something of

Figure 3.6 Hero, standard logo of the Player's branch of Imperial Tobacco.

an uncle figure for potential women smokers.[49] If the combination of these elements was unintentional, it held implicit meanings that became increasingly obvious the more sophisticated advertising creation became. A 1960 *Guardian* article was able to point to the potential effectiveness of youthful representations surrounding the 'familiar bearded sailor'.[50] The accompanying slogan, 'Player's Please' (almost always alongside the picture of Hero), was alliterative, memorable, and geared for the point-of-sale transaction, and the activity it suggested for the consumer was potentially inclusive of the entire mass market. The image and the adage were repeated in the advertising for most of Player's leading brands, to the extent that brands no longer had to be mentioned. The huge commercial success of Player's in the interwar years has been largely attributed to this image, and Wills struggled constantly to create a comparable all-embracing promotional image.[51]

In all the above examples the manufacturer as economic modernist used the advertisement to communicate directly to the mass of consumers and to embrace as many people as possible around the commodity. In this sense, the manufacturer positions himself as part of an elite, somehow physically above the marketplace. This is never shown more clearly than in the language of the mass that business leaders employed in their advertisements and other publications. Newspapers' titles, such as *The People* and *News of the World*, made it clear for how many readers they could cater, and certain retailers, most obviously Universal Provider, used trading names that showed their intended customer base.

In the rhetoric of advertising, the 'world', the 'universe' and 'everybody' featured regularly. In 1932, Wills claimed its Capstan brand 'suit[ed] everyone',[52] while much earlier Ogden's boasted that its Guinea Gold cigarettes had the 'largest sale in the world'.[53] The image of the world was even used in its advertisement to express the 'universal' nature of their sales. In a 1901 image, the globe is the home of the mass of consumers, whereas Ogden's, and its products, reside in the clouds above, paternalistically looking down on the world of consumption (Figure 3.7). This mass base was not confined to tobacco products. Hudson's soap was 'for the people',[54] Peter's Milk Chocolate was 'sold everywhere',[55] 'thousands of families' used Beecham's Pills,[56] and a variety of baking powders, cocoas, chocolates, patent medicines and other common household goods claimed to have 'world-wide popularity'.[57] The language of the many, the world, the universal, the mass, pervades the advertising that can be found in the popular press and periodicals from the turn of the century. A development of this was to show the variety of situations in which the consumer could use a product. Advertisements for Wills's Gold Flake in 1935 asked if 'you' smoke 'in bed', 'when you are busy', 'in your bath', 'to relax', 'to think', 'when you're worried' and in a variety of other moods and situations.[58] A year later, Wills's Star cigarettes were shown, with corresponding pictures, 'between the dances', 'before you turn in', 'between the acts' and 'before supper's served' because, 'There's always time for a Star.'[59] Not only did the manufacturers hope that the cigarette would permeate as much geographical space as possible within the marketplace; they also hoped to penetrate further into the temporal space of each particular smoker.

At the same time as attempting to create the mass, advertisers also identified the individual within it. D. L. LeMahieu refers to the 'paradox of mass communication', in which the most effective strategy adopted by the mass media, cinema and radio in communicating with millions of individuals was to adopt a style that was 'intimate, personal and subjective'.[60] The same style was adopted in advertising, as frequent references were made to the personal: 'You smoke a good cigarette for pleasure alone, it satisfies you . . .'.[61] The consumer was both an individual and a part of the mass. In a 1932 advertisement for Gallaher's Park Drive, there is a clear celebration of the mass, a statement that the huge crowd of

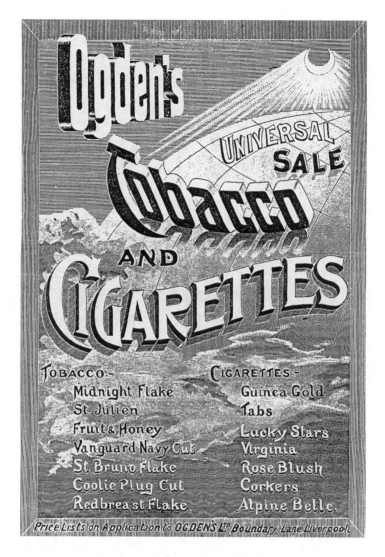

Figure 3.7 Universal sale, Ogden's advertisement, 1901.

football fans are all potential Park Drive smokers: 'The crowd in the advertisement, far from symbolising urban alienation, represents a community of consumers' (Figure 3.8).[62] But in the bottom left corner of the mass, a spotlight focuses on just a few members of the crowd. This seems to highlight the individual in the mass, recognizing his existence but at the same time demonstrating his relationship with the collectivity of Park Drive smokers. Again, the light shining on the crowd has as its source the manufacturer, Gallaher, looking down as the only true rational individual upon the mass of consumers below.

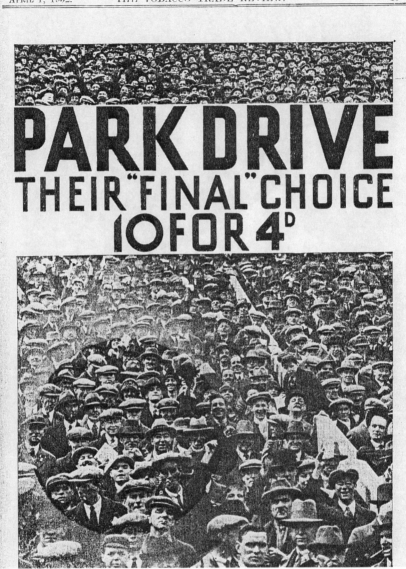

Figure 3.8 Their 'final' choice, Gallaher Park Drive advertisement, 1932.

However, there are a number of important qualifications to be made. Some market segmentation did continue to take place, and manufacturers were never able to create a truly 'universal' cigarette. The creation of a mass through advertising was an ideal; the masses as perceived did not always behave as each company's advertising sought to direct them. Consequently, there are numerous points at which manufacturers had to take into account the actual consumption patterns occurring in the marketplace. In particular, local and traditional markets continued to exist, often based around a form of employment. Wills were therefore still supplying chewing tobaccos to South Wales miners (it was permitted on the job) in the 1960s, and their Press and Poster Committee constantly discussed regional variations. An analysis of sales in 1930 led the Committee to restrict advertising for Bulwark Cut Plug (a dark solid tobacco) to certain rural and heavy industrial areas.[63] Later, to take just one of many examples, Capstan's provincial press advertising was concentrated on Scotland and the North of England except for a number of ports in the South.[64] Such examples also raise the question of class differences. These allowed Capstan to be advertised in the most popular press; but Three Castles cigarettes, also manufactured by Wills, were pushed rather in the 'quality' papers, such as *The Times* and the *Telegraph*.[65] In 1930, it was further decided by Wills to use a certain amount of copy in the Gold Flake advertising that was to be placed in the 'quality' papers, though a more direct message was required for the readers of 'ordinary' papers.[66]

Just as class and region continued to play a role in the mass market, so too did conceptions of femininity and masculinity, with perhaps only Player's Medium being a truly androgynous cigarette. Although women smoked for a variety of reasons beyond the pressures of advertising, there was nevertheless a deliberate attempt to appeal directly to women in the 1920s and 1930s. Craven 'A' became a particularly feminine smoke, and Carreras had to make considerable efforts to overcome this stereotype.[67] Many cigarettes also remained essentially masculine in their associations. Despite the advertising to women by Player's Weights, the cheap cigarette range (Wills's Woodbines, Carreras' Clubs, Gallaher's Park Drive, sold at five for one penny before the First World War and at twopence until 1939) was mainly seen as masculine. Indeed, there is a celebration of the male working class in Woodbine's advertising, and Carreras mobilized the concept of mass masculinity with a 1932 advertisement for Clubs that featured the following endorsement from Alex Jackson, the Chelsea Captain and Scottish football international: 'I fully agree with Alex James that CLUBS is a 'he-mans' cigarette – a small smoke with a big kick and certainly no penalties – in fact the best at its price I have ever smoked and I know good cigarettes.'[68]

The mass was also constructed as a given, enabling other cigarettes in the middle price-range (10 for 3d. before the First World War and 10 for 6d. after: that is, although not the cheapest, they were still affordable on a mass basis) to step rhetorically outside it, offering instead a cigarette that allowed ordinary smokers to enter the world of the 'real' smoker, the direct descendant of the Victorian bourgeois male. De Reszke advertisements appealed to the 'educated palate . . . – the cigarette for the few'.[69] Calling itself the 'aristocrat of cigarettes', De Reszke informed their potential customers that:

The secret of pleasurable smoking lies in the fragrant aroma of pure, properly matured tobacco leaf and the subtleties of skilful blending, which are qualities exclusive to the good cigarette. You smoke a good cigarette for pleasure alone, it satisfies you, and therefore you smoke in moderation. That is why a good cigarette is more economical than a 'gasper'.[70]

De Reszke cigarettes were not expensive (ten for 6d.) and there was no financial reason why they should not be a part of that mass from which they tried to distinguish themselves. Yet they appealed directly to the emulative tendencies within the market, and were mirrored by the similarly priced cigarettes of Sarony ('above the usual standard') and Greys (the 'gentleman in the 10 for 6d. cigarette world').[71]

But, besides these qualifications, one can discern an attempt by many large-scale manufacturers to create as wide a market as possible for their products, which, collectively, served to modify the language of the mass.[72] In this project they acted as a type of modernist, or an economically motivated version of a Leavisite 'minority culture', attempting to shape individuals' lives according to a master plan. Their technological innovations and marketing developments not only mirrored the broader modernist project, but actually served to direct the cultural formations of various artistic and intellectual elites, in the same way that Frederic Jameson has argued that the decentred nature of multinational capitalism has shaped the cultural developments within postmodernity.[73] The rise of the mass market provoked numerous cultural reactions, with some individuals celebrating the political and social potential that the machine could bring about if channelled into appropriate areas, and others panicking against the homogeneous conformity it was perceived to instil in the general population. Both reactions, though, positioned the masses below, with the cultural commentator raised, metaphorically, above.

As Marshall Berman has argued, many of these twentieth-century radical modernists sought to create an elitist vanguard that could step outside modernity and lead society to a new utopia. Their mistake, according to Berman, was not to look to the internal dynamism of modernity – as Marx did – which could in itself promote change.[74] Thus modernist projects failed, most dramatically in the architectural styles of figures such as Le Corbusier, who offered grandiose schemes for urban regenerations that tragically took little account of the existing society (and its population) from which they emerged.[75] The economic modernists of monopoly capitalism, however, offered no such alternative vision of society. The rational goal at which they aimed existed very much in the capitalist world in which they found themselves in the late nineteenth century. The world of the commodity that their advertising promoted was a world that had arguably existed since the eighteenth century, at least for certain sections of the population. They merely extended the economic structures they found themselves in, but, because of certain technological and financial developments, were able to form a capitalist vanguard, speeding up the economic processes of the nineteenth century and creating a greater division between producer and consumer.

Together, the thousands of advertisements issued by Wills, Carreras, Players and Gallaher all attempted to create a nation-wide community of smokers with as many individuals as possible, according to the economic interests of each particular manufacturer, smoking the same brand of tobacco or cigarette. It has not been the concern of this chapter to demonstrate the success or otherwise of the manufacturers' attempt to mould the mass market. Rather, it has been to argue that the tobacco advertisement was the image of modernity presented to ordinary men and women in their everyday lives. In this sense, then, advertising was and is the modernist aesthetic of social history.

Notes

1 Anon [Historicus], 'Pipes and politics', translated and republished in *Living Age*, 323, 11 October 1923, pp. 98–100.
2 These ideas are explored at greater length in M. Hilton, *Smoking in British Popular Culture, 1800–2000* (Manchester: Manchester UP, 2000).
3 D. Harvey, *The Condition of Postmodernity: An Enquiry into the Origins of Cultural Change* (Oxford: Blackwell, 1989); M. Horkheimer and T. Adorno, 'The Culture Industry: Enlightenment as Mass Deception', in *Dialectic of Enlightenment* (London: Allen Lane, 1973), pp. 120–67; M. Berman, *All That Is Solid Melts into Air: The Experience of Modernity* (London: Verso, 1983); J. Habermas, 'Modernity: An Incomplete Project', in H. Foster (ed.), *Postmodern Culture* (London: Pluto Press, 1985), pp. 3–15.
4 R. Williams, *Culture and Society, 1780–1950* (London: Chatto & Windus, 1967), p. 300. Williams further points out that 'To other people, we also are masses. Masses are other people.'
5 M. Hilton, 'Retailing History as Economic and Cultural History: Strategies of Survival by Specialist Tobacconists in the Mass Market', *Business History*, 40 (1998): 115–37.
6 The names were obtained from the price lists collected and filed in the Bristol Record Office: W. D. & H. O. Wills archive (hereafter Wills), 38169/Pr/i/a, *Pricing records*.
7 *Tobacco Trade Review* (hereafter *TTR*), 20(233) (May 1887): v.
8 A. V. Seaton, 'Cope's and the Promotion of Tobacco in Victorian England', *Journal of Advertising History*, 9:2 (1986): 5–26.
9 A. Forty, *Objects of Desire: Design and Society 1750–1980* (London: Thames & Hudson, 1986), pp. 62–3.

10 J. M. Barrie, *My Lady Nicotine* (London: Hodder & Stoughton edn, 1902).

11 The Papers of John Fraser, University of Liverpool Special Collections (hereafter Fraser), 680.

12 Fraser, 1105. See also the unpublished MA dissertation held at the Fraser collection: S. F. E. Scott, 'A Good Joke and a Good Smoke: Tobacco Advertising Ephemera in the Fraser Papers', May 1995.

13 R. D. Altick, 'Cope's Tobacco Plant: An Episode in Victorian Journalism', *Papers of the Bibliographical Society of America*, 45 (1951): 333–50.

14 *Cope's Tobacco Plant*, 1(1) (March 1870): 12 (Fraser, 665); Fraser 680.

15 Fraser, 630–42.

16 M. Hilton and S. Nightingale, '"A Microbe of the Devil's Own Make": Religion and Science in the British Anti-tobacco Movement, 1853–1908,' in S. Lock, L. Reynolds and E. M. Tansey (eds), *Ashes to Ashes: The History of Smoking and Health* (London: Rodopi, 1998), pp. 41–77.

17 *Cope's Tobacco Plant*, 1(32) (November 1872): 377 (Fraser, 665).

18 G. F. Todd, *Statistics of Smoking in the United Kingdom*, 4th edn (London: Tobacco Research Council, 1966).

19 B. W. E. Alford, *W. D. & H. O. Wills and the Development of the UK Tobacco Industry* (London: Methuen, 1973), pp. 143–50.

20 G. Barraclough, *An Introduction to Contemporary History* (Harmondsworth: Penguin, 1967), pp. 43–64.

21 Alford, *W. D. & H. O. Wills*; M. Dempsey, *Pipe Dreams: Early Advertising Art from the Imperial Tobacco Company* (London: Pavilion Books, 1982); M. Corina, *Trust in Tobacco: The Anglo-American Struggle for Power* (London: Michael Joseph, 1975); Parliamentary Papers, The Monopolies Commission, *Report on the Supply of Cigarettes and Tobacco and of Cigarette and Tobacco Machinery*, Cmd. 218, 1961.

22 R. Batchelor, *Henry Ford: Mass Production, Modernism and Design* (Manchester: Manchester UP, 1994), especially Chapter 4: 'Believers, heretics and innocents'; J. Jervis, *Exploring the Modern: Patterns of Western Culture and Civilisation* (Oxford: Blackwell, 1998).

23 S. Strasser, *Satisfaction Guaranteed: The Making of the American Mass Market* (New York: Pantheon, 1984).

24 S. Bronner, 'Introduction', in S. Bronner (ed.), *Consuming Visions: Accumulation and the Display of Goods in America, 1880–1920* (New York: W. W. Norton, 1989), p. 2.

25 The links between the aesthetics of modernism and advertising and design have been made by a number of historians writing on the US consumer economy. See T. Smith, *Making the Modern: Industry, Art and Design in America* (Chicago: University of Chicago Press, 1993); J. Meikle, *Twentieth Century Limited: Industrial Design in America, 1925–1939* (Philadelphia:

Temple University Press, 1979); R. Marchand, *Advertising the American Dream: Making Way for Modernity, 1920–1940* (Berkeley, CA: University of California Press, 1985); P. Johnston, *Real Fantasies: Edward Steichen's Advertising Photography* (Berkeley, CA: University of California Press, 1997).

26 C. L. Pass, 'Coupon Trading – An Aspect of Non-price Competition in the UK Cigarette Industry', *Yorkshire Bulletin of Economic and Social Research*, 19(2) (1967): 124–35; Alford, *W. D. & H. O. Wills*, pp. 335–51; Corina, *Trust in Tobacco*, pp. 163–4.

27 Monopolies Commission, *Report on the Supply of Cigarettes*, p. 83; *The Statist*, 'The Trust Movement in British Industry, XXIV: Combines in the Tobacco Industry', 25 August 1923, pp. 271–3.

28 R. S. Tedlow, 'The Fourth Phase of Marketing: Marketing History and the Business World Today', in R. S. Tedlow and G. Jones (eds), *The Rise and Fall of Mass Marketing* (London: Routledge, 1993), pp. 8–35.

29 T. Richards, *The Commodity Culture of Victorian England: Advertising and Spectacle, 1851–1914* (London: Verso, 1991); L. A. Loeb, *Consuming Angels: Advertising and Victorian Women* (Oxford: Oxford University Press, 1994).

30 *TTR*, 34(408) (December 1901): 41–2.

31 Cartophilic Society, *The Tobacco War Booklet* (London: Cartophilic Society, 1951). See also the two cigarette card collections of B. R. Lillington and M. L. Horn, held at the John Johnson Collection, Bodleian Library, Oxford.

32 *The People*, 19 December 1915, p. 2.

33 Players, DD PL 6/22/1, *Storekeeper's file containing details of advertising archive*.

34 Richards, *Commodity Culture*, p. 158.

35 *TTR*, 57(680) (August 1924): 25; Wills, 38169/M/8/(o), *Press and Poster Committee Reports*, 16 October 1933.

36 E. S. Turner, *The Shocking History of Advertising* (Harmondsworth: Penguin, 1965), p. 170.

37 Richards similarly refers to the autonomy of the commodity when discussing patent medicine advertising: *Commodity Culture*, p. 197.

38 John Johnson Collection, *Tobacco Box No. 3*.

39 Richards, *Commodity Culture*, especially Chapter 4; Loeb, *Consuming Angels*.

40 *Tit-Bits*, 28 January 1922, p. iv.

41 *Daily Express*, 21 November 1901, p. 6.

42 *Daily Express*, 28 January 1930, p. 2. Another advertisement in the series featured a woman with a similar shadow and the same copy except for the first sentences: 'The comely, shapely curves of the modern figure are ever-appealing. Ugly fat, caused by over-indulgence – eating between meals, soon ruins the charm of these soft outlines': *Daily Express*, 22 January 1930, p. 3.

43 *TTR*, 53(625) (January 1920): 45.

44 *Sunday Express*, 23 February 1935, p. 3.

45 Loeb, *Consuming Angels*, pp. 54–5.

46 Johnston, *Real Fantasies*, especially Chapter 5, 'The Modern Look in Advertising Photography and Product Design', pp. 105–31.

47 P. Greenhalgh, 'The English Compromise: Modern Design and National Consciousness, 1870–1940', in W. Kaplan (ed.), *Designing Modernity: the Arts of Reform and Persuasion, 1885–1945* (London: Thames & Hudson, 1995), pp. 111–39.

48 Dempsey, *Pipe Dreams*, p. 32.

49 This is a view held by many female respondents to a Mass-Observation questionnaire. See Mass-Observation File Report 3192, *Man and His Cigarette*, 1949, p. 163, in *The Tom Harrisson Mass-Observation Archives* (Brighton: Harvester Press Microform Publications, 1983).

50 *Guardian*, 10 August 1960, p. 9.

51 Alford, *W. D. & H. O. Wills*, p. 362.

52 *Tit-Bits*, 12 March 1932, p. i.

53 Dempsey, *Pipe Dreams*, p. 34.

54 *Tit-Bits*, 27 February 1892, p. i.

55 *Daily Express*, 23 November 1901, p. 9.

56 *Tit-Bits*, 22 February 1902, p. i.

57 Loeb, *Consuming Angels*, p. 143.

58 Wills, 38169/M/8/(r), *Press and Poster Committee Reports*, 15 January 1935.

59 Wills, 38169/M/8/(t), *Press and Poster Committee Reports*, 25 March 1936.

60 D. L. LeMahieu, *A Culture for Democracy: Mass Communication and the Cultivated Mind in Britain Between the Wars* (Oxford: Clarendon Press, 1988).

61 The copy is taken from an advertisement appearing in the *Daily Mail* or *Daily Express*, 2 November 1922, held in Wills, 38169/P/1/(b), *Press Cuttings, 1921–1927*.

62 Loeb, *Consuming Angels*, p. 143. Loeb is referring to an advertisement for Bovril, displayed in 1907, which adopted a similar format.

63 Wills, 38169/M/8/(j), *Press and Poster Committee Reports*, 6 November 1930.

64 Wills, 38169/M/8/(l), *Press and Poster Committee Reports*, 16 April 1932.

65 Wills, 38169/M/8/(h), *Press and Poster Committee Reports*, 19 April 1930; 38169/M/8/(i), 28 April 1930; 38169/M/8/(l), 6 January 1931.

66 Wills, 38169/M/8/(i), *Press and Poster Committee Reports*, 22 April 1930.

67 For example, in 1926 they used the caption, 'Most men like them': *Tobacco*, 546 (June 1926): 55.

68 *Tit-Bits*, 27 February 1932, p. 735.

69 *Tobacco*, 547 (July 1926): 37.

70 Wills, 38169/P/1/(b), *Press Cuttings, 1921–1927*.

71 *Daily Express*, 31 January 1930, p. 13; *Daily Express*, 30 January 1930, p. 11.

72 The idea that the masses were now 'targeted' within the system arises from two essays by Asa Briggs: 'The Language of "Class" in Early Nineteenth-century England', and 'The Language of "Mass" and "Masses" in Nineteenth-century England', in A. Briggs, *The Collected Essays of Asa Briggs, Volume I: Words, Numbers, Places, People* (Brighton: Harvester Press, 1985).

73 F. Jameson, *Postmodernism, or, the Cultural Logic of Late Capitalism* (London: Verso, 1991).

74 Berman, *All That Is Solid*, p. 29.

75 R. Hughes, *The Shock of the New: Art and the Century of Change* (London: Thames & Hudson, 1991), pp. 164–211.

4

Occultism and the 'Modern' Self in *Fin-de-Siècle* Britain

Alex Owen

The concept of a modern self, rather like the individual terms it employs, is a slippery and perhaps inherently unsatisfactory way of attempting to locate in recent Western culture precisely what is signified by the 'I'. To speak of the self is still to accept the premise that there is an individual embodied consciousness through which an expressive language of self, the 'I', emerges. It also implies that this 'I', however much subjected to and structured by the multiple forces of history, culture, and language, represents a unique human being as well as that which is uniquely human. In this sense, selfhood is both experienced and registered as personal and individual, even though we might simultaneously acknowledge the demise of the infamous humanist individual and give the nod to the long-awaited death of Man. Somewhere, and perhaps more to the point, somehow, the experiential 'I' of the personal self remains to subvert and exceed the rhetoric of the decentred subject. This is the 'I' of personal identity which, however unstable and fleeting, and however constituted, is nevertheless understood by each and every one of us to stand at any given moment for human particularity. The 'I' of the self is unique, for all that it is formulated in interaction with others and intrinsically bound up with shared historicized social identities. It is also interiorized and private. Indeed, it is this notion of reclusive inner singularity that distinguishes the concept of self so markedly from that of social identity. The language of the modern self is a language of interiority.

Interiority, of course, is nothing new. The sense of an experiential inner self was evident in the spiritual *travails* of early medieval Europe, and was central to both Catholic and Protestant practices of pious introspection throughout the early modern period.[1] What was new was the implicit challenge to a spiritualized concept of self that emerged during the seventeenth century with the formulations of René Descartes and John Locke. The subsequent attempt to distinguish the self from anything approaching the notion of the soul and to identify it instead with the autonomous thinking 'I' has been one of the hallmarks of modern culture.[2] It is this newly imagined self, a self conceived as mind and consciousness, that must be placed at the centre of narratives of cultural modernity; that is, modernity as it is conceptualized, experienced, and lived.

The nature and parameters of modernity have become the focus of intense debate in recent years, but for all its differently charged valences the idea of modernity as synonymous with secularization has had remarkable staying power. Whether conceived as a useful periodizing device, descriptive account of massive and interrelated structural processes, a discrete set of social practices, or particular kinds of lived experience and their representation, accounts of post-Enlightenment modernity remain closely associated with a perceived commitment to Reason and the eradication of religious superstition. Max Weber famously pointed to precisely this during the course of a speech delivered in 1917, when he spoke of *Entzauberung* or 'disenchantment' to identify one of the major social and cultural indicators of modernity.[3] His argument was more broadly directed towards the ambiguous liberation implied by a triumph of 'instrumental rationality', but his assertion that Western modernity has been characterized by the impossibility of 'living in union with the divine' has been hugely influential. Historians have traditionally understood the nineteenth century partly in terms of the secularizing process, and regarded the Victorian period as a watershed in the transition to a modern secular society.

We might expect, then, that cultural modernity would be exemplified by an increasingly secularized idea and sense of self. Indeed, it is just this self that emerged from the late nineteenth-century colonization of the self by medical psychology and the new sciences of the mind.[4] This newly psychologized self represented an assault on what were perceived as the speculative formulations of theologians and philosophers. Gone was the sense of the self as a transcendental entity, a single applied consciousness conceived in the tradition of affective individualism, but one with an everlasting aspect – the soul. In its place was a variously conceived but invariably fragmented or multiple self, formulated through complex processes of remembering and forgetting, and one in which the conscious 'I' of the moment is inherently unreliable or unstable. The psychologized self as it emerged at the turn of the century appears to be characterized by the exchange of a non-rational spiritual dimension (the soul) for a secularized irrational (the unconscious) as integral to the process of self-constitution.

And yet the shift to a psychologized self was implicated in all kinds of different ways in those fraught attempts to redefine a Christian world-view that we associate so strongly with the late-Victorian period. For whilst there is no doubt that the nineteenth century witnessed a steady decline in the power and centrality of organized religion, that is, a religion invested with public authority and operating at the heart of the social fabric, this did not necessarily guarantee the cultural dominance of a secular outlook. That is why over twenty years ago Owen Chadwick cautioned historians to 'beware of the word Entzauberung'.[5] Far from the rationalizing credos of the mid-century heralding the demise of 'the divine', what occurred in late-Victorian Britain was a series of initiatives and adjustments that spoke to the on-going search for a spiritual dimension to life. What is recognizably modern about the post-1880 period is not so much its disenchantment as the evident unresolved tension between the spiritual and secular. The competing concepts and accounts of the self at the turn of the century sustained and elaborated this tension.

In this chapter I will argue that *fin-de-siècle* occultism was deeply involved in a renegotiation of self that was directed towards the reconciliation of secular imperatives and spiritual desire. The discussion presented here is part of a broader project in which I examine the British development and elaboration of nineteenth-century pan-European occultism, and argue for its significance in terms of a national experience of modernity. I sustain that theme in the following discussion by arguing that advanced occult theory and practice represented an acute engagement with the concept and experience of self that underscored the self's multiplicity and contingency, and exemplified the modern elision of self and consciousness. Indeed, it is the extreme modernity of this occult self that is so striking. On the other hand, in elucidating the occult's resistance to a secularized formulation of human consciousness and its simultaneous commitment to a rationalized experience of the spiritual, the chapter develops the theme that the occult constituted a crucial enactment of one of the ambiguities of 'the modern'. I sketch the broader parameters of this ambiguity in my necessarily brief treatment of the relationship between the intensive occult investigation of self and some of the most avant-garde debates of the day, showing how closely related some secular undertakings were to the spiritualized investments of occultism. Ultimately, then, the argument presented here works to support my broader contention that the occult represented a particular articulation of the multivalent processes through which *fin-de-siècle* modernity was constituted.[6]

* * *

One of the trends commonly remarked at the *fin de siècle*, but perhaps the least investigated and understood by historians, is the rise of interest in what contemporaries loosely referred to as 'mysticism'. Owen Chadwick noted the 'breath of spirit' that swept through late nineteenth-century Europe, and Jose Harris has recently drawn attention to an Edwardian 'rising tide of interest in mystical religion'.[7] There is, however, little developed sense among historians of what this 'rising tide' might mean. For late Victorians, however, the use of a term like mysticism was both familiar and closely identified with what contemporaries called the new 'spiritual movement of the age'. They meant by this the proliferation of spiritual groups and identities that emerged during the late 1880s and 1890s both within heterodox religious circles and in a more conventional Christian context. In particular, they were thinking of a revived interest in medieval and Renaissance Christian mysticism, 'esoteric' or unorthodox expressions of inspirational Christianity, and a non-denominational (often non-Christian) interest in 'esoteric philosophy' or occultism. These trends were perhaps most clearly illustrated in orthodox terms by William Ralph Inge's famous lectures at Oxford ('Inge's Bamptons' of 1899), in which, while claiming exemption from the vagaries of Neo-Platonism, the future dean of St Paul's Cathedral spoke of the connections between Christian mysticism and the pagan Greek Mysteries. A decade later those with a finger on the cultural pulse of the nation acknowledged that a general 'spiritual renaissance' and 'mystical revival' were part of the general *milieu* and a mark of the times.[8]

When Holbrook Jackson published his classic account of *fin-de-siècle* art and ideas in 1913, he looked back to the exhilarating decade of the 1890s – with its inescapable sense of intense social and cultural change, its literary Decadence, and its proliferation of new religious movements – as the quintessential moment in the generation of a truly New Age. In particular, Jackson identified the 1890s with 'the beginning of the revolt against rationalism and the beginning of the revival of mysticism'.[9] Interestingly, he spoke of this in terms of 'the development of a Transcendental View of Social Life', and undoubtedly had in mind the close association of a new, often heterodox, spirituality with radical socialist politics.[10] But he was also making an explicit connection between transcendentalism and an Emersonian metaphysics that combined rejection of Puritan orthodoxies and an attack on materialistic philistinism with the concept of self-realization. It was this 'idea of self-realization, as old as Emerson, and older', Jackson states, that 'was at the root of the modern attitude'. If 'the modern attitude' is itself a slippery concept, and Jackson notes the contemporary preference for '*fin de siècle*' or 'new' 'to indicate extreme modernity', his observation nevertheless goes straight to the heart of the matter. By the end of the century, the idea of the self as perhaps the supreme source of value and judgement was gaining ground, and with it the notion that 'the highest of all things' was what Jackson called 'the individual ego'. These are views that were to be popularized during the first decade of the twentieth century by those interested in the ideas of Nietzsche and Stirner; but they were already the audacious intellectual currency of the 1890s. A new self-consciousness, a preoccupation with consciousness and self that manifested itself in some of the leading artistic work, thought, and inquiry of the day, was the hallmark of the *fin-de-siècle* 'modern'.[11]

An acute cultural critic like Holbrook Jackson was aware that behind much of the intellectual and cultural ferment that marked the 1890s lay a new attitude towards what we would now call issues of subjectivity. For him, the 'idea of self realisation' lay at the heart of 'the modern attitude'. Later in the century, and with the benefit of hindsight, what Jackson had defined as the *fin-de-siècle* expression of 'extreme modernity' came to be seen as part of a broader and 'distinct stylistic phase' in literature and the arts known as Modernism. For all the continuities and discontinuities in the catalogue of international Modernist production, Modernism is usually taken to be typified by 'a new consciousness, a fresh condition of the human mind'. Literary critics discuss this 'fresh condition of the human mind' in terms of an awareness of the 'multiplicity of consciousness', the kind of 'quickened, multiplied consciousness' to which Walter Pater referred in the 1870s, but which became emblematic of cultural modernity at the *fin de siècle*.[12] New work in European literature and drama that emphasized the complexities of individual psychologies, and the 'split and vacillating', 'uncertain, disintegrated' human figures who were increasingly to populate the modern landscape, now seized the imagination of the British avant-garde.[13] By the early 1900s a generation of British, French, and American writers were seeking to probe the inner lives of their characters, emphasizing the distinction between appearance and reality, and the differences between perceived time and space and the temporal geography of the psyche. They did so in part through those 'strategies of inwardness' that literary critics associate so closely with the canonical lexicon of literary Modernism, as they elaborated, often in experimental but also in disciplined and recognizable form, the opaque, elusive, mysterious inner world of the self.[14]

At the turn of the century, however, these aestheticized developments were only one aspect of a broader investigation of the nature of subjectivity, consciousness, memory, experience, and sensation. As Sigmund Freud worked towards the theorization of a dynamic model of the mind that stressed the relative importance of conscious awareness, others began to postulate a psyche that might best be understood in terms of division and fragmentation rather than unitary wholeness. It began to appear that the mind was a vast labyrinth possessed of a hidden but frighteningly powerful realm that interacted with everyday consciousness, and what all of this amounted to was an implied assault on the undisputed authority of the autonomous rational self as personified by the 'I' of personal identity. A commonality of themes exemplified not only by an interest in and awareness of the complexity of the mind but also by the complications wrought by an appreciation of the subjectivity of cognition manifested themselves across the disciplines concerned with human behaviour and values. The contemporary questioning of cognitive and moral absolutes raised new concerns about the contingency of 'truth' and the role of subjective appraisal in determining the codes by which life is understood and lived; while developments in sociology, psychology, and philosophy stressed the interrelationship of subject and object and brought into question the concept of an irreducible reality existing independently of human perception and understanding. What H. Stuart Hughes referred to as 'the problem of consciousness' lay at the heart of much of this innovative inquiry and debate, and with it the related issues of the constitution and experience of modern subjectivity moved to the fore.[15] What cognitive modernism in the human sciences shared with idealist philosophy and canonical Modernism was a pre-eminent concern with consciousness and the modern experience of self. And it is this engagement with self and self-consciousness that some scholars have deemed the 'truly central insight of modernity'.[16]

* * *

It was in this intellectual and cultural climate that the 'mystical revival' of the late-Victorian and Edwardian years occurred, and central to this revival was a reconfigured interest in the occult. A general fascination with the occult was a marked aspect of Victorian culture. Spiritualism had enjoyed a huge boom after the mid-century, but during the 1880s and 1890s a new range of occult groups began to appear that drew on spiritualism's belief in invisible but real spirit forces while reinterpreting its explanation of and emphasis on the exoteric.[17] By far the largest, most famous, and outwardly successful of these groups was the Theosophical Society, which was inaugurated in New York in 1875 by Madame Helene Petrova Blavatsky and her close associate, Colonel Steel Olcott. Madame Blavatsky, an enigmatic and charismatic figure with a suitably mysterious past, appropriated the term 'theosophy' (meaning 'divine wisdom' or 'wisdom of the gods') and adapted an occult concept with venerable roots in Western philosophical and religious thought to her own personal brand of Eastern-oriented metaphysics. Many of those who joined the Theosophical Society were or had been practicing spiritualists, but during the final two decades of the century a steady stream of spiritual seekers passed in and out of the Theosophical Society as they made their way into various rival or complementary groups. One of the most notable of these was the small but influential Hermetic Society, established in 1884 by Dr Anna Kingsford and her close friend and spiritual collaborator, Edward Maitland. Kingsford and Maitland considered themselves to be deeply committed Christians, but their brand of 'esoteric Christianity' bore little relation to conventional Christian teaching. They believed that much of Christian theology should not be understood in a literal sense, but as metaphor for the esoteric wisdom of the Pagan mysteries as interpreted by the Western occult tradition. Their message appealed to Christian spiritualists, Theosophists with Christian as opposed to Buddhist leanings, and non-Christian occultists; and the Hermetic Society had an influence that belied its mere two years of formal existence.

What linked these two groups and epitomized an occult 'esoteric philosophy' was a belief in what might loosely be called an animistic understanding of the universe in which all of creation is interrelated and part and expression of a universal soul or cosmic mind. In practice this could be translated into the pursuit of a hidden realm of spiritual reality and wisdom, and this was perhaps most evident in the closely guarded study of the theory and techniques of ritual or ceremonial magic – so-called practical occultism. Anna Kingsford dabbled in ritual magic, and several magicians were active in the Hermetic Society; while Madame Blavatsky's establishment in 1888 of a special Esoteric Section of the Theosophical Society, a private, privileged, and powerful inner sanctum, became a proving ground for some who wanted to venture into the practice of the occult arts. Madame Blavatsky drew a distinction between Theosophy as a metaphysical and spiritual path and that aspect of the occult tradition that emphasized ritual magic; but some of her followers did not.[18] After her death in 1891, and particularly after Annie Besant was elected President of the Theosophical Society in 1907, the Esoteric Section became heavily involved with practical occultism.

The most important and influential of the late-Victorian magical societies, however, was the secret and hierarchical Hermetic Order of the Golden Dawn, established in the late 1880s and often remembered only in connection with its most famous initiate, the Irish poet and playwright W. B. Yeats.[19] The Order represented an ingenious reworking of seventeenth-century Rosicrucian learning, and its teaching, with its roots in Jewish mysticism, Hebrew-Christian sources of ancient wisdom, and the powerful 'Egyptian' writings of Hermes Trismegistus, was marked by the elaborate interplay of the philosophical or spiritual with the practical and magical. The Order's name spoke to the realization of a Rosicrucian rebirth, the regeneration of the old, corrupt world and dawning of a new spiritually enlightened age – timely notions for many at the *fin de siècle*.[20]

There were strong ties, in terms of both personnel and teachings, between the Hermetic Order of the Golden Dawn, the Hermetic Society, and the Theosophical Society, and while these groups differed in orientation they held in common two of the key characteristics of the new occultism: the move towards subtle and complex metaphysical teachings and an explicit emphasis on self-transformation as the route to an understanding and experience of spiritual realities. In both respects this marked a distinct break with spiritualism, which prided itself on its straight-forward message and non-elitist practice, and was suspicious of complex notions of the self. Spiritualists were particularly hostile to any theory that might suggest that spirit communications originated within the mind rather than from a separate entity outside it, and espoused the idea of a single temporal self that passed in death from the earthly body to the spirit Summerland.[21] The new occultists, on the other hand, while accepting the existence of spirit life on other planes, worked with a more complex notion of self and often laid stress on the role of inner processes of exploration and change in the attainment of spiritual wisdom and perfection. The occult endeavour was increasingly represented as an interiorized undertaking that pre-eminently took the form of an inquiry into the meaning and mutuality of self and consciousness.

Indeed, occultism at the *fin de siècle* was deeply invested in a distinctively 'modern' elision of the concepts of consciousness and self, and was intent on exploring what occultists took to be the limitless spiritual potential of that personal consciousness. This was always articulated in metaphysical terms, and in general occultists distinguished between a temporal and a divine self. Theosophists, for example, referred to the distinction between the earthly 'personal Self' or 'personal Ego' (the 'I') and a timeless 'permanent Self' or 'Spiritual Ego' that is continuously incarnated in human form until finally perfected and released from the wheel of karma. According to Blavatsky, the personal Self or Ego represents merely the temporary personality of a particular human incarnation. It is the Permanent Self, that which survives death to be continuously incarnated, that constitutes 'the real individuality' – the 'real' self.[22] But Madame Blavatsky also spoke of an impersonal and ungendered Higher Self, a third self, and this was a concept that assumed great importance in *fin-de-siècle* occult circles. The Higher Self was represented in strict Theosophical terms as the universally diffused 'divine principle' within every human being and akin to that spark of divinity that signifies 'the God within us'. The Theosophical Higher Self, then, is 'one with the Universal Soul or Mind' and constitutes an inner manifestation of 'the Universal Spirit'.[23] Theosophists knew the importance of reaching an understanding of the Higher Self, and advanced occultists within the Theosophical Society recognized that their goal was experience of 'the God within'.

Many of the senior members of the Hermetic Order of the Golden Dawn similarly conceived of what the Order variously referred to as the Higher (sometimes Highest) Self, Angelic Self, or Genius, as a God-like Self that must be nurtured and developed through advanced occult practice. The Golden Dawn taught its senior Adepts how to achieve what the Order called knowledge of or 'conversation' with the Higher Self, and underlined the importance of a complete awareness of the implications of self as a prelude to approaching not only 'the God within' but divinity itself. One Golden Dawn document states that 'Perfect knowledge of Self is required in order to attain Knowledge of Divinity, for when you can know the God of yourself it will be possible to obtain a dim vision of the God of All . . .'.[24] The rich interrelatedness of occult personnel meant that the concept of a Higher Self (like that of God) underwent transmutation, but all serious students of the occult understood that occult study and practice were in part dedicated to the full knowledge and understanding of 'Self' in each of its different manifestations.

This was summed up in the Hermetic Order of the Golden Dawn by the Renaissance admonition to 'Know Thyself'.[25] Florence Farr, the Ibsenite actress and muse of George Bernard Shaw, and a senior official in the Golden Dawn, drew upon the traditional imagery of alchemy when she suggested that an ultimate self-consciousness achieved through the refining processes of occult practice is one of the highest goals of the Adept: 'consciousness of Being is the name we give to the white tincture which the adept distils from his human form in the alembic of the mind.'[26] The notion of an all-encompassing 'consciousness of Being' as an essence distilled from the 'human form', however, was not meant to suggest a materialist interpretation of mind. Occultists acknowledged the interrelationship of mind and body while resisting any theory that reduced either mind or consciousness to the mechanistic workings of the brain. They argued for the autonomy of mind, and regarded consciousness as a mental field that could not be correlated with physiological or neurological functions. On the other hand, as Farr indicated, occultists were well aware of the importance of mind–body interaction in the production of a full 'consciousness of Being'. Advanced occultists were taught the various techniques through which such consciousness might be achieved – meditation, incantation, ritual, and forms of self-hypnotism, for example – and stressed the importance of the creative partnership of mind and body in aspiring to occult wisdom.

Most importantly, however, occultists believed that a fully realized consciousness implies an understanding of the limits of everyday self-awareness. For occultists, a fully elaborated consciousness involved far more than simply that interiorized experience of the mundane self that we call the 'I'. Annie Besant asserted that this is one of the major lessons of occultism, and in her role as leader of the Theosophical Society after Blavatsky's death stressed the unity of consciousness whilst explicating its different manifestations. Besant taught that those unschooled in esotericism have only limited awareness of the full potential of human consciousness, and mistakenly assume that a unifocal 'waking-consciousness' is synonymous with a fully realized self. Like all Theosophists and many other serious occultists, Besant was acutely aware that Eastern religions had long been familiar with the operation of different states of what she called 'super-consciousness', or 'the consciousness above the waking consciousness', and stressed the superiority of the Eastern tradition in this respect. She was perfectly *au fait* with European studies of multiple personality and trance states, and readily acknowledged the seemingly parallel preoccupations of psychology and occultism, but argued that while all but a few 'advanced psychologists' tended to view anything other than the consciousness of the waking state as 'abnormal', 'sub-conscious', 'inconscient', and necessarily 'disorderly', the East (and, by implication, occultism) regarded such states as 'higher than the waking state' and sought to reproduce them at will. She pointed, too, to the difference between the induced hypnotic trance produced at 'the Salpêtrière and elsewhere' and the willed altered consciousness of the Yogî or Adept. Most significantly, Besant argued that 'The Spiritual Man' who accesses the trance state at will via a range of meditative techniques moves into a higher but fully self-conscious mode of being in which 'he' can access planes beyond the earthly and temporal.[27]

Other occultists, while differing on the cosmological details, placed similar emphasis on gaining entry to non-temporal reality, and what this often amounted to in practice was the willed movement between different levels of consciousness, which in turn facilitated the sense of multiple selves. Fledgling magicians, for example, were trained to move between two levels of consciousness, the magical and the mundane, and experimented with a variety of self-hypnotic and ritualized techniques designed to produce the sense of a second initiated or magical self. Furthermore, senior magicians in the Golden Dawn (and subsequently also members of the Esoteric section of the Theosophical Society) were instructed in the occult clairvoyant practice known as Astral Travel, which relied on a complex set of mental techniques to effect the sense of a timeless and travelling 'I' that would then explore what magicians called the Astral Light. The Astral Light was conceived in the Golden Dawn as a great web of otherworldly planes or orders of existence that interpenetrate the world of earthly perceptions, and exploration of these planes came to assume an important (indeed an addictive) role in occult practice for many magicians.[28]

An occult elite was taught how to produce an intense sense of a personal double, a materialized replica of an embodied self, which left the temporal body of the occultist and journeyed at length in Astral realms. Golden Dawn adepts were taught how to formulate their own 'Sphere of Astral Light', which would replicate their person and, to a certain degree, initiated consciousness. In other words, a complete second self, conceived as a subtle replica of the original, was created in the mind, and it was this second self that travelled in the Astral Light. The astral self was therefore conceptualized in physical terms and possessed a consciousness of its own, even though it was subject to ultimate control by the magician's Will – the focused intent of the initiated self. In effect, what this type of magical practice taught was a highly refined system of dual or even triple consciousness. The mundane self, the initiated magical self, and the 'Sphere of Astral Light' apparently operated at different levels of consciousness, and at the very least this exercise involved a double displacement of the 'I' as a necessary preamble to travel in Astral realms.

Astral Travel was based on the precept, 'Believe thyself to be in a place, and thou art there', and the projection of a 'Sphere of Astral Light' worked in conjunction with an accepted code of occult symbolism to effect an intense extra-terrestrial experience.[29] Nevertheless, Victorian adepts were well aware that at one level Astral Travel was an interior journey conducted within the mind. They knew that practices like Astral Travel relied upon a series of intricate manoeuvres of personal consciousness, just as they understood that the power of the structured imagination was crucial to the success of any magical undertaking – whether conceived as exploration of Astral realms or in terms of more temporal concerns. In fact, what magicians referred to as 'the magical process' was entirely under-written by the power of the mind and of the prepared imagination.[30] Intense concentration effected the transformation of the mundane into the magical self; the application of specific techniques produced a heightened consciousness or changed sense of 'I'; and an imagination attuned to complex symbolic representations of occult reality worked to create the vivid visualizations so necessary for effective practical magic. As magicians acknowledged, the 'Cultivation of the imaginative faculty' and 'means of attaining to intuition' are central to the attainment of magical or 'supra-normal powers'.[31]

This did not mean, however, that a powerful magical experience like the movement of a transformed sense of self across a range of non-earthly realms of existence was taken to be a purely subjective or interiorized phenomenon. Far from it. Advanced occultists accepted that in theory as in practice magic blurred the usual distinctions between inner and outer and subjective and objective, while never doubting the absolute reality of the magical experience. Indeed, they conceived of the entire occult endeavour as the search for a veiled or hidden reality, but a reality that transcends temporal and seemingly physical limitations. Different occult groups each taught a form of psychospiritual metaphysics that emphasized the relationship between different aspects of the self and levels of other worldly and Divine consciousness. Occultists understood that teachings that spoke of the 'Realization of the Microcosm as a representation of the Macrocosm' were directing attention to a direct correspondence between the fully realized 'inner' kingdom of the self and the 'outer' realities of the Cosmos. Similarly, they recognized that the 'merging of the Ego into the realm of Macrocosmic beings' referred to the interrelationship of 'inner' and 'outer'.[32] This, the correlation of the different inner worlds or levels of self-consciousness with the outer worlds of non-temporal reality, was one of the great secrets imparted to advanced occultists. And much advanced occult activity was dedicated to mapping this relationship as adepts sought to perfect a disciplined, controlled, and fully self-realized consciousness capable of acknowledging and transversing the permeable boundary between the personal self and the spiritual 'other' of the other world.[33]

When magicians were taught, then, to 'Believe thyself to be in a place, and thou art there', the meaning of both 'believe' and 'there' was closely circumscribed. Although the entire panoply of phenomena associated with other worldly realms was at one level recognized to be a subjective emanation, it was also conceived as part of a hidden reality existing beyond but also in relationship with the inner world of the individual self. Rather than worrying about the precise location (inner/outer) or status (subjective/objective, real/unreal) of the Astral Light, Golden Dawn magicians assumed a correspondence between microcosm and macrocosm and concerned themselves with an array of procedural devices intended to probe the authenticity of occult experience. They were taught how to conduct themselves in the Astral Light, recognize different astral planes and beings, 'test' their experiences by reference to magical signs and passwords, and protect themselves in hazardous situations. Astral journeying was acknowledged by magicians to be potentially dangerous. Their understanding, based on experience, was that the planes were not always welcoming, just as celestial or other beings were not always friendly or easy to read. Early journeys were often fraught affairs, and novices returned exhausted from their forays. But those who were knowledgeable and expert in Astral Travel, and familiar with the means of astral defence and attack, could maintain a two-hour astral journey without undue stress. What is more, advanced Adepts were capable of lengthy shared journeys in the Astral Light – sojourns during which magicians travelled together in their Astral bodies and communicated freely with each other whilst encountering identical Astral conditions and phenomena.

These remarkable journeys, which some sophisticated Golden Dawn Adepts regarded as a kind of experiential metaphor, reinforced the conviction held by all occultists that their experience of the 'phenomena of consciousness occurring on super-physical planes' spoke to more than the power of mutually reinforcing fantasy or the exquisite inventiveness of the personal self.[34] Florence Farr's 'Consciousness of Being', the alchemical 'white tincture', involved not only an 'occult' awareness of the full dimensions of the self but also its relationship with and place in the wider order of creation. Furthermore, like all occultists, Farr conceived of the highest manifestation of an occult development of self as 'a state of consciousness in which all our powers become supernatural'.[35] In an apparent reversal of that formulation, but one that amounts to the same thing, Annie Besant stated: 'Whatever forces may be latent in the Universe at large or in man in particular, they are wholly natural . . . This repudiation of the supernatural lies at the very threshold of Theosophy: the supersensuous, the superhuman, Yes; the supernatural, No.'[36] Initiates of the Golden Dawn echoed Besant's sentiments when they agreed that 'Supernormal events may be, but nothing is supernatural.' As Florence Farr expressed it, 'Magic power only implies a power not limited by common experience.'[37] It was the 'supernormal' and 'superhuman' to which advanced occultists aspired at the turn of the century, and the cultivation of imagination, the honing of the Will, and the successive refinement of a particular understanding of self were the means by which that might be achieved.

Occultists, of course, conceived of the initiated 'superhuman' 'spiritual man' within a framework of esotericism, but the kind of esotericism privileged at the *fin de siècle* was specific and contemporary in tone. As some occultists recognized, there was a sympathetic resonance between an occult theorization of self and pursuit of an experience of 'Being' and other highly influential avant-garde ideas. Nowhere was this more obvious than in the modern Nietzschean and Bergsonian vogue, and no one did more to promote the ideas of Nietzsche and Henri Bergson than A. R. Orage. Orage, a Theosophist and friend of Holbrook Jackson, had an acute sense of what was important as well as new in *fin-de-siècle* art and letters. The work he supported and commissioned for his periodical the *New Age* often stood at the cutting edge of innovative European ideas, and it is this that makes the periodical so important as one of the cultural touchstones of the early twentieth century. A. R. Orage regarded Nietzsche as an inspired mystic, was personally active in promoting his ideas, and incorporated a Nietzschean perspective in the statement of aims for the *New Age*.[38]

Leading influential occultists were similarly quick to claim a kinship with a Nietzschean 'egoistic philosophy'. Nietzsche's insistence on the sovereignty of the self as creator and arbiter of all 'truths', his emphasis on the all-powerful will, and his notions of the highly-evolved 'superman' spoke with great immediacy to occult endeavours. Annie Besant saw the Nietzschean superman as directly related to the 'superhuman' occultist and a Theosophical understanding of spiritual development, views supported by A. R. Orage.[39] Similarly, Florence Farr shared Orage's enthusiasm for Nietzsche and on the recommendation of George Bernard Shaw was recruited to write for the *New Age*. Like Orage and other occultists, Florence Farr was also interested in the views propounded by the Eugenic Education Society, and both she and Orage undoubtedly saw eugenics as paralleling occultism's emphasis on the development of the self-realized 'Perfect Man'. Florence Farr had been taught in the Golden Dawn that 'It must be our object then, to become that Perfect Man', and that 'one of our aims should be the Regeneration of the Race of the Planet'.[40] She and other Golden Dawn magicians had worked together on a spiritual level towards that goal. The reactionary and racist implications of these ideals went unacknowledged and were possibly not recognized by either Farr or Orage who, in common with many occultists and early twentieth-century eugenicists, held politically progressive views. The proto-fascism inherent in certain strands of occult thought was later to become more developed, but at the dawn of the new century the elaboration of this line of thinking lay in the future.[41]

Nietzsche was claimed by occultists as a fellow traveller, but it was Henri Bergson who came closest to articulating an 'occult' philosophy. A. R. Orage's *New Age* was as active in promoting Bergson as it was Nietzsche, and published T. E. Hulme's seminal introductory articles on Bergson. T. E. Hulme, whom Holbrook Jackson also greatly respected, was an admirer of Bergson and translated his *Introduction to Metaphysics* (1903). Hulme was himself emblematic of the symbiotic relationship between occultism and advanced ideas. An intellectual and an embryonic poet, Hulme formed a small discussion group that met during 1909 to discuss 'a new "dry and hard" poetic', and constituted a forerunner of the Imagist movement.[42] He was deeply attracted to Bergson's anti-positivist vitalism, which constituted part of that European 'breath of spirit' noted by Owen Chadwick, and borrowed from Bergson's metaphysics to conceptualize his own theory of poetry as 'intuited truth'.[43] Hulme's concern with the poetic image as a non-discursive representation of intuited reality also owed a great deal to French Symbolism, and both vitalism and Symbolism had direct relevance for *fin-de-siècle* occultism – particularly magic, with its Kabbalistic references to the conjoined power of words and images. Arthur Symons's important book *The Symbolist Movement in Literature* (1899), which was dedicated to W. B. Yeats, slightly pre-dated the Bergsonian craze in Britain, but recognized the relationship between what Symons called Mysticism and major Symbolist assumptions about the power of the poetic image.[44] Yeats as both poet and prominent Golden Dawn magician was to become a major source of the transmission of Symbolist and occult ideas to other seminal twentieth-century poets, and it is significant that Yeats, Florence Farr, T. E. Hulme, and the poet Ezra Pound were moving in the same avant-garde literary circles by 1909.[45] Indeed, Florence Farr was to inspire Ezra Pound's 'Portrait d'une Femme'.

It is possible that Florence Farr received her introduction to Henri Bergson's ideas through her association with T. E. Hulme, but in a further personal twist she would also have known that Bergson was the brother of Moina (born Mina Bergson) MacGregor Mathers – the wife of the head of the Golden Dawn and the Order's chief inspiration and priestess. Certainly W. B. Yeats met Henri Bergson in 1894 when he visited the Mathers's in Paris, and was aware that MacGregor Mathers was irritated by his inability to impress his brother-in-law with his magic.[46] But if Henri Bergson showed no interest in magic, he was nonetheless deeply concerned with matters relating to spirit and consciousness. He espoused a critical vitalist philosophy with roots in a long and venerable European history, of which the Renaissance hermetic tradition is a part, and with links both to German *Naturphil-osophie* and Nietzschean ideas.[47] Bergson's notion of an *élan vital*, a vital force or impulse that permeates the universe and everything in it, bore a distinct relationship to animistic occultism; but it was not solely his neo-vitalism that resonated with an occult perspective. Bergson's concern with the mystery of existence, engagement with the phenomena of consciousness, assertion that the 'intellect is characterized by a natural inability to comprehend life' and consequent valorization of intuition, had clear implications for early twentieth-century occultism.[48]

Bergson argued for the importance, intensity, and reality of inner experience, and proposed the interrelationship not only of inner and outer realities but also of body and spirit. In a striking parallel with occult thought, Bergson argued that matter and spirit are not opposites but part of a whole. Furthermore, he conceived of the origins of matter, and of life itself, as an effect of 'supra-consciousness'. The primacy he accorded consciousness, and by implication the suggestion that the real is an effect of consciousness, was enormously appealing to occultists for whom access to alternative realities was bound up with changes in consciousness. Equally, his views had immediate relevance for all those who accepted the notion of an evolving spiritual Self with an existence that defies the limitations of temporality, and in a wider permutation could be taken as confirmation of the movement between individual and 'cosmic' consciousness to which Theosophists and magicians referred. Perhaps most importantly, Bergson valorized intuition over what he maintained were the rationalizing and therefore necessarily limiting strategies of the intellect. It is only consciousness in its fullest sense, he argued, a consciousness characterized by the development of the intuitive faculties and allied to the wellsprings of creativity, that can truly encounter the essence of all things and apprehend reality itself.[49] Indeed, Bergson postulated a reality that could be 'known' only in flashes of experiential inspiration by the developed intuitive faculties as they connected with the great life forces that animate the universe. Although occultists often aspired to far more than a mere flash of experiential knowledge of a hidden but ultimate real, Bergson's emphasis on intellect illuminated by intuition as the means of 'knowing' reality was similar in tone and substance to the acknowledgment by occultists of the role of the consciously controlled and developed 'imagination' in magical practice.[50]

These claims and preoccupations seem far removed from the concerns of the innovative late-nineteenth-century practitioners of the new sciences of mind. And yet at the end of the nineteenth century medical psychology had not entirely shaken itself free of a traditional association between philosophical inquiry and issues of the self or of the equally traditional metaphysical implications of that inquiry. Indeed, the ideas of Bergson, the psychologically-inclined philosopher, bore some relation to those of William James, the highly influential philosophically-inclined psychologist, who gave credit to Bergson's elaboration of the concept and role of consciousness in the development of his own ideas. More to the point, Pierre Janet, the medical psychologist whose work on multiple personality was so influential at the turn of the century (and was followed with such interest by occultists like Annie Besant), held doctorates in both philosophy and psychology and maintained a close friendship with Bergson and an association with William James. Furthermore, all three men, in common with many of the leading European medical psychologists of the day, were members of the Society for Psychical Research.[51] The tensions inherent in these various affiliations, however, were severe. In particular, medical psychologists were highly sensitive to any suggestion that their professional field was related to the occult. Although they readily acknowledged that the states of consciousness that constituted their object of study were correspondingly often those of the spiritualist medium, the struggle for scientific recognition and validation was in part bound up with the effort to rid psychology of any taint of the occult arts.

Many practitioners were uncomfortably aware that the term 'psychology' was used by spiritualists and followers of the 'esoteric philosophy' to describe their investigations in the seance room and elsewhere, and all recognized the mesmeric and occult precursors of the hypnotic techniques then employed in the consulting room and medical theatre. Certainly Freud knew all too well the occult connotations of his early use of hypnosis, of his interpretative work on dreams, and, indeed, of many of the phenomena of consciousness that interested him. His simultaneous fascination with the occult and vigorous attempts to distance himself from it are matters of record. Freud feared that the occult, which he referred to in 1910 as 'the black tide of mud', would compromise the respectability of psychoanalysis. But his early immersion in *Naturphilosophie*, his friendship with men like Wilhelm Fleiss, his investigations of mediumistic phenomena with Sandor Ferenczi, his legendary superstitious anxieties, his mixed response to the occult interests of some of his followers, and his great rift with Carl Jung over just such matters, suggest, if only in the briefest outline, the parameters of the tensions inherent in Freud's position.[52]

But if Freud sought to distance psychoanalysis from charges of occultism, this was not the case for some occultists. By 1910 certain advanced occultists had become interested in Freudian psychoanalytic theory, and indeed claimed that occultism anticipated the insights of psychoanalysis. Dedicated occultists found it perfectly possible to accept that certain occult experiences rely upon an intimate relationship with the personal unconscious, while refusing the notion that occult reality is simply a subjective unconscious effect. Occultists who were sympathetic to psychoanalytic insights remained unshaken in their belief in the efficacy of practical magic and a verifiable occult reality. In a different vein, W. B. Yeats felt that it was his early experience with magic that convinced him 'that images well up before the mind's eye from a deeper source than conscious or subconscious memory'.[53] This idea of a 'deeper source' as the wellspring of inspiration, wisdom, and noumenal or mystical experience, was explored during the earlier part of the twentieth century by Jung, whose concept of a collective unconscious has clear and acknowledged implications for magical practice. Jung, whose early career was marked by a professional interest in spiritualist mediumship, went on to explore the relevance of Eastern, mystical, and occult teachings as potential keys to a more spiritualized 'self-realization' than was possible within Freudian psychoanalytic theory. His deep interest during the interwar period in sixteenth-century hermetic literature led him to propose a psychologized reading of alchemy similar to that espoused by occultists at the *fin de siècle*. Indeed, Jung thought of Renaissance alchemy as 'the historical counterpart of my psychology of the unconscious'.[54]

But while Jung acknowledged his debt to Renaissance magic, some pre-war occultists embraced psychoanalytic theory, and *fin-de-siècle* occultism itself remained deeply implicated in the contemporary innovative elaboration of subjectivity, there were significant differences between the occult and allied enterprises. Occultism was conceived in quite different terms and dedicated to different ends. Late-Victorian magicians were undertaking what we might think of as remarkable and sustained explorations of the psyche, and extraordinary experimentation with the powers of the human mind; but they were absorbed in the magical enterprise and expressed the endeavour in these terms. Adepti were aware that at its most sophisticated, advanced magical practice exposed the limited nature of the personal 'I' of conscious identity, but were concerned less with probing the limits of subjectivity than with exploring and establishing the reality of occult realms. The seeming parallels with the psychoanalytic project are startling, but although Magical Orders were teaching adepts how to develop a magical self that could conduct lengthy forays into real but hidden worlds that interpenetrate our own, occultists spoke not of psyche but of Planes; and in practical terms, of Astral Travel rather than of investigations of the repressed components of the unconscious. Additionally, magical practice relied upon a development of multiple selves that did not constitute a problematic splitting of the 'I' or represent a crisis of personal identity. It taught *willed* access to the Astral Light, and emphasized mutuality of experience and the ability to take control and 'change' certain facets of Astral existence. This, then, represented a developed and controlled engagement with personal consciousness that was quite distinct from the kinds of mental states investigated and pathologized by late-Victorian medical psychology and Freudian psychoanalysis; distinct even from the hermeneutic processes of 'actualization' favoured by Jungian analytical psychology. Magical practice was an undertaking that operated on a different scale and in a different register.

Fin-de-siècle occultism was like a shadow-play of synchronicity. It mirrored broader cultural trends and preoccupations, but in key respects magnified and outstripped them. For all that, though, the occult remained a child of the historical moment. Occult reality was conceptualized in the nineteenth-century tradition of an all-embracing and universalized explanatory system, and occultism confirmed the prestige of the rational self-referential 'I' even as it assumed the power and importance of the occluded realms of personal consciousness. Advanced occultism addressed in its own unique way the contemporary exploration of the limits of the rational self while predicating self-realization on the notion of a boundless but acutely self-aware 'I' with ultimate referral to a stable and controlling consciousness. Occultism defined consciousness in a way that might not have been amenable to scientific criteria, or provable in any positivist sense, but was nevertheless conceived as infused with rationality even as it postulated a self that could traverse the dichotomized fault lines established by the rationalizing intellect. After all, the rationalizing intellect was not jettisoned during occult voyages of discovery. It was actively at work. Occult 'strategies of inwardness' were still strategies, designed to shift the sense of self beyond the limits imposed by everyday 'waking consciousness' and towards a full 'Consciousness of Being'. This was a self that transcended in graphic terms those conceptual dualisms of subject/object and inner/outer that had recently come under attack from the secular disciplines, and at the same time epitomized that faith in rationality upon which those disciplines depended. Most crucially, however, like the new sciences of mind, an occult metaphysics of self represented an identifiably modern (if unorthodox) attempt to bring consciousness to a particular 'understanding of itself'.[55]

In the name of the unravelling of the mystery of 'Being', the occult generated a language of selfhood that implicitly countered the modern association of spirituality with irrationality while pursuing a spiritualized formulation of a distinctively modern secularized understanding of the complexity of human consciousness and the significance of the irrational domain. In so doing it sought to negotiate that seemingly oppositional relationship between the spiritual and the secular that was so often expressed in the modern period through anxieties about the irrational. However, while occultists conceived of a refined and spiritualized 'Consciousness of Being' in which all the dimensions of consciousness were known, a 'self-realization' that stood in stark contrast to the fragmented psyche postulated by Freud and the medical psychologists, an occult consciousness of self was representative of a modern sensibility that remained immured in and fascinated by the performance of the irrational even as it sought to measure, understand, and to some extent control or manipulate it. As the new century got under way and neo-vitalism was played out in often tragic circumstances, European perspectives on modernity increasingly incorporated the recognition of the necessity for and the frailty of a *rapprochement* with the unconscious.[56] Freud's analysis of the cost of 'civilization', the often devastating eruption of all that must be repressed in the name of rationality, order, and respectability, comes close, as Marshall Berman suggests, to 'a definitive vision of the inner contradictions and ultimate fragility of modern life'.[57]

Not least of these inner contradictions at the turn of the century was the uneasy co-existence of a distinctively modern Weberian disenchantment and a converse aspiration to noumenal experience. This unresolved tension between the spiritual and secular, with all that it implied for the modern subject, now emerged as constitutive of a new dialectic of modernity. As I have argued in this chapter, occultism addressed this tension and sought to negotiate the oppositional deployment of a contingent and transcendent self as formulated through competing accounts of subjectivity. It is in this sense that occultism constituted a crucial enactment of the ambiguities of 'the modern'. The occult conceived of divinity as bound up in complex ways with the secularized self, just as occult practice sought direct experience of both divinity and a spiritualized real through a unique understanding and exploration of subjective consciousness. Occultists repudiated the notion of a transcendent godhead existing beyond the forces of nature, preferring instead the formulation of the supernatural as 'a state of consciousness'. In proposing the immanence of the self-referential subject, the occult articulated a unique expression of both the modern drive for 'self-realization' and a contemporary impulse towards spirituality. Ultimately, occultists sought in the infinite realms of subjective consciousness an alternative source and repository of self-understanding and spiritual purpose. In effect, then, occultism taught modern men and women how to create new spiritualized meanings 'out of the resources of the self'. As Florence Farr expressed it: 'I stood naked in a bleak and dark eternity and filled it with my exultation.'[58] This was the 'modern' enchanted self.

Notes

1 For recent helpful accounts of the self during the Renaissance, early modern, and Enlightenment periods, see the essays in Roy Porter (ed.), *Rewriting the Self: Histories from the Renaissance to the Present* (London: Routledge, 1997).

2 I am using the term 'modern' here to indicate that classic second phase of modernity, approximately the nineteenth and early twentieth centuries. See Marshall Berman, *All That Is Solid Melts Into Air: The Experience of Modernity* (Harmondsworth: Penguin Books, 1988), p. 17.

3 Max Weber, 'Science as a Vocation' [1919], in *Max Weber: Essays in Sociology*, trans. and ed. H. H. Gerth and C. Wright Mills (Oxford: Oxford University Press, 1958). For a discussion of the date of Weber's Munich University lecture, traditionally thought to have been given in 1918, see Wolfgang Schluchter, 'The Question of the Dating of "Science as a Vocation" and "Politics as a Vocation"', in Guenther Roth and Wolfgang Schluchter, *Max Weber's Vision of History: Ethics and Methods* (Berkeley, CA: University of California Press, 1979), pp. 113–16.

4 Michel Foucault, *The Order of Things: An Archaeology of the Human Sciences* (London: Tavistock, 1970), is the influential precursor of an important literature on the psychologized self. See, for example, Nikolas Rose, *Governing the Soul: The Shaping of the Private Self* (London: Routledge, 1990); Ian Hacking, *Rewriting the Soul: Multiple Personality and the Sciences of Memory* (Princeton, NJ: Princeton University Press, 1995).

5 Owen Chadwick, *The Secularization of the European Mind in the Nineteenth Century* (Cambridge: Cambridge University Press, 1975), pp. 239, 258.

6 These arguments are developed in my forthcoming book, *Magic and Modernity: Occultism and the Culture of Enchantment in Fin-de-Siècle Britain*.

7 Owen Chadwick, *The Secularization of the European Mind*, pp. 239, 258; Jose Harris, *Private Lives, Public Spirit: A Social History of Britain 1870–1914* (Oxford: Oxford University Press, 1993), pp. 173–4. Chadwick notes that this 'breath of spirit' was exemplified by work in the arts, literature, and philosophy.

8 See Edward Maitland, *Anna Kingsford. Her Life, Letters, Diary and Work* (London: George Redway, 1896), Vol. 2, p. 379, for a discussion of the new spirituality as a phenomenon of the 1890s. Edward Maitland and Anna Kingsford are considered briefly hereafter. Jose Harris, *Private Lives, Public Spirit*, p. 174, comments that on the eve of the First World War *The Times* religious correspondent was using the terms 'spiritual renaissance' and 'mystical revival' to define the explosion of interest he saw around him.

9 Holbrook Jackson, *The Eighteen Nineties: A Review of Art and Ideas at the Close of the Nineteenth Century* (1913; reprint edn, New York: Capricorn Books, 1966), p. 132. Jackson briefly co-edited with A. R. Orage the prescient periodical the *New Age*, which was revived in 1907. My reliance on Jackson's analysis is not idiosyncratic. *The Eighteen Nineties* is a superb (and in some respects unsurpassed) piece of literary and cultural criticism. As John Stokes *In the Nineties* (Chicago: University of Chicago Press, 1989), p. 167, notes: 'It remains unchallenged in its scope.'

10 Holbrook Jackson, *The Eighteen Nineties*, p. 27.

11 Holbrook Jackson, ibid., p. 132, 21, 133. Max Stirner's *Der Einzige und sein Eigentum* (1844) was published in English as *The Ego and His Own* in 1907 and became the basis for a Stirner revival in Britain. Stirner (whose work had languished in obscurity until the end of the nineteenth century) anticipated in extreme form some of the central ideas of Bergson and, more especially, Nietzsche.

12 Malcolm Bradbury and James McFarlane, 'The Name and Nature of Modernism', in Bradbury and McFarlane, (eds), *Modernism 1890–1930* (1976; reprint edn, Harmondsworth: Penguin Books, 1991), pp. 22, 30, 32-3. I am indebted to this seminal discussion of Modernism. Bradbury and McFarlane cite the distinguished critic Frank Kermode (in his 'Modernisms', in *Modern Essays*, London, 1971), as placing the antecedents of Modernism in the 1890s. Walter Pater's famous 'Conclusion' to the first edition of *The Renaissance* (1873) was often read against the grain, and became an important influence on *fin-de-siècle* Decadence. See Holbrook Jackson, *The Eighteen Nineties*, pp. 59–61.

13 August Strindberg, 'Preface' to *Miss Julie* (1888), cited in James McFarlane, 'The Mind of Modernism', p. 81, and Bradbury and McFarlane, 'The Name and Nature of Modernism', p. 47, both in Bradbury and McFarlane, *Modernism 1890–1930*. The work of Baudelaire, Ibsen, Maeterlink, and Strindberg exemplified this attention to a 'disintegrated' modern subjectivity .

14 Frederic Jameson, *Fables of Aggression, Wyndham Lewis, the Modernist as Fascist* (Berkeley, CA and Los Angeles: University of California Press, 1979), p. 2. See Ricardo J. Quinones, *Mapping Literary Modernism: Time and Development* (Princeton, NJ: Princeton University Press, 1985) p. 249. The writers I have in mind here are Henry James, Yeats, Gide, and Proust, followed by Eliot, Pound, Lawrence, and Joyce.

15 H. Stuart Hughes, *Consciousness and Society: The Reorientation of European Social Thought, 1890–1930* (1958; reprint edn, Brighton: Harvester Press, 1979).

16 David A. Hollinger, 'The Knower and the Artificer, with Postscript 1993', in Dorothy Ross (ed.), *Modernist Impulses in the Human Sciences 1870–1930*

(Baltimore, MD and London: The Johns Hopkins University Press, 1994), p. 41, makes this point. He is quoting Paul de Man, who grouped various categories of thinkers and writers together 'as exemplars of his modernism'. See Paul de Man, 'What Is Modern?', *New York Review of Books*, 26 August 1965.

17 Spiritualists believe that the spirits of the dead not only survive but are capable of communicating with the living, and during the nineteenth century these beliefs attracted many thousands of adherents across a broad class and ideological spectrum in Britain, Europe, and the United States. Spiritualists tended to favour democratic ideals and the values of rational, empirical inquiry, but often came close to an identifiably 'occult' view of the universe as promulgated by the Theosophical Society and other esoteric groups. For the more recent literature on nineteenth-century British spiritualism, see Geoffrey K. Nelson, *Spiritualism and Society* (London: Routledge & Kegan Paul, 1969); Janet Oppenheim *The Other World: Spiritualism and Psychical Research in England, 1850–1914* (Cambridge: Cambridge University Press, 1985); Logie Barrow, *Independent Spirits: Spiritualism and English Plebeians, 1850–1910* (London: Routledge & Kegan Paul, 1986); and Alex Owen *The Darkened Room: Women, Power and Spiritualism in Late Victorian England* (London: Virago Press, 1989).

18 See, H. P. Blavatsky, *Practical Occultism and Occultism versus The Occult Arts*, reprinted from *Lucifer*, April and May 1888, (London: The Theosophical Publishing Society, 1912). Annie Besant's early position was similar. See Annie Besant, *Occultism, Semi-Occultism and Pseudo-Occultism*, a lecture delivered to the Blavatsky Lodge, London, 30 June 1898, (Adyar, Madras: Theosophical Publishing House, 1920, 2nd. edn).

19 The term 'hermetic' is derived from the vast body of occult literature ascribed to Hermes Trismegistus, thought by the Renaissance magi to be an ancient Egyptian priest. This corpus was probably the work of various unknown Greek authors, but is nevertheless often referred to as 'Egyptian' in the modern Western occult tradition. Isaac Casaubon (1559–1614) first revealed the Hermetic writings to be more modern in origin than ancient Egyptian, and scholars currently assume dates ranging from AD 100 to 300. See Garth Fowden, *The Egyptian Hermes,* (Cambridge: Cambridge University Press, 1986); Frances A. Yates, *Giordano Bruno and the Hermetic Tradition* (Chicago: University of Chicago Press, 1964), pp. 2–3; and Anthony Grafton, *Defenders of the Text* (Cambridge: Harvard University Press, 1991), p. 163.

20 The history of the Rosicrucian tradition is a vexed one, but we know that a secret Rosicrucian Masonic Order, the Societas Rosicruciana in Anglia, was founded in England in 1865. Its membership was involved in the formation of the Hermetic Order of the Golden Dawn. Frances A. Yates, *The Rosicrucian*

Enlightenment, (London: Routledge & Kegan Paul, 1972), suggests that the seventeenth-century Rosicrucian movement was in part an allegory for a renewed 'general reformation' based on a strengthened Protestant alliance with Frederick V, Elector Palatine of the Rhine, at its centre. For an account of Rosicrucianism written by an early member of the Hermetic Order of the Golden Dawn, see, Arthur E. Waite, *The Brotherhood of the Rosy Cross* (London: W. Rider & Sons, 1924). Several reliable and relatively recent studies of the Hermetic Order of the Golden Dawn have helped to throw light on its organizational structure and membership. Particularly valuable because they include or draw upon privately printed and unpublished sources, and are written by scholarly enthusiasts (rather than enthusiastic occultists), are: Ellic Howe, *The Magicians of the Golden Dawn: A Documentary History of a Magical Order, 1887–1923,* (London: Routledge & Kegan Paul, 1972); R. A. Gilbert, *The Golden Dawn: Twilight of the Magicians* (Wellingborough: The Aquarian Press, 1983); and R. A. Gilbert, *The Golden Dawn Companion: A Guide to the History, Structure, and Workings of the Hermetic Order of the Golden Dawn* (Wellingborough: The Aquarian Press, 1986). W. B. Yeats' scholarship has been enormously helpful in unravelling the complexities of the Golden Dawn, and contextualizing it in literary and intellectual terms; see, for an early influential example, George Mills Harper, *Yeats's Golden Dawn* (London: Macmillan, 1974).

21 A minority of British spiritualists favoured the idea of reincarnation as developed by the French spiritist Allan (sometimes Alain) Kardec, whose *Le Livre des Esprits* (1856) took a very different view of spiritual evolution from that prevalent in Britain and America.

22 H. P. Blavatsky, *The Key to Theosophy being a clear exposition in the form of question and answer of the Ethics, Science and Philosophy for the Study of which the Theosophical Society has been Founded* (1889; reprint edn, London: Theosophical Publishing House, 1968), pp. 130–6.

23 H. P. Blavatsky *The Key to Theosophy,* pp. 131–5.

24 Vestigia Nulla Retrorsum (Moina Mathers), Flying Roll No. XXI, 'Know Thyself', in Francis King (ed.), *Astral Projection, Ritual Magic and Alchemy* (London: Neville Spearman, 1971), p. 137. 'Know Thyself' was originally delivered as a lecture on 24 September 1893. Moina Mathers was married to the Hermetic Order of the Golden Dawn's 'Chief', Samuel Liddell MacGregor Mathers, and was instrumental in the development of the Order's teachings. The Flying Rolls were teaching documents prepared by high officials within the Order.

25 Vestigia Nulla Retrorsum (Moina Mathers), Flying Roll No. XXI, 'Know Thyself', in Francis King (ed.), *Astral Projection, Ritual Magic and Alchemy,* pp. 137–45, establishes that the adept must seek to understand and reconcile

the 'I' of three levels of consciousness: Human Consciousness, Spiritual Consciousnesses and Divine Consciousnesses. See Francis King's helpful introduction to the Kabbalistic basis of the esoteric psychology taught in the Golden Dawn as elaborated in Flying Roll No. XX, 'Constitution of Man', originally delivered as a lecture by S. L. MacGregor Mathers on 23 September 1893, *ibid.*, pp. 129–35. Mary K. Greer, *Women of the Golden Dawn: Rebels and Priestesses* (Rochester, VT: Park Street Press, 1995), p. 134, also provides a brief and useful explanation of the Golden Dawn system.

26 See Florence Farr, 'The Rosicrucians and Alchemists', *Occult Review,* Vol. 7, No. 5 (January–June 1908): 259–64.

27 Annie Besant, *A Study in Consciousness. A Contribution to the Science of Psychology* (1904; London: Theosophical Publishing Society, 1915 [2nd edition], pp. 224, 221–2, 225–6, 229, 232. See also Annie Besant, *Theosophy and the New Psychology* (London: Theosophical Publishing Society, 1904).

28 The Golden Dawn followed Eliphas Lévi, the French occultist, in referring to planes other than the physical as the Astral Light. Madame Blavatsky also referred to the Astral Light, but the term should not be confused with the 'astral plane' of the Theosophists, which refers simply to one occult dimension close to that of the physical. See, Francis King, *Modern Ritual Magic: The Rise of Western Occultism* (Bridport: Prism Press, 1989), p. 56.

29 'Ritual U', *The Secret Wisdom of the Lesser World or Microcosm which is Man*, Part 5: Of Travelling in the Spirit Vision, reproduced in R. A. Gilbert *The Golden Dawn: Twilight of the Magicians,* p. 130. 'Ritual U' provided Adepts with the theoretical basis of Astral Travel.

30 See *A Short Enquiry Concerning the Hermetic Art* by a Lover of Philalethes, Preface by Non Omnis Moriar [William Wynn Westcott], An Introduction to Alchemy and Notes by S.S.D.D. [Florence Farr] (London: Theosophical Publishing Society, 1894), Introduction, p. 11.

31 William Wynn Westcott, 'A Recent Spiritual Development', S.R.I.A., *Transactions of the Metropolitan College* (1917), pp. 18–25. Reproduced in R. A. Gilbert *The Magical Mason. Forgotten Hermetic Writings of William Wynn Westcott, Physician and Magus* (Wellingborough: The Aquarian Press, 1983), pp. 294–5.

32 William Wynn Westcott, 'A Recent Spiritual Development', reproduced in R. A. Gilbert, *Magical Mason*, pp. 294–5.

33 This process of mapping relied on another complex magical procedure, associated in the Golden Dawn with an imaging technique involving a Sphere of Sensation and the Kabbalistic Tree of Life. See Mary K. Greer, *Women of the Golden Dawn*, p. 428, footnote 26.

34 See Annie Besant *A Study in Consciousness*, pp. 208–9; and Annie Besant, *The Reality of the Invisible and the Actuality of the Unseen Worlds*, reprinted

from *The Theosophical Review*, Vol. XXXVI, No. 216 (August 1905) (Adyar, Madras: Theosophical Publishing House, 1921), *passim.*

35 Florence Farr, *The Solemnization of Jacklin: Some Adventures on the Search for Reality* (London: A. C. Fifield, 1912), p. 157.

36 Annie Besant, *Why I Became a Theosophist* (London: Theosophical Publishing Society, 1891), p. 17. The pamphlet was written in July 1889.

37 William Wynn Westcott, 'Man, Miracle, Magic. From the Ancient Rosicrucian Dogmata', a paper read to members of the Isis Temple of the Golden Dawn, undated, in R. A. Gilbert, *The Magical Mason*, p. 66; Florence Farr, 'The Magic of a Symbol', *The Occult Review*, Vol. VII, No. 2 (February 1908): 86

38 See 'The Future of the New Age', *New Age*, 1 (2 May 1907), p. 8. See also Note 9 of the present paper for Holbrook Jackson's connection with Orage.

39 See, for example, Annie Besant, 'On the Watch-Tower', *The Theosophical Review*, XXVII, September 1900–February 1901, 101–2. See also A. R. Orage, *Consciousness: Animal, Human, and Superman* (London: Theosophical Publishing Society, 1907).

40 Vestigia Nulla Retrorsum, Flying Roll No. XXI, 'Know Thyself', in Francis King (ed.), *Astral Projection, Ritual Magic and Alchemy*, pp. 140, 141.

41 Joy Dixon, 'Gender, Politics, and Culture in the New Age: Theosophy in England, 1880–1935', Ph.D., Rutgers, The State University of New Jersey, January 1993, develops this theme. For an elaboration of the fascist theme, see N. Goodrick-Clarke, *The Occult Roots of Nazism: The Ariosophists of Austria and Germany* (Wellingborough: Aquarian Press, 1985).

42 Natan Zach, 'Imagism and Vorticism', in Bradbury and McFarlane (eds), *Modernism*, p. 229.

43 This is Frank Kermode's phrase. See Frank Kermode, *Romantic Image* (New York: Chilmark Press, 1961), p. 128, and his discussion of T. E. Hulme, pp. 119–37.

44 Frank Kermode, *Romantic Image*, considers these issues in his chapter on Arthur Symons, pp. 107–18, and was influential in establishing the importance of the hermetic tradition (and specifically Magic) for Romantic, Symbolist, and early twentieth-century post-Symbolist aesthetics.

45 See Timothy Materer, *Modernist Alchemy: Poetry and the Occult* (Ithaca, NY: Cornell University Press, 1995), for a full consideration of the impact of occultism on twentieth-century poetry.

46 W. B. Yeats, *Memoirs* (London: Macmillan, 1972), p. 73.

47 For a helpful introduction to vitalism, see George Rousseau, 'The Perpetual Crises of Modernism and the Traditions of Enlightenment Vitalism: with a Note on Mikhail Bakhtin', in Burwick and Douglass (eds), *The Crisis in Modernism: Bergson and the Vitalist Controversy* (Cambridge: Cambridge University Press, 1992), pp. 15–75.

48 Henri Bergson *Creative Evolution,* trans. Arthur Mitchell (1911; reprint edn, London: Macmillan, 1960), p. 174. The 1911 edition was the first available English translation of *L'Evolution créatrice* first published in French in 1907. In his 1903 article, 'Introduction to Metaphysics', Bergson identifies two kinds of knowledge – analysis and intuition. He develops his theme in *Creative Evolution*, where he distinguishes intuition from both 'intellect' (or 'intelligence') and 'instinct'. Bergson's definition of intuition is elusive, but he argues that it is conscious, reflective, and capable of grasping 'life'. In this sense, intuition outstrips intellect and instinct (to which it is related). For a helpful if partial exposition of Bergson's ideas published in 1926 by a long-time friend, see J. Chevalier, *Bergson*, trans. L. A. Clare (London: Rider, 1928).

49 See Henri Bergson, *Creative Evolution*, pp. 281–2, 241. For a helpful discussion of these issues, see Jurgen Klein, 'Vitalism, Empiricism, and the Quest for Reality in German and English Philosophy', in Burwick and Douglass (eds), *The Crisis in Modernism*, pp. 190–229.

50 In fact, Bergson's position was close to that of Madame Blavatsky, who asserted that 'the infinite cannot be known by the finite', and emphasized that 'superhuman knowledge' of 'the divine essence could be communicated to the higher spiritual Self in a state of ecstasy'. See H. P. Blavatsky *The Key to Theosophy*, p. 10.

51 Some of the most renowned international psychologists, including Bernheim, Janet, Richet, Lombroso, Schrenck-Notzing, William James, and subsequently, Freud, were members of the late-Victorian Society for Psychical Research. The Society for Psychical Research was founded in 1882 by a group of well-educated men dedicated to the goal of objective investigation of paranormal phenomena. William James served as president of the Society during 1894–5, and Freud finally became a Corresponding Member in 1911. Bergson also served as a pre-war president of the Society.

52 For a discussion of Freud and occultism, see Ernest Jones, *The Life and Work of Sigmund Freud*, Vol. 3 (New York: Basic Books, 1957), pp. 375–407; and James Webb, *The Occult Establishment* (La Salle, IL: Open Court Publishing Company, 1976), Chapter 6. Freud referred to the occult as 'the black tide of mud' in an exchange with Jung and appeared to be using the term synonomously with psychical research. For his remarks, see C. G. Jung, *Memories, Dreams, Reflections*, recorded and edited by Aniela Jaffe, trans. Richard and Clara Winston (London: Fontana Press, 1993), p. 173.

53 W. B. Yeats, *Autobiographies*, 'The Trembling of the Veil' [1922] (London: Macmillan, 1979), p. 183.

54 C. G. Jung, *Memories, Dreams, Reflections*, p. 231.

55 Paul de Man, 'What is Modern?', p. 12, argues that modern thought 'at its best' has been characterized by 'the persistent attempt of a consciousness to reach an understanding of itself'.

56 These were themes that were to be explored later in the century by members of the Institut für Sozialforschung (Institute of Social Research), now commonly referred to as the Frankfurt School. Figures associated with the Institut include Max Horkheimer, Theodor W. Adorno, and Walter Benjamin. The Frankfurt School's Critical Theory addressed idealist philosophy and reviewed *fin-de-siècle* notions of the self in its own blend of Marxist and psychoanalytic theory. Given Theodor Adorno's trenchant critique of occultism during the 1940s and 1950s, it is poignantly instructive of the ongoing purchase of *fin-de-siècle* 'Mysticism' that as the human tragedy of the First World War unfolded the young Walter Benjamin was immersing himself in Symbolist writing and preparing to move on to mystical philosophy, apocalyptic prophecy, and the Jewish Kabbalah.

57 Marshall Berman, 'Why Modernism Still Matters', in *Modernity and Identity*, ed. Scott Lash and Jonathan Friedman (Oxford: Basil Blackwell, 1992), p. 42. For Freud's reckoning with the horrors of the Great War, see 'Thoughts for the Times on War and Death' (1915), and *Civilization and its Discontents* (1930, 1931).

58 Florence Farr, *The Mystery of Time. A Masque* (London: The Theosophical Publishing Society, 1905), Preface.

5

Psychology and the 'Consciousness of Modernity' in Early Twentieth-century Britain

Mathew Thomson

It has long been assumed that a disjuncture in psychological theory, associated in particular with the work of Sigmund Freud, was a key component in a reconceptualization of consciousness within the intellectual and artistic modernism of the early twentieth century. What has attracted less attention is the impact of a much broader, concurrent permeation of psychological knowledge into the culture, the social fabric, and the mentality of the era. It was becoming difficult to conceptualize or describe consciousness without drawing on the models and language of psychology, and this was reinforced by the emergence of a series of everyday practices for the management and development of this psychological self. Although this mediating role can be traced back to the eighteenth century, both the social extent of psychology's influence and its pre-eminent authority over alternative secular and religious frameworks for locating the self in the world were unprecedented.[1]

Social and cultural historians have paid surprisingly little attention to this development within the British context. And the work of historians of medicine has tended to emphasize resistance towards Freud, particularly by contrast with a warmer reception in the United States. They point out that his theories were criticized as over-dogmatic, lacking a firm empirical basis, dangerously demoting the power of will over base instinct, and lacking balance and good taste in their single-minded emphasis on the sexual drive. And psychoanalysis was attacked as exposing patients to abuse when under hypnosis, opening the field to untrained quacks, and establishing a kind of semi-mystical cult. The psychodynamic practice that did slowly emerge was of a suitably modified, moderate and more eclectic version.[2] Recent work on the impact of Freud among the educated reading public provides a more enthusiastic though still ambivalent picture.[3] However, there is still a tendency, as within broader social histories, to dismiss from serious consideration the evidence of fairly widespread interest in both a bastardized and watered-down Freudianism and a series of non-Freudian psychologies on the medical, occult, and religious fringes. Indeed, the latter have invariably been dismissed as intellectually superficial and faddish, and regarded as further evidence of the relative weakness of modernist thought within the broader culture.[4] In sum, though still blinkered by the Freudian paradigm, historians are beginning to construct a more complex picture of the culture of psychoanalysis; but we still know very little in practice about consciousness among the majority or about the vast mass of non-Freudian psychological theory that circulated within popular culture.

The potential for radically broadening our approach to psychological culture is highlighted by recent work that takes seriously the place of psychological theory within the occult movement of the era.[5] It would be wrong, however, to limit such an argument to fairly elitist occult sects. For instance, the engagement with the problem of consciousness and a serious interest in the latest psychological theory can be traced among much broader coteries of theosophists, spiritualists, Christian Scientists, and followers of the New Thought movements who occupied what was during this period a highly active and large territory between the poles of orthodox religion and the occult.[6] Popular fascination with and eagerness to explore the hitherto unknown realms of the mind also led to the formation of a series of 'practical psychology' movements in the first decades of the century. The exact influence of this loosely-knit movement is almost impossible to measure; it certainly reached considerably further than the active membership of the affiliated clubs that emerged in many of the country's major towns and cities. Regular subscription journals, correspondence courses, public meetings, and clinics brought both theory and practice to a much more extensive audience. Clubs emerged from the start of the century in London, where they attracted what appears to have been a Bohemian audience already immersed in a culture of vegetarianism and diet reform, eurhythmics, and eastern mysticism – the 'people in the van', as H. G. Wells put it.[7] The idea that some 90 per cent of mental power lay beyond consciousness, but might be accessed through the modern techniques of psychology, brought the prospect of a new capacity for mental sensitivity and in turn for exercising greater control over the body. This provided a natural, holistic bridge with these other cultures of self-development and also with a burgeoning commodity culture centred around them; indeed, the new popular science of consciousness had strong claims to being the key to development of body as well as of mind. Drawing on a somewhat different social constituency, appealing to middle-class and lower-middle-class aspirations for self improvement, clubs gradually emerged in other areas of the country, particularly the North-West and North-East, and growth accelerated in the 1920s. By 1939 the British Union of Practical Psychologists had expanded to the extent that it was organized into four regional federations (Northern, Yorkshire, Lancashire and British), and its fifty-three clubs stretched from as far afield as Torquay and Worthing, to Glasgow and Dundee.

The vast majority of the population, who did not actively enter into or directly encounter this associational culture, were nevertheless increasingly likely to be regularly exposed to a similar language, similar assumptions about human nature, and similar promises of a better life on the basis of psychological guidance and insight. The Blackpool-based Mr A. Myddleton, a teacher and the publisher of manuals like *Suggestion that Wins*, *Life Building*, *How to Analyse Yourself*, and *Psychology in Business*, as well as the editor of the journal *Practical Psychology*, was not alone in recognizing this in the mid-1920s:

> Psychology is everywhere; week by week it is more and more in evidence in almost every walk of life, and in wider and still wider circles it is frequently on the lips of public speakers. Preachers take some phrase of psychology as the subject of an attractive sermon. Magazines are full of it – and now we find our evening newspapers devoting a leading article to its consideration; the dailies print articles from prominent psychologists; on every hand, in fact, as an esteemed correspondent writes: "Psychology is going with a bang".[8]

A much more general and deeply entrenched self-help culture was becoming increasingly psychological in tone. Albeit in a form radically transmuted from orthodox academic theory, innumerable manuals and advice columns would offer the psychological secrets of perfect health, happiness, and business success. This latter audience was a particular target for the self-improvement manual. During the interwar period women also became an increasingly important audience, as was reflected in the growing volume of titles published on the psychological problems of child-rearing.[9] And everyday phenomena were redefined as problems of psychological self-management.[10] Psychology also extended its influence within the sex manuals that began to reach best-selling status during this period. Although the psychology within many of these texts, for instance Marie Stopes's *Married Love*, which sold half a million copies between 1918 and 1924, has been dismissed by historians as 'sub-Freudian', superficial and vaguely mystical, it clearly appealed to contemporary sensibilities, and as such its meaning and significance deserve more careful consideration.[11] An active interest in the psychological perspective was also spreading from the occult and spiritualist fringe into increasingly orthodox religious circles, where it appeared to meet a need for a new spirituality of personal development, a modernist openness to the discoveries of science, and a reinvigorated practical pastoralism, and where it was diffused with evangelical zeal in sermons, prayer gatherings, radio broadcasts, and Sunday School teaching.[12] In sum, not only were new languages and theories of consciousness being diffused to a truly mass audience, but the interactive nature of courses, manuals, advice columns, and public meetings and services was reinforcing the shift of understanding through everyday practice.

There is an equally strong case for moving away from the narrow Freudian paradigm towards recognizing a much broader shift in the understanding of consciousness when we turn to academic psychological writing and its influence on other disciplines. Here, well before any significant awareness of Freud – which only developed, and then hesistantly, after the first English translation of his work in 1911 – there was a fundamental reconceptualization of human psychology in the last decades of the nineteenth and the first decades of the twentieth centuries. In short, the role of mind in mediating between experience and action or knowledge was radically problematized, and in the process the architecture of consciousness was opened up as a territory for exploration, with implications for all areas of human understanding. The utilitarian model of man as a psychological hedonist, whose actions were determined by rational, self-interested calculations of resulting pleasure and pain, became untenable. In this post-Darwinian era, an appreciation of the role of instinct in animal psychology was extended to the human species. Early anthropological study of 'primitive races' and their beliefs and of folklore within Western culture encouraged this shift in thinking. The human mind was recognized as having a mind of its own: it was now a purposive agent, not simply reacting to its environment, but dynamically interacting with it as instinct and emotion were tamed and channelled by will, sentiments, and ideals. Mind was also reconfigured as complex and layered, containing deep within itself the mental traces of a more primitive, impulsive past. Confidence in a unitary, rational self was on the wane; belief in a multidimensional and potentially irrational self was on the rise. Such a shift was further encouraged by the rejection of a merely introspective approach to the study of mind (which was naturally predisposed to focus on conscious, rational thought) and the reorientation towards the 'practical' study of behaviour and scientific research into psychopathology and the 'psychic'. Phenomena such as hysteria, split personality, crowd behaviour, hypnosis, and mental sensitivity to the thoughts of others, including the dead, all suggested the existence of a vigorous subliminal mental world and called into question the primacy of the rational, individual consciousness. What had earlier been regarded as an irrationality confined to the mad was increasingly accepted as something that was integral to the normal mind, manifesting itself in everyday phenomena such as the dreams of sleep. In an era in which physical science was discovering new invisible forms of energy, it seemed only reasonable to consider the possibility that minds might occupy a sea of mental energy, thoughts might travel from mind to mind, and personalities might survive bodily death. And in an era in which physicists were replacing a world of Newtonian certainty with relativity, it is unsurprising that there was a loss of confidence in a mechanistic sensationalist psychology or in a consciousness that was fixed in time or space.

On an international scale, the response of British intellectuals and academics to this reframing of consciousness may have been muted, typically moderate, and modified in line with a powerful prevailing faith in man's potential for rational and moral action; but reframed in response to new ideas about consciousness it still was.[13] Assumptions about human psychology in a broad range of academic studies in the decades after 1900 would reflect this, particularly within the social sciences, where disciplinary boundaries were still relatively fluid. In his influential and broadly read, *Introduction to Social Psychology* of 1908, William McDougall argued that psychology's new insights into the nature of man were essential for the study of politics, economics, sociology, anthropology and history, as well as for effective government – for any subject that depended on the science of man.[14] This grandiose vision for social psychology was never fully realized, and many of its theoretical assumptions about group behaviour would subsequently attract more criticism than admiration; but it is important to recognize the ways in which the insights, the questions, and the language of McDougall and fellow psychologists did nevertheless influence work in the other disciplines. In an era of syndicalism, jingoism, the emergence of mass politics, and descent into world war, political scientists, for instance, could scarcely overlook the fact that psychology had cast into doubt the rational nature of their subjects;[15] even if, like the pioneer of the subject in Britain, Graham Wallas, they still attempted to defend a rational politics and were critical of the growing alarm about the loss of individual consciousness in mass society.[16] The interwar experience of the attractions of apparently irrational demagoguery, xenophobic nationalism, and extremism would reinforce the case for recognizing consciousness as a political problem.[17] The mind of the economic subject was similarly problematized in a retreat from classical theory; most notably, John Maynard Keynes would draw on psychological theory to recognize the irrationality of economic man and the importance of the 'pleasure principle' in motivating action.[18] Others would recognize the economic and political value of psychology in developing a more sophisticated understanding of the behaviour of consumers, employers and owners, and workers and their unions.[19] Anthropology, in its formative first decades at the start of the century, was almost impossible to separate from psychology, with figures such as C. S. Myers, W. H. R. Rivers, C. G. Seligman, McDougall (all members of the seminal Torres Straits expedition of 1898), and B. Malinowski straddling or at least connecting the two disciplines and turning the anthroplogical field into a psychological laboratory for under-standing the 'savage within' of civilized man.[20] In the nascent field of academic sociology, the considerable space devoted to psychology within the new *Sociological Review*, founded in 1908, attests to the seriousness attached to the question of consciousness. Even in the writing of history, there were those who consciously attempted to integrate and explore a new model of human psychology;[21] and it can be assumed that the majority who did not were at least more aware than their forebears of a new difficulty in interpreting the actions and motivations of their historical subjects.

If Britons inhabited an increasingly psychological world after 1900, in what sense can consciousness within this world be regarded, not only as 'psychologized', but also as peculiarly, and because of the psychological dimension, the 'consciousness of modernity'? One approach to this question is to study contemporary self-perceptions. These are easiest to trace among the intellectuals of the period. Here, there is clear evidence that a belief that psychology offered new keys to understanding human consciousness was often an essential part of a sense of being modern. Virginia Woolf's observation that 'On or about December 1910 human character changed' captures this self-consciousness. Although her specific reference-point was a shift in visual representation at the first London exhibition of work by Manet and the Post-Impressionists, she was also drawing a parallel with the contrasting views of human psychology manifested in the move from the Edwardian to the Georgian generation of novelists.[22] No Freudian herself, Woolf still clearly saw herself as modern because of a new understanding of consciousness; though others within her Bloomsbury world did tie themselves more closely to the Freudian mast in constructing a modernist identity.[23] Even the generation dismissed by Woolf for an outdated understanding of human psychology were themselves both increasingly fascinated by the subject and well aware of its potential for self-transformation. In his *Secret Places of the Heart* of 1922, for instance, H. G. Wells highlighted the coupling of psychology and the modern, with his portrayal of Dr Martineau and his attempt to find a new source of meaning amidst the stresses of modern life in his aptly titled 'The Psychology of the New Age'.[24] It was no coincidence that journals with titles such as the *New Age* and the *New Era* would become advocates for the new understanding of mind.

The very language and scientific pretensions of psychology projected an aura of modernity. When people spoke of the 'New Psychology', as they did by the first decades of the century, they acknowledged their self-consciousness of a break with the past.[25] This was reinforced by a series of more specific linguistic markers of psychological progress. Perhaps the most important of these was the spatial model of the discovery of new 'levels' of mind. In the old world, attention had largely been limited to conscious thought; in the new world, understanding had broken through to an altogether different stage of what was variously described as the subconscious, unconscious, subliminal or superconscious.[26] The idea that the new realms were much vaster and thus potentially more powerful than the old caused unsurprising excitement. On the popular fringe, the idea that through tapping into this power, the human mind could become sensitive to a hitherto hidden world of thought and sensation – that absorbed constantly outside of consciousness – suggested not only a break with the past, but also a path into the future via a new stage of mental evolution and the development of a 'higher' consciousness. Even at the level of more mainstream academic thought, there was considerable excitement about psychology's revolutionizing the human sciences and being harnessed to guide mind – now recognized as highly dynamic and malleable – in a new era of mental evolution.

This sense of the modern was magnified by the way psychological discourse drew on the broader experience of modernity, both as its subject-matter and as a fund of metaphor. In self-improvement literature, the pace, complexity, artificiality, and sheer bombardment of the senses in modern life (acting on a mind now recognized by psychologists as highly prone to such influences because of its innate 'suggestibility') framed the diagnosis of a consciousness in need of new vitality, harmony, and authenticity. And in social psychology, the emergence of the 'great society', with its intensified systems of communication and its concentration of individuals into crowds and organizations was recognized as a fundamenally transformed environment for individual consciousness. The growing awareness of 'primitive' societies through anthropology acted to heighten this sense of civilization's own modernity. In terms of language, popular psychology was rich in metaphor drawn from recent developments in technology and science. The mind, for instance, was compared to a radio: projecting as well as receiving. Thought was imagined as a form of wave energy, like the recently discovered X-ray, invisible to the human eye. And the 'storehouse' of unconscious memory was compared to the phonograph: everything a person had ever experienced made an imprint on mind, like musical vibrations carving grooves in a record, and though this imprint might now be stored away deep within the unconscious, like a record it might one day be retrieved and played back. More than anything else, however, in popular and academic psychology alike, it was the power of scientific language that was most important in positioning knowledge as modern. A series of vague and purely speculative concepts about mind were given authority by their location within systems of mental classification. The paradoxical concept of the unconscious, for instance, was turned into part of a new biological-style topography of layers of mental evolution. Likewise, the focus on instinct – again, a conceptual field that in fact lacked a firm empirical basis – assumed authority as it spawned a new project of anatomizing the multiple instincts of man, their interrelation, and their order of dominance and subordination. New models of consciousness, in sum, were modern because they appeared to have been placed, at last, on a scientific basis. The ability to draw on the growing reputations of figures such as Freud, Jung and Adler, even when there was, as so often, a profound gap between theory and popular interpretation, added a final dimension to this modernist, scientific aura.

The problem with an analysis of the consciousness of modernity that is limited to contemporary self-perceptions is that to a degree all eras see themselves as modern. Of course, one can argue that some periods have a more acute sense of being modern than others, and that this together with the coincidence of a sense of radical innovation in psychological theory provides the early twentieth century with claims to a particular significance. However, it is also surely necessary to engage with the use of modernity as an analytical marker of a particular stage of historical development: both one associated with a particular form of consciousness, and a form that was the product of the broader conditions of modernity.

Reframed in these terms, although the origins of a modern, individualist consciousness must clearly be located much earlier, the psychologizing process of the early twentieth century can be conceptualized as pushing this development to a new and accentuated stage.[27] For instance, the opening up of a more extensive internal topography of the self furthered an interiorization of identity. With self increasingly to be discovered within, and with self-development increasingly a project of managing one's own psychic economy and 'personality', rather than simply an issue of public conduct and 'character', the individualism, and in turn potentially the atomization and narcissism, that have been associated with the experience of modernity were all encouraged. The heightened awareness of mind's role in mediating between experience and reality both placed the individual at the centre of the world and presented knowledge of this world as relative, contributing much towards that self-reflexivity that has been regarded as such a central feature of modernity. Finally, a fragmentation of mind into multiple levels of consciousness, and an acknowledgement of the power of the irrational in instincts and the suggestive force of the unconscious brought a new potential for complexity to self-identity. A minority of modernists would respond by embracing the irrational and the dissolution of a fixed self. However, the project of self-realization more often looked towards these powers of the mind being harnessed and channelled in tandem with the rational. Only then, with the full self working in harmony, might the highest form of consciousness be attained. In that sense, the irrational consciousness of radical modernism was to a large degree tamed within the more general culture of psychological self-development.

The new psychological models, languages, and practices can also be seen as responses to broader processes of modernization. This can help to explain the often remarkable similarities between ostensibly disparate occultist, popular, and academic psychologies; discourse refracting a modernist reality, rather than acting as the spark that alone created it. Perhaps the most important of these modernizing processes was secularization. Psychology can be seen as helping to re-enchant life, replacing the meaningless void left by the supplanting of a God-centred by a materialist world-view with an apparently scientific yet still humanistic path to a higher state of being.[28] The wonder once provided by divine salvation was now to be found in the search for a transcendent level of personal consciousness. The ethics of scripture made way for the ethics of the psychologically healthy life as laid out in countless manuals. And the confessional gave way to varieties of psychoanalysis. Not only was such a faith attractive to those who had rejected religion altogether; it was also fundamental to the myriad spiritualist and 'new thought' movements of the day, and it reinvigorated a more orthodox Christian constituency, which responded to secularization by modernizing religion. Moreover, the idea that transcendence could be found through development of consciousness was taken very seriously within the work of respected academic psychologists well into the interwar period.[29]

Economic modernization was the second key prerequisite for the expansion of this psychological culture. The extension, beyond the wealthy – to whom anxieties over neurasthenia earlier in the nineteenth century had largely been restricted – to lower-middle- and working-class self-improving constituencies of a culture of worrying about and cultivating the psychological domain of the self and its relationships, and the development of a mass therapeutic industry of cures, advice manuals, and courses were facilitated as the availability of surplus time and money extended to new social groups and as a culture of commodification reached further into the recesses of private life.[30] The even more pronounced development of a psychotherapeutic culture in the United States during this period can be explained in part by the fact that such socio-economic conditions were earlier and more highly developed there.[31]

Clearly, an appreciation of the psychological perspective helps to illuminate what was peculiarly modern about consciousness in the new century. However, it must also be recognized that the culture of the new psychology looked to the past as well as the future and often reacted against the modernity of the present. It looked to re-embed the atomized 'modern' self in the tradition and culture of the social. And in its construction of new languages and practices of self-development, it often built on, rather than rejected, more traditional discourses of self. In sum, the consciousness of the era was not exclusively progressive, individualist, or new: if it was the 'consciousness of modernity', it was a modernity rooted in this type of contradiction.[32]

The emphasis on inheritance of instincts within British psychological theory was one way in which the primitive past was conceptualized as still lying within the civilized, unconscious mind. William McDougall, for instance, constructed a model of consciousness that revolved around the intelligent modification of the instincts of flight, repulsion, curiosity, pugnacity, self-abasement, self-assertion, reproduction, acquisition and construction, and the parental and gregarious instincts.[33] Others included a religious instinct. Most typically, variants on three instincts – sex, self-centredness, and sociability – took centre stage. Though the past was thus recognized in the present, it was also distanced from it through an appreciation of the way intelligence and environment had civilized and repressed instinct in its original form. In the tension between this civilizing, repressing process and the innnate desire to satisfy instinctive impulse lay, it was realized, one of the fundamental roots of the unease, dissatisfaction. and mental conflict within modern life. To many followers of the new psychology, therefore, the search for a reinvigoration of modernity – for the 'New Life', as many put it – depended on an acceptance and rediscovery of the primitive dimension of consciousness hidden within.[34]

Theories of memory, since they dealt with more specific, recent and meaningful traces of the past, were even more important in this process of re-embedding the modern consciousness. The idea that all experience was recorded in memory, albeit in a memory often hidden from the conscious mind and expressed through the influence of the unconscious, opened up the possibility of a rich but hidden past identity. In particular, it located the past of a preconscious childhood within the adult personality, and thus helped turn the search for the lost mind of the child into one of the century's great sources for identity and psychotherapeutic salvation.[35] Commonly at a popular level, and less commonly in the realms of academic theory, since it demanded acceptance of a largely discredited Lamarckian model of inheritance, though with notable exceptions such as the Jungians with their theory of archetypes and the influential McDougall with his concept of a 'Group Mind', it was also proposed that the memories of former generations were inherited by the present. Like the behavioural pattern of the instinct, generation after generation of common experience, it was argued – dictated for instance by local climate, geography, and cultural tradition – left an imprint in consciousness that was passed on as organic memory.[36] Within the unconscious, this common experience also stimulated a common set of myths, dream images, and archetypes that became embedded in the psyche of a people. The individual consciousness, as such, was integrally tied to the communal consciousness of past generations; more particularly, the English consciousness looked back to the history, traditions and culture of the nation.[37]

The idea that a disposition to act as a member of the nation – or of other manifestations of the social, such as the crowd, class, or the political public – was embedded in individual consciousness could also draw on the theory that a variously named social, gregarious or herd instinct was intrinsic to human consciousness. At an unconscious level, humans were naturally disposed to orientate their behaviour towards the dictates of the group. Pessimistic conclusions about the inherent irrationality of mass politics and mass culture could be drawn from this; though others, more optimistically, would recognize the importance of the social instinct as a force for cohesion and co-operation in mass society, if it was effectively managed. The emphasis on a social instinct would wane in the interwar period; but it would make way for a cultural environmentalism that, in recognizing that consciousness was always modified by its location within the social, concluded that there was no such thing as individual psychology: all psychology was necessarily 'social psychology', and there was no such thing as an exclusively individual consciousness.

The model of a disjuncture between the traditional and the modern is also at odds with the clear continuities or at least evolutionary links between dominant nineteenth-century discourses of self and the new psychological models of consciousness. One of these links, that of the reshaping though persistence of a spiritual dimension, has already been highlighted.[38] A second, that of the evolution from a discourse of character to one of personality development, will now be developed. Woolf's vocabulary, in describing the shift in human consciousness, had been doubly significant: not only had an understanding of 'character' changed, but a framing of the question in these terms was being cast into doubt. A discourse of character had dominated the Victorian culture of self-development.[39] It emphasized moral conduct and public duty, rather than an internal psychological struggle or journey. Samuel Smiles, for instance, directed individuals towards 'truthfulness, mercifulness; and with these integrity, courage, virtue, and goodness in all its phases'.[40] There was little sense, here, of an interiorized journey, apart from the stress on maintaining self-control through rational will over lower, animal impulses. Clearly, the eventual acceptance of these impulses and the emergence of psychological strategies to co-ordinate and harness fully the multiple internal qualities of self constituted a fundamental shift, and this was signified by the growing prominence of a language of 'personality'.[41] However, the ethics of the character discourse were not displaced. Analysis of popular psychological movements, for instance, reveals that public 'service' was invariably regarded as integral to the healthy personality (particularly in the light of theories of thought transference and social instinct, which directly situated the social within the self and the self within the social). Indeed, British practical psychologists were able self-consciously to counterpose their service-orientated model of personality to that prevalent in the United States in these very terms. The same naturalization of an ethics of public conduct – of the importance of good character – was embedded in the psyche within academic psychologies. McDougall, for instance, recognized that his instinct theory, emphasizing as it did the dynamic organization and modification of impulses and their channelling towards higher sentiments, was far from pointing towards a new immorality, and could instead complement the stress on character development of the influential Idealist philosopher T. H. Green.[42] Psychological self-development, in sum, remained a moral and social project, and in its early twentieth-century manifestation, at least, it did not necessarily point towards a 'culture of narcissism'.[43] The psychological reconfigured but still embraced democratic subjectivity.[44]

This chapter has been implicity critical of a counter-narrative of modernity that concentrates on the restriction of freedom through a new 'iron cage' of disciplinary knowledge and bureaucratic regulation. Instead, it has highlighted some of the ways in which psychology provided a tool for the self-fashioning of new identities in response to the opportunities but also the anxieties brought by modernity. On the other hand, any analysis of the consciousness of modernity would remain grossly incomplete without acknowledging and briefly assessing what was clearly in many ways the outstanding development of the era: the regulation of the psychological subject from above. Indeed, even if individuals themselves remained ignorant and uninterested in the psychological perspective, as many no doubt did, they inhabited a world in which their consciousness was beginning to be measured, classified, and managed with direct consequences for their life opportunities whether they knew about it or not.[45]

In the nineteenth century the state had taken a very early interest in this area, the insane emerging as one of its primary recipients of welfare. As such, the bureaucrats, doctors, and lawyers who administered these institutions did help to delineate the boundaries of mental illness, and in doing so influenced broader conceptions about healthy states of consciousness.[46] But whether the huge increase in the number of institutionalized insane over the century can be exclusively attributed to the imposition of a more prescriptive view of normality is debatable; recent research, for instance, questions professional power or independence and highlights the role of families who could not cope with dependants in defining categories of mental disorder. The Mental Deficiency Act of 1913 would add an extra dimension to this policing role, focusing as it did not only on the intellectually subnormal, dull and backward, but also on the socially ineffective and the 'morally defective' sections of the population.[47] Although together these systems of institutional care covered little more than 150,000 inmates by the middle of the interwar period, the influence of the threat of segregation and of systems of early detection within the community, and within schools in particular, should be recognized as considerably broader. The consciousness of modernity, as such, occupied a space whose boundaries were delineated by heavily stigmatized and public markers of mental pathology.

The most fundamental development in the state's role during this period, however, was not the already well-established function of policing boundaries, but the recognition that a dynamic model of consciousness opened the door to new possibilities of shaping human nature. The state's most important response, by far, was in the redesign of the education system. Psychological tests measured and ranked specific mental aptitudes and general intelligence, not only as a eugenic screen to weed out the mentally defective, but also to fit education to the abilities of the child.[48] The movement towards a child-centred education went furthest at the nursery and primary school levels, under the influence of the educational psychology of figures like Maria Montessori. In their training, future teachers were encouraged to understand the world through the developing consciousness of the child. Learning among infants, for instance, was reconceived as an active process, in which doing was more important than being told. Rote learning was gradually rejected. Play, to release instinctive energy, was encouraged and was certainly no longer to be repressed. And the cultivation of creativity and imagination in young children was recognized as just as vital as the development of rational thought.[49] In the reality of the schoolroom, the advance of a psychological perspective fell a long way short of such visions.[50] Nevertheless, one should not underestimate the significance of the educational experience in modifying and moulding the consciousness of this generation of children and future adults.

The comparative success of the state in reaching the mind of the child contrasts with its influence over the adult population. Only in specific institutional sites, such as prisons, some factories, and the army, was adult consciousness prone to psychological observation and possible manipulation. Even in these regulated spaces, however, there remained considerable limitations. For instance, although the First World War shell-shock experience is often seen as the key turning-point in the British acceptance of the new psychology (a perspective in its broader cultural sense that has been implicitly called into question in this chapter's exploration of a more fundamental relationship between modernity and a new view of consciousness), it is also important to note that psychologists faced resistance from military authorities when they suggested that soldiers were suffering from shell-shock, and that their influence within the armed forces virtually disappeared in peacetime.[51] Here, as in the factory or the prison, the problem with a psychological diagnosis was that it challenged more traditional and more institutionally and culturally powerful explanatory systems: the broken-down soldier and the mentally drained worker were still more likely to be regarded as malingerers. Thus, though the initial steps were taken during the first decades of the century, it was not until the Second World War and after that these sites would be fully redesigned in the light of the consciousness of their subjects.[52]

The emergence of the psychological clinic, through the activities of the state, the medical profession, and voluntary organizations was once again a significant departure, and represented the most advanced engagement of organized modernity with new theories of consciousness. However, because of limited resources and expertise, such clinics could never reach more than a small minority of the population; and many continued to cater for private patients alone. Perhaps more significant, therefore, was the fact that general practitioners were beginning to pay more attention to the psychological dimension of illness – though, again, this interest in the psychosomatic would proceed much further after the Second World War. In fact, if a psychotherapeutic culture was emerging already in the first decades of the century, as has been argued in this chapter, it was more a product of activities within the popular sphere; in part, the medical profession's tentative movement in this direction was a response to the challenge of this broader culture's non-orthodox claims to therapeutic efficacy.

In sum, despite the clear significance of organized modernity's growing interest in consciousness, the reach and practical effects of the state's 'psychological complex' should not be exaggerated. Psychology's main advances in shaping and articulating a language to describe the consciousness of modernity came from the activities and ideas of movements within popular culture as much as if not more than being imposed from above. Ultimately, these movements would become increasingly institutionalized, and in the second half of the century their ideas and most importantly their strategy of spreading the psychological perspective through internalization and self-government would be appropriated and tamed by the medical profession, advertisers, managers, and psychological specialists to position the modern consciousness within a matrix of psychological assumptions.[53] However, this chapter has argued that the central position of a psychological perspective within consciousness – the consciousness of modernity, not just of modernism – was already being pioneered in the first decades of the century, well beyond the parameters of organized modernity and the psychological discipline.

Notes

1 On the permeation of psychology into culture since the late eighteenth century see G. J. Barker-Benfield, *The Culture of Sensibility: Sex and Society in Eighteenth-Century Britain* (Chicago and London: University of Chicago Press, 1992); and J. Oppenheim, *Shattered Nerves: Doctors, Patients, and Depression in Victorian England* (New York and Oxford: Oxford University Press, 1991).

2 On the British reception: Oppenheim, *Shattered Nerves*, pp. 304–11; T. Turner, 'James Crichton-Browne and the Anti-Psychoanalysts', in H. Freeman and H. Berrios (eds), *150 Years of British Psychiatry. Volume II: The Aftermath* (London: Athlone, 1996), pp. 144–55; and M. Pines, 'The Development of the Psycho-dynamic Movement', in H. Freeman and G. Berrios (eds), *150 Years of British Psychiatry* (London: Gaskell, 1991), pp. 206–31. On the readiness of North Americans to adopt an (optimistically) modified Freudianism: N. Hale Jr., *Freud and the Americans: The Beginnings of Psychoanalysis in the United States, 1876–1917*; and *The Rise and Crisis of Psychoanalysis in the United States: Freud and the Americans, 1917–1985* (New York and Oxford: Oxford University Press, 1995).

3 D. Rapp, 'The Early Discovery of Freud by the British General Educated Reading Public, 1912–19', *Social History of Medicine*, 3 (1990): 217-45; D. Rapp, 'The Reception of Freud by the British Press: General Interest and Literary Magazines, 1920–1925', *Journal of the History of the Behavioural Sciences*, 24 (1988): 191–201; and S. Ellesley, 'Psychoanalysis in Early Twentieth Century England: A Study in the Popularisation of Ideas' (unpublished Ph.D. thesis, University of Essex, 1995).

4 R. Graves and A. Hodge, *The Long Weekend: A Social History of Great Britain, 1918–1939* (London: Penguin, 1971), pp. 98–100.

5 Alex Owen, 'Occultism and the ''Modern'' Self in Fin-de-Siecle Britain', paper to the symposium on 'The Consciousness of Modernity', University of London, 1998 in this volume. See also her 'The Sorcerer and His Apprentice: Aleister Crowley and the Magical Exploration of Edwardian Subjectivity', *Journal of British Studies*, 36 (1997): 99–133.

6 On the emergence of an interest in the 'psychological' within nineteenth-century spiritualism: J. Oppenheim, *The Other World: Spiritualism and Psychical Research in England, 1850–1914* (Cambridge: Cambridge University Press, 1985), pp. 238–9. Oppenheim estimates that there were between 10,000 and 100,000 active spiritualists by the First World War, and some 200 local spiritualist lyceums: *The Other World*, pp. 50, 103. See also: R. Hayward, 'Popular Mysticism and the Origins of the New Psychology, 1880–1910', (unpublished Ph.D. thesis, University of Lancaster, 1995).

7 H. G. Wells, *Ann Veronica* (London: T. Fisher Unwin, 1909).

8 Editorial, *Practical Psychology* (Blackpool, Sept. 1925), p. 2.

9 For instance: Mary Chadwick, *Chapters about Childhood: The Psychology of Children from 5–10 years* (London, 1939); and Robert Ladell, *The Parents' Problem: or How to Tell Children about Sex* (London, 1941).

10 See for instance the series of practical psychology handbooks published by the *Psychologist* magazine between the mid 1930s and the early 1950s. In 1936 alone these included: W. J. Macbride, *The Conquest of Fear through Psychology* (London, 1936); W. J. Macbride, *The Inferiority Complex: Its Meaning and Treatment* (London, 1936); Wilfred Northfield, *Curing Nervous Tension* (London, 1936); Howard Littleton Philp, *Memory: How To Make the Most of it* (London, 1936); and 'Psychologist', *Nervousness: Its Cause Prevention and Cure* (London, 1936).

11 M. Stopes, *Married Love* (London: Putnam, 1918). Suggesting that the psychology usually came in a bowdlerized form: R. McKibbin, *Classes and Cultures: England, 1918–1951* (Oxford: Oxford University Press, 1998), p. 299; L. Hall and R. Porter, *The Facts of Life: The Creation of Sexual Knowledge in Britain, 1600–1950* (New Haven, CT and London: Yale University Press, 1995), p. 189; and J. Weeks, *Sex, Politics and Society: The Regulation of Sexuality since 1800* (Longman, 1981), pp. 152–6.

12 S. Mews, 'The Revival of Spiritual Healing in the Church of England, 1920–26', in W. J. Shiels (ed.), *The Church and Healing* (Oxford: Basil Blackwell, 1982), pp. 299–331; and J. C. Travell, 'Psychology and Ministry With Special Reference to the Life, Works and Influence of Leslie Dixon Weatherhead' (unpublished Ph.D. thesis, University of Sheffield, 1996). For examples of the diffusion: E. Waterhouse, *An ABC of Psychology: For Sunday School Teachers and Bible Students*, 4th edition (London: Magnet Press, 1933); and E. Waterhouse, *Psychology and Religion: A Series of Broadcast Talks* (London: Elkin, Matthews and Marriot: London, 1930).

13 R. Soffer, *Ethics and Society in England: The Revolution in the Social Sciences, 1870–1914* (Berkeley, CA and London: University of California Press, 1978).

14 First published by Methuen in 1908, *An Introduction to Social Psychology* had been reprinted thirty times by 1960. See also his proposal to place

psychology at the centre of anthroplogical and historical analysis: *Anthropology and History* (Oxford: Oxford University Press, 1920). For a critique of his vision of psychology as a new tool of government: R. Soffer, 'New Elitism: Social Psychology in Pre-War Britain', *Journal of British Studies*, 8 (1969): 111–40.

15 W. H. Greenleaf, *The British Political Tradition: Volume I. The Ideological Tradition* (London and New York: Methuen, 1983), pp. 273–86; and P. Crook, *Darwinism, War and History: The Debate over the Biology of War from the 'Origin of Species' to the First World War* (Cambridge University Press, 1994).

16 Soffer, *Ethics and Society*, pp. 190–213. See also Michael Freeden's discussion of the exploration but ultmate rejection of a psychological stress on instinct among interwar liberals, not least L. T. Hobhouse, first Professor of Sociology at the London School of Economics and himself an author of studies of animal psychology: *Liberalism Divided: A Study in British Political Thought, 1914–1939* (Oxford: Oxford University Press, 1986), pp. 228–39.

17 M. Thomson, 'Before Anti-Psychiatry: "Mental Health in Wartime Britain"', in M. Gijswijt-Hofstra and R. Porter (eds), *Cultures of Psychiatry and Mental Health Care in Postwar Britain and the Netherlands* (Amsterdam: Rodopi, 1998), pp. 43–60. For one example: S. Brooke, 'Evan Durbin: Reassessing a Labour "Revisionist"', *Twentieth Century British History* 7 (1996): 40–1.

18 R. Skidelsky, *John Maynard Keynes: The Economist as Saviour* Vol. II (London: Macmillan, 1991), pp. 88–9, 236–41; T. Winslow, 'Keynes and Freud: Psychoanalysis and Keynes's Account of the "Animal Spirits of Capitalism"', *Social Research*, 53 (1986): 549–78.

19 See for instance C. Delisle Burns and his *Industry and Civilisation*, discussed in Freeden, *Liberalism Divided*, pp. 239–41.

20 H. Kuklick, *The Savage Within: The Social History of British Anthropology, 1885–1945* (Cambridge: Cambridge University Press, 1991), pp. 119–81; M. Thomson, '"Savage Civilisation": Race, Culture and Mind in Britain, 1898–1939', in W. Ernst and B. Harris (eds), *Race, Science and Medicine, 1700–1960* (London: Routledge, 1999), pp. 235–58.

21 See for instance: L. Colley, *Namier* (London: Weidenfeld and Nicolson, 1989), pp. 21–45; and C. White, 'The Strange Death of Liberal England in its Time', *Albion* 17 (1985): 425–47.

22 Her remark originally came in a talk on 'Character in Modern Fiction' and was subsequently published in the essay 'Mr Bennett and Mrs Brown'. For accounts of the Exhibition's impact on Woolf and fellow modernists: H. Lee, *Virginia Woolf* (London: Chatto and Windus, 1996), pp. 287–91; and C. Harrison, *English Art and Modernism, 1900–1939* (New Haven, CT and London: Yale University Press, 1981), p. 251.

23 B. Caine, 'The Stracheys and Psychoanalysis', *History Workshop Journal*, 45 (1998): 145–69.

24 H. G. Wells, *The Secret Places of the Heart* (London: Cassell, 1922).

25 A. G. Tansley, *The New Psychology and its Relation to Life* (London: George Allen and Unwin, 1920). D. Rapp claims that the publisher printed 19,000 copies of this book and that it received more reviews than any other psycho-analytic study: 'The Reception of Freud by the British Press', p. 201.

26 The roots of this discovery of the unconscious can however be traced back much further: H. Ellenberger, *The Discovery of the Unconscious: The History and Evolution of Dynamic Psychiatry* (New York: Basic Books, 1970).

27 A. Giddens, *Modernity and Self-Identity: Self and Society in the Late Modern Age* (Cambridge: Polity Press, 1991).

28 For a useful discussion of the Weberian concept of disenchantment and its relationship to holism in German culture, which had clear parallels in Britain's popular therapeutic culture of the era: A. Harrington, *Reenchanted Science: Holism and German Culture from Wilhelm II to Hitler* (Princeton, NJ: Princeton University Press, 1996).

29 See, for instance: William Brown, *Mind and Personality: An Essay in Psych-ology and Philosophy* (London: University of London Press, 1926).

30 T. Richards, *The Commodity Culture of Victorian England: Advertising and Spectacle, 1851–1914* (London: Verso, 1990); and G. Cross, *Time and Money: The Making of a Consumer Culture* (London: Routledge, 1993).

31 T. J. Jackson Lears, 'From Salvation to Self-Realization', in R. W. Fox and T. J. Jackson Lears (eds), *The Culture of Consumption: Critical Essays in American History, 1880–1980* (New York: Pantheon, 1983), pp. 3–38; and L. Birken, *Consuming Desire: Sexual Science and the Emergence of a Culture of Abundance, 1871–1914* (Ithaca, NY and London: Cornell University Press, 1988).

32 Such a tension lies at the heart of Marshall Berman's influential *All That Is Solid Melts into Air: The Experience of Modernity* (London: Verso, 1988).

33 W. McDougall, *Social Psychology* (London: Methuen, 1908).

34 For instance: E. Carpenter, *The Art of Creation: Essays on the Self and its Powers* (London: George Allen and Unwin, 1904); and S. Rowbotham and J. Weeks, *Socialism and the New Life: The Personal and Sexual Politics of Edward Carpenter and Havelock Ellis* (London: Pluto, 1977). The relationship between psychology, the 'new life' and socialism will also be explored in M. Thomson, 'Mind in Socialism: Montague David Eder, Socialist, Psycho-Analyst, and Zionist', in R. Cooter and R. Viner (eds), *Socialism in Anglo-American Medicine, 1850–1950* (forthcoming).

35 For an account that traces the earlier roots of this source of interiority: C. Steedman, *Strange Dislocations: Childhood and the Idea of Human Interiority, 1780–1930* (London: Virago, 1995).

36 For analysis of this theme from a literary/historical perspective: L. Ottis, *Organic Memory: History and the Body in the Late Nineteenth and Early*

Twentieth Century (Lincoln, NE and London: University of Nebraska, 1994).

37 W. McDougall, *The Group Mind: A Sketch of the Principles of Collective Psychology with Some Attempt to Apply them to the Interpretation of National Life and Character* (Cambridge: Cambridge University Press, 1920); and M. Thomson, 'Savage Civilisation'.

38 On the persistence of this strain within modernity: P. Heelas, *The New Age Movement: The Celebration of the Self and the Sacralization of Modernity* (Oxford: Blackwell, 1996).

39 S. Collini, *Public Moralists: Political Thought and Intellectual Life in Britain, 1850–1930* (Oxford: Oxford University Press, 1991), p. 94.

40 S. Smiles, *Character* (London, 1871), p. vi.

41 The *Oxford English Dictionary* reports the use of 'personality-type' (1919); 'personality-traits' (1921); 'personality-defect' (1927); 'personality tests' (1927); 'personality factors' (1932); 'personality disorder' (1938); and 'personality structure' (1939).

42 *Social Psychology*, pp. 329–30.

43 For a critique of the emergence of such a culture in later twentieth-century America: C. Lasch, *The Culture of Narcissism* (New York: Norton, 1978).

44 On the development of an identity framed in terms of democratic values: P. Joyce, *Democratic Subjects: The Self and the Social in Nineteenth-Century England* (Cambridge: Cambridge University Press, 1994).

45 N. Rose, *The Psychological Complex: Psychology, Politics and Society in England 1869–1939* (London: Routledge, 1985).

46 A. Scull, *The Most Solitary of Afflictions: Madness and Society in Britain, 1700–1900* (New Haven, CT: Yale University Press, 1993).

47 M. Thomson, *The Problem of Mental Deficiency: Eugenics, Democracy and Social Policy in Britain, 1870–1950* (Oxford: Oxford University Press, 1998).

48 A. Wooldridge, *Measuring the Mind: Education and Psychology in England, c.1860–1990* (Cambridge: Cambridge University Press, 1994).

49 See for example Carolyn Steedman's study of Margaret McMillan: *Childhood, Class, and Culture in Britain: Margaret McMillan, 1860–1931* (London: Virago, 1990).

50 G. Sutherland, *Ability, Merit and Measurement* (Oxford: Oxford University Press, 1984).

51 M. Stone, 'Shellshock and the Psychologists', in W. F. Bynum, R. Porter, and M. Shepherd (eds), *The Anatomy of Madness. Volume 2* (London: Tavistock, 1985), pp. 242–71; and R. Cooter, 'Malingering in Modernity: Psychological Scripts and Adversarial Encounters during the First World War', in R. Cooter, M. Harrison, and S. Sturdy (eds), *War, Medicine and Modernity* (Stroud: Sutton, 1998), pp. 125–48.

52 N. Rose, *Governing the Soul: The Shaping of the Private Self* (London: Routledge, 1989).

53 Rose, *Governing the Soul*.

Part II
The Historical Dimensions of British Modernity

−6−

The Consciousness of Modernity?
Liberalism and the English National
Character, 1870–1940[1]

Peter Mandler

In this chapter I want to propose that the invocation and elaboration of an English 'national character' was one of the principal, enduring means by which the cultivated elites in England came to express a consciousness of their own modernity in the late nineteenth and early twentieth centuries. The dominant view of the English 'national character', I will suggest, was moulded from the mid-nineteenth century onwards primarily by liberals and radicals who wished to project the English as a model for all nations in a rapidly changing world: egalitarian, self-governing, enterprising and adaptable. At a time when in other European countries organic conservatives were taking over from liberals the aggressive promotion of nationality, British conservatives shunned organic and populist modes of thought and left the definition of national character (though not patriotism) in liberal hands. When, in the interwar period, British conservatives did finally move towards an embrace of the idea of nation, they inherited much of the liberal legacy, and with it a posture of optimism towards modernity. Right up to the point in the 1930s when the very concept of a 'national character' began to lose its lustre, the English 'national character' was widely felt to be an asset in dealing with modernizing forces – urbanization, democracy, economic development – with which other European countries were coping less successfully.

To propose the language of 'national character' as a key discourse of British modernity, right up until the Second World War, may not seem entirely natural. Although there has been some acknowledgement of the liberalism of English thought on nationality in the high Victorian period, there has been a general tendency to emphasize – I would say, over-emphasize – its exclusive, anxious, even neurotic qualities. Even more pronounced, though not universal, is the view that after the turn of the century the liberal understanding of 'Englishness' curdled, either retreating from modernity pell-mell into a swooning nostalgia for 'Old England', or slowly crumbling in the face of the twentieth-century challenges of mass democracy, urbanization and collectivism.[2]

I respond to these views here by shifting slightly the focus of inquiry.[3] The English 'national character' is not precisely the same thing as 'Englishness', at least as 'Englishness' has been defined in the recent historical literature. The idea of a 'national character' is the idea of a cultural, psychological or biological essence that all individuals in a nation share in common, and that directs – somewhat abstractly – all manifestations of national life; it may, however, be latent or only partially visible in any given sphere. 'Englishness', in contrast, is normally taken to refer to attempts to define a national style in some or all of these manifestations – it may be art, or literature, or the constructed landscape. It may in fact be almost anything, as a national or ethnic style can be detected in practically any representational activity (much as we nowadays liberally assign gender or socio-economic co-ordinates to all spheres of representation). 'National character' is thus a narrower but also a more fundamental category than 'Englishness'. If the literate public saw its own national character as modern, progressive and adaptable, it would be unlikely to accept as 'essentially English' depictions, however enjoyable otherwise, of English art or landscape that were nostalgic, conservative and static.

The discourse of 'national character' that I examine here is drawn from a body of writing by figures close to the political and intellectual establishment – pamphlets, tracts, textbooks and public lectures by statesmen, Churchmen, Fleet Street journalists – and especially by well-known figures from the English universities. This body of writing constitutes a peculiar genre with its own internal conventions and exclusive boundaries; it is not – any more than the writings of the fledgling heritage industry or of the folk-song movement or of the first teachers of English literature at the ancient universities – a comprehensive statement of the English national identity. But I would contend that as a window on to dominant conceptions of what it meant to be English it has a better claim to representativeness and impact than those other genres and institutions adopted to portray 'Englishness' as anti-modern, anti-urban and anti-democratic.

Today the very idea of 'national character' is in disrepute as a serious category of social analysis, and rightly so, not least because of the trivial and exploitative use journalists make of alleged changes in 'national character' to 'explain' a change of government, the mourning of a princess, or the result of a devolution referendum. But the decline (which one can trace back to the 1930s) of 'national character' as a touchstone for systematic assessments of the English scene should not obscure its centrality during the preceding century for expressing a sense of what English life was all about and for expressing, too, a consciousness of its modernity.

I

When and why did 'national character' emerge as a respectable and necessary category of analysis? The answer to the first part of the question, I would argue, lies in the middle of the nineteenth century, and the answer to the second must no doubt start with the acceleration of social, economic and political change across Europe after the French Revolution. There is, however, no reason to see such responses, particularly in Britain, as inevitably frigid and reactionary. British intellectuals had by the middle of the nineteenth century put down layer upon layer of explanation for changes of all sorts, with which they had become intimately familiar and even comfortable. The Scottish Enlightenment's stadial theories provided explanation for the march of commerce and manners; the great Whig historians, gloriously climaxing with Macaulay, had traced the unfolding of liberty by yoking Enlightenment theories of progress to Burkean themes of continuous development; and in the 1850s and 1860s social-evolutionary themes, not limited to those inspired by Darwin, helped further to explain why some societies developed out of a primitive state while others seemed to remain stationary.[4]

What was new in the middle of the nineteenth century was not the explanation of change, but the explanation of change in terms of national character, for none of these earlier intellectual systems made much provision for nationality. The stereotyping of national characteristics is an ancient parlour game, played by all nations at all times.[5] But 'national character' did not feature prominently in the serious discourse of public life in England in the eighteenth or early nineteenth centuries; in this respect, England differed markedly from France and Germany. There was no English Herder; no English Grimm; no English Savigny; no English Thierry or Michelet; the nearest British equivalent was a Scot, the eponymous Sir Walter, whose thinking on nationality was more influential in France than in England, where it had some impact on popular-radical but hardly any on elite circles.[6] In England, as John Burrow has shown, Enlightenment traditions of a universal human nature and cosmopolitan politics persisted well into the nineteenth century, and when the nineteenth-century Whig thinkers grafted on Burkean themes that stressed continuity and tradition, they still looked to wise, adaptive leadership rather than the common action of the collectivity to guide progress. As late as Macaulay's *History*, Burrow shows, the Whig hero is not the people but the legislator, the Augustan public servant who might now seek to cultivate the 'character' of the whole of the people as well as his own virtue, but who does not feel *as one* with the people or even representative of them.[7] Nor did social-evolutionary thinking necessarily help to accentuate attention to national difference, for in Britain evolutionary thought sought to explain in a fairly linear way how primitive societies became 'civilized' but not how civilized societies diverged and differentiated – a point to which we will return.[8]

Two linked ideas, impinging increasingly upon British intellectual life after the revolutions of 1848, gradually forced British Enlightenment and Whig categories to make room for national difference: these were the ideas of nationalism and democracy. The intensity of national feeling in the revolutions of 1848, and the mounting evidence that nationalist political movements were to be the revolutions' chief legacy in ensuing decades, made a deep impact on sympathetic British observers. So, belatedly, did the historical writing of the likes of Grimm and Michelet, which sought to explain contemporary effusions of nationalism in terms of deep-seated processes long antedating the eighteenth or nineteenth centuries. To many socially-conscious observers coming to maturity in the years after 1848, the Enlightenment's comparative carelessness about pre-modern history, and the way it could generate lasting patterns of difference, began to seem a profound weakness.[9] This perception was then fortified by growing interest in 1848's other big idea, democracy. Here the British could feel that they were leading, not following the Continent. By 1867, liberal Britons could claim that they were approximating to a democracy more closely and better than Bismarckian Prussia or Napoleonic France, or practically anywhere else on the Continent, for that matter. Trying to understand Britain as a democracy again cast doubt on existing models of social analysis, particularly the elite-leadership model of the Whig historians, which still placed so much emphasis on the virtue of the legislator and so little on the character of the people.

Of course, 1848 and 1867 were not bound to stimulate British intellectuals to think more positively about nationality and democracy, and we can readily develop long lists of people who had pretty much the opposite reaction. But those who *did* start to develop an idea of the 'English national character' as a determining force in social development *were* precisely those advanced liberals who were most inspired by the nationalist and democratic projects and most eager to show how centrally the English could figure in them. The pioneer – unsurprisingly, in this light – was John Stuart Mill, who put what he called 'ethology', or 'the Science of Character . . . including the formation of national or collective character as well as individual', at the centre of his *System of Logic* of 1843: 'Of all the subordinate branches of the social sciences, this is', he complained, 'the most completely in its infancy . . . Yet . . . it must appear that laws of national (or collective) character, are by far the most important class of sociological laws.'[10]

Mill himself never wrote his ethology. That task was left to one of his followers, highly celebrated and immensely influential at the time (though nearly forgotten today), H. T. Buckle. This self-educated son of a wealthy merchant, an acolyte of Mill's and like him an egalitarian feminist, died young and left behind him one great work, the *History of Civilization in England*, which appeared in two volumes in 1857 and 1861. The *History of Civilization* was probably the most widely read and appreciated work on the English national character in the second half of the nineteenth century. Its fundamental purpose, Buckle noted in his journal, was to reveal that 'the history of every country is marked by peculiarities which distinguish it from other countries, and which, being unaffected, or slightly affected, by individual men, admit of being generalised'; in other words, Mill's 'ethology' or 'science of character'.[11] Beyond Buckle, the science of national character was also pursued by that whole generation of university-educated liberals for whom Mill's *Logic* was the Bible in the 1850s and who were passionate believers in the English democracy they felt had been institutionalized in 1867, but whose roots could be traced far into the past. These 'University Liberals', as they have been called, were responsible for most of the other major treatises on the 'English national character' written between 1867 and the turn of the century: among those to which I will be returning are the famous collective volume, *Essays on Reform*, of 1867, James Bryce's writings on the evolution of democracy, Edward Freeman's and J. R. Green's English histories, J. R. Seeley's bestselling *Expansion of England* of 1883, and Mandell Creighton's Romanes Lecture for 1896, which actually bore the title, *The English National Character*.

One reason for the monopoly these advanced liberals held and (for a long time) kept upon the idea of the national character was that conservatives, on the whole, stood fastidiously apart from it. Continuing to occupy the elite-leadership ground of the Whig tradition, they denied that national cohesion or democratic participation in Britain had ever gone or need ever go much beyond loyalty to established institutions (patriotism, in short). Their unwillingness to embrace any notion of true national character is poignantly illustrated by the case of Walter Bagehot, who thought that, in *Physics and Politics* (1872), he was writing a treatise on national character that would replace and make more scientific Buckle's *History of Civilization*. Yet the text of *Physics and Politics* actually repeats and fortifies old views that discount national character: the Enlightenment view that commercial societies were essentially uniform and cosmopolitan, mingling ideas and breaking down old creeds; and the Whig view that nations played 'follow the leader', adopting the character of their leading statesmen.[12] Here is the theoretical underpinning for Bagehot's famous idea of deference as the key to the English Constitution – but it is not a notion of national character at all.

Bagehot, it might be argued, was not *enough* of a conservative to have a vision of the nation. Yet the same presupposition of the adequacy of the elite-leadership model applies to those on his right. A true conservative like W. H. Mallock also objected to discussions of 'the people' as 'merely a synonym for the inhabitants taken as a whole'; any meaningful sense of 'the people' would have to be of 'a narrower and more incisive kind', which accepted the fundamental distinction between the masses and their leaders.[13] Those conservatives who did see in religion (or, rather, Churchmanship) a binding force for the nation put their emphasis on the spiritual leadership of the Church rather than on the spiritual commonalities of the people.[14] Even figures like Carlyle or Froude, as close to organic conservatives as British intellectual life gets, tended to base their theories of history on the ability of 'strong men' to form the national character at will; that is, they were paternalists rather than true organicists.[15] None of these conservatives had enough confidence in the character of the people even to accept the concept of 'national character', much less to celebrate it.

In associating the idea of national character so closely with advanced-liberal ideas of nationality and democracy, I am deliberately discounting what might have been another important mid-century stimulus to thinking on national character, the idea of race. Although much recent work on mid-Victorian intellectual life has striven to demonstrate the impact of the new biological thinking about race, on liberals as on everyone else, I do not think a close scrutiny of the writing on 'national character' will bear this out.[16] Mill's influence was again paramount. He was about as clear in his rejection of biological race as it is possible to get. In a well-known passage of the *Principles of Political Economy*, he protested, 'Of all vulgar modes of escaping from the consideration of the effect of social and moral influences on the human mind, the most vulgar is that of attributing the diversities of conduct and character to inherent national differences.'

This passage is not only well known today, but was well known to contemporaries, 'cordially subscribe[d]' to by Buckle at the very outset of the *History of Civilization*, and just as cordially excoriated by those (like physical anthropologists) who had a vested interest in the biologizing of difference. For Mill, like most of the liberals who came after him, the science of national character was part of the 'revolt of the nineteenth century against the eighteenth' – that is, the revolt of particularity against uniformity, and of continuities against obliterating progress – but they being British liberals, their revolt was more of a gentle rebuke than a full-scale revolution. They did not junk Enlightenment psychology altogether; they retained its belief in the *essential* uniformity of the human mind and its malleability over time. What Mill sought in the *Logic* was the *minimum* possible addition to the principles of human psychology that could explain real historical variations between peoples. He and Buckle and most other liberals were persuaded – both by their prejudices and by their study of national character – that national character was itself too fluid (not perfectly fluid, but not static enough either) to admit any correlation to biological race.[17]

It would be foolish to suggest that biological race had no impact on educated opinion, but it hardly entered into this liberal discourse about national character, which in turn has some claim to being *the* master narrative of national character in the late Victorian period and beyond. The discourse of national character did not, therefore, necessarily dovetail with two contemporary and related discourses that were more heavily biologized. First, of course, there was an imperial language of racial difference that drew stricter biological distinctions between Europeans, Africans and Asians. But it was very common for the strongest believers in black–white difference to deny flatly any biological basis for intra-European difference. Among other problems, European civilization was seen as too recent to have been affected much by biological change, even by a bio-fanatic like Francis Galton;[18]

for another, Europeans were thought to be too mobile and thus interbred for any notion of racial purity, to be meaningful; again, even fanatical anthropometricians were seeking to document diversity rather than purity and rarely drew psychological conclusions from their measurements.[19] Second, a popular language of racial difference within the British Isles – the language of Teuton and Celt – was also pretty well shunned by writers on national character. The English were, most of these writers held, a compound of Anglo-Saxon and Celt and of various other nationalities. Those who did believe in the 'Teutonic' foundation of the English national character still felt that this 'Teutonic' character could, with the passage of time, be acquired by the Welsh or the Scots or even the Irish and the Jews, as was passionately desired by Victorian liberals as otherwise different as Edward Freeman, Matthew Arnold and John Stuart Mill.[20]

If the English national character was not, in this discourse, based on race, what did form it? As some French thinkers proved, climate and geography could serve as a basis for national character almost as deterministic as race; but most British liberals rejected this source of fixity, too.[21] Buckle was sometimes interpreted as a geographical and especially a climatic determinist, because he opened his *History of Civilization* with a geographical explanation for differences between tropical and northern peoples (sharing with Mill an aversion for basing even this gross distinction upon biology). But Buckle argued for a diminishing influence of physical conditions as civilization advanced, so that everywhere in Europe – and, gradually, elsewhere in the world – national distinctions were narrowing down to the crucial, non-physical sources of variety.[22] Thus divesting themselves of the certainties of race and geography, Victorian liberals went in search of national character in the more congenially flexible realm of history – and not always to the distant past.

Starting from common primitive origins, they argued, the nations of the world branched and diverged. Language was one early marker of difference, so early that it could easily (but shouldn't be) mistaken for an essential, biological difference. But linguistic differentiation was only the first change in the making of a national community. Subsequent variations could be triggered by a variety of factors, which had in common only that they affected all classes of the community rather than the ruling classes alone. Following Whig instincts, political institutions and legal structures were seen to be crucial, but only where they genuinely reflected communal rather than elite practices. Moral traditions, especially those rooted in popular religion, could also be formative of national character. So, too, could literary and historical traditions, again if rooted in popular religion and thus available to the masses even in a largely pre-literate state. What we have here, in short, is something not unlike Benedict Anderson's 'imagined community', but one that English liberals backdated to pre-modern times by conceiving of law, government, popular morality, religion, literature and history as substitutes for the mass communications and modern forms of popular mobilization that Anderson considers necessary for a true nationalism to emerge. Indeed many Victorian liberals used a language similar to Anderson's, Freeman speaking of race as 'an artificial doctrine, a learned doctrine' and Seeley of nationality as a kind of fictive kinship.[23]

II

So far I have argued that the idea of 'national character' developed, in elite culture, not among conservatives seeking to fix an essential English national character in biology or geography as a bulwark against change, but rather among liberals seeking to explain change by reference to national, popular characteristics, which previous liberal accounts had omitted or depreciated. But it is not only in this epistemological sense that the category of 'national character' was a product of modernity. In looking back on the historical emergence of their 'imagined community', English liberals also assigned specific characteristics to it that explained, in their view, England's peculiar ability to adapt and prevail in the rapidly changing world of the late nineteenth century. In matching so carefully English national characteristics to the challenges of the modern world, these liberals sketched out their own consciousness of what modernity was.

There has probably never been a list of English national characteristics that did not have 'liberty' at the top of it, and the Victorian liberals' list was no exception. Yet each generation and each class has its own idea of liberty. For Victorian liberals, to qualify as a genuine primary national characteristic, liberty had to be enjoyed by the whole of the people as far back as the national character could be traced. It could not therefore be located in modern institutions only, as the Whig tradition insisted, nor could it be given a merely nominal history by some Burkean means such as 'virtual representation'. To Victorian liberals, English liberty was not so much an attribute of the English Constitution as of the English constitution, a habit of mind favouring free discussion, voluntary association and respect for law. As to the reasons for or date of genesis of these habits, opinion differed. There were some, notably Freeman, who traced English liberty back to Teutonic origins, associating it with local government practices based on free discussion and voluntary association. Perhaps surprisingly, Mill also on occasion endorsed this view, taking his cue from Guizot.[24] But more common was an acceptance that English liberty in any recognizable sense could not be traced back much further than the sixteenth century. If there was one seedbed that was generally acclaimed as the source of English nationality by Victorian liberals, it was not the primeval soup of the Aryans nor the misty forests of the Teutons nor the folkmoot of the Anglo-Saxons but rather the dawning of post-feudal order under the Tudors. The Whigs' traditional hostility to the Tudors as authoritarians who tried to do without Parliament could be ignored if, far beneath Parliament, the rule of law and the sway of free discussion could be seen to be brewing amongst the people. This was the way many Victorian liberals saw it: from the fifteenth century onwards, Buckle claimed,

> the people imbibed that tone of independence, and that lofty bearing, of which our civil and political institutions are the consequence, rather than the cause. It is to this, and not to any fanciful peculiarity of race, that we owe the sturdy and enterprising spirit for which the inhabitants of this island have long been remarkable.[25]

To Buckle's rationalist account of English liberty J. R. Green's *Short History of the English People* (1874) added more enduringly popular themes of Protestantism and prosperity to help explain how liberty could sink its roots into the souls of the people at a time when their rulers were doing everything in their power to limit it. In Green's passionate, colourful account modern English readers were meant to recognize themselves coming into spiritual existence in the century between Elizabeth's accession and the 'triumph of Naseby', when 'Modern England, the England among whose thoughts and sentiments we actually live, began'.[26]

As Green's history demonstrates, one of the advantages of tracing English liberty no further back than the Tudors was that it could more plausibly be interpreted as an apprenticeship for (or even the real historical practice of) democracy. For reasons already explored, it was terribly important to the University Liberals to show that the English national character was not only suited to – but, amongst all Europeans, pre-eminently suited to – democracy. The failure of democracy on the Continent in 1848 could be explained, they felt, by the lack of national traditions of discussion, tolerance and association, and they took comfort in Alexis de Tocqueville's similar analysis. By the same token, they argued in *Essays on Reform* in 1867, the English national character was ideally formed for democratic decision-making.[27] In this respect, they were ahead of Mill, who in his later years had developed a more abstract understanding of liberty that no national character could sustain and that it required institutional checks and balances to guarantee. The younger University Liberals, in contrast, dwelt upon the mutual tolerance and sense of equity that had long been latent in English liberty and that now qualified the whole of the nation for formal democratic powers. To them, democracy simply *was* the fullest expression of English liberty, not, as the enemies of democracy insisted, the formless mêlée that passed for democracy elsewhere. Thus John Morley protested against the alternative view that 'democracy must be fragile, difficult, and sundry other evil things, because out of fourteen presidents of the Bolivian Republic thirteen have died assassinated or in exile', by demonstrating with the English example how well democracy worked when yoked in tandem with the right kind of national character.[28]

Second only to liberty, and its modern corollary, democracy, on the list of English characteristics was the national propensity for hard work and material accumulation. Even before liberty, materialism was the first point of the national character to interest Mill. As early as 1829 he had identified materialism as both the best and the worst point in the English character, engendering prosperity but also 'that exclusive and engrossing selfishness which accompanies it'.[29] For Mill as for many later commentators, the propensity for hard work and accumulation was intimately linked to English liberty, which gave the maximum scope and reward to individual initiative, in contrast to the despotisms of the Orient and the Mediterranean, which inculcated 'submission', 'endurance' and 'envy'.[30] Of course, there was a down side to English materialism, which worried Mill especially, the national inability to appreciate higher abstractions such as art, music, speculative thought and the 'greater good'; but Mill was unusual in this, and most late Victorian portrayals of English materialism accepted it as a brutal yet useful force of nature. As Miles Taylor has shown, the *Punch* caricaturists transformed the very image of John Bull from the puny victim of early nineteenth-century Old Corruption into the stouter, smugger, more pugnacious embodiment of national prosperity and commercial growth.[31]

While it might be thought that the propensity to labour was also prone to the near-racial Teutonic interpretation, in fact the reverse was true – the Angles and the Saxons were not known to be hard workers.[32] As Seeley pointed out, as late as the fifteenth century the English were widely reputed to be 'indolent and contemplative . . . preeminent in urbanity and totally devoid of domestic affection'. The true turning-point, he felt, was again the Tudor era, when, Mandell Creighton agreed, '[t]he modern Englishman came into definite existence' and 'all the characteristics of the modern Englishman' materialized: 'an adventurous spirit, practical sagacity, a resolve to succeed, a willingness to seek his fortune in any way, courage to face dangers, cheerfulness under disaster, perseverance in the sphere which he has chosen'. There was little agreement, however, on what precisely happened in the Tudor era to unleash this national work-in: Seeley threw in a bit of geographical determinism by emphasizing the westward exposure to the sea and the stimulating effect of the discovery of the New World; Creighton echoed him, but also put weight upon Protestantism in catalysing the English sense of difference, isolation and self-reliance; Mill gave equal emphasis to Protestant modes of thought and the more recent development of a political system that rewarded wealth.[33]

Seeley's view that the discovery of the New World triggered the English development of enterprise reminds us that, for some late Victorian commentators, expansion – that is, overseas colonization – was another central trait of the English national character, a natural concomitant of the propensity for self-reliance and hard work. Though liberals, many of these commentators on national character were imperialists. Their high opinion of the English national character caused them to expect it to triumph in many different settings, and their non-racial, assimilationist understanding of it provided the mechanism by which it could do so. They expected that the English, where they mingled with other Europeans, would anglicize them or at least provide the dominant character in the mix, as Mill had himself advocated for Ireland and observed approvingly in America.

The ability of the English to project themselves and then root themselves successfully all over the world could be taken as the ultimate test of the modernity of Englishness, its ability to survive and thrive on the world stage of the late nineteenth century. Such powerful believers in Englishness as J. R. Seeley and Charles Dilke lingered lovingly on the successful implantation of English communities in North America, Australia and New Zealand. But, reflecting their confusion about race outside the European context, they were less certain how to view expansion into those parts of the world where the English encountered non-European peoples and proved, at least in the short term, unable to mix with or alter them. India was the obvious sticking-point; neither Seeley nor Dilke, as has often been noticed, ever came up with a satisfactory explanation of what the English were doing in India.[34] One answer to this problem was a frankly anti-imperialist view of the English national character, one that argued that English 'independence' or 'insularity', as the University Liberal Goldwin Smith put in 1878, 'precludes not only fusion, but sympathy and almost intercourse with the subject races'.[35]

Empire therefore became a divisive factor in the discussion of national character – most evident in 1886, when the University Liberals divided over Irish Home Rule, in unpredictable ways, Goldwin Smith and Seeley on one side, Freeman and Bryce on the other. These divisions over Empire, widening from 1886, may perhaps be signs of a general crumbling of consensus over the nature and fate of the English national character. Here we come, in some ways, to the crux of the argument. For believers in an essentially anti-modern, anti-democratic idea of Englishness tend to nominate these *fin-de-siècle* and immediate pre-war years as the crucible. Even those, it could be, who had constructed the liberty-loving, democratic, industrious, accumulative and expansionist idea of the national character in the sunny light of the Victorian high noon might have had second thoughts in the twenty years before the First World War. They might in old age have recoiled from the democracy they had in their youth put on a pedestal. They might have doubted whether the national character could endure in the face of collectivism, urbanization, migration, population control and other degenerative forces. In this reactionary turn they might well have been joined by conservatives who had never believed in an English national character in the first place, but may have now been willing to participate cynically in the reconstruction of an idea of national character on a more properly hierarchical basis. But in the remainder of this chapter, I want to argue against this view and for the considerable persistence of the liberal idea of national character established in the late Victorian period.

III

As the Victorian liberals aged, many did grow more conservative. One of the contributors to *Essays on Reform* in 1867, Charles Pearson, wrote a gloomy screed in 1893 on *National Life and Character* that fits in nearly every respect the counter-argument I have just sketched out: urbanization and over-civilization had weakened the English race, and the national characteristics of independence and enterprise that had prevailed since the sixteenth century were terminally on the wane. There was an explicitly biological language here that marks a new element in the writing of Pearson and his peers. Even James Bryce, always one of the more optimistic of his generation (and to his dying day, in 1922, a Liberal), wrote to Pearson that he shared some of his forebodings.[36] Against this, however, Mandell Creighton's Romanes Lecture on the English national character – which, from the lips of a highly respectable bishop of Pearson's generation, simply repeated the older liberal recipe in pure form – followed Pearson's tract three years later and was probably intended as a direct rebuttal of it; Creighton's lecture in turn became one of the most widely cited authorities on the English national character over the next thirty years and inspired further direct refutations of Pearson into the 1920s.[37]

After Creighton, in fact, the discourse of national character goes quiet for a time. It is most striking that, at and just after the turn of the century, a period when Britain (along with the rest of Europe) was gripped by anxiety about international competitiveness and the need to pursue a maximally 'efficient' economic and military policy, the language of national character was *not* often employed to express or allay that anxiety.[38] I think this attests to the persistent weakness of national thinking in Britain, especially among Conservatives (the governing party from 1895 to 1906), and specifically the inutility of national thinking when dealing with the problems of a multinational empire. What we see instead in the 1890s and 1900s, as J. H. Grainger has sensitively documented, is a whipping-up of *patriotism*, of deference to traditional national symbols (flag, Constitution, military leadership), rather than of sentiments of organic English nationality.[39] Not many British Conservatives followed the Continental move of the New Right towards a more organic or collectivist conception of the people; instead, they continued in a recognizably whiggish way to focus on the link of deference or obedience between the masses and the elite. As Ewen Green has shown, there was a weak, late appearance of collectivism in British Conservative thinking about economics and empire, but no perceptible movement towards thinking about democracy or other collective manifestations of the nation.[40] The idea that democratic politics must or should reflect the rooted 'instincts' of the mass – an increasingly widespread notion on the Continent – was still shunned by British Conservatives and embraced by Liberals mainly in the comparatively anodyne, optimistic form that they had hammered out since the 1850s.[41]

Positive appeals were therefore not often couched in terms of English nationality, nor were anxieties about economic and military weakness so presented, but rather in class, familial or imperial forms. And, as has been widely noted, even British eugenicists considered the degeneration of the stock in class rather than in national terms: they were interested less in the overall character of the English people than in the specific problems of the professional elite.[42] Furthermore, to put turn-of-the-century anxieties in perspective, few governments in Europe had less time for notions of degeneration and eugenic solutions than the British.[43] When Arthur Balfour delivered the Sidgwick Memorial Lecture of 1908, he may have taken up the subject of 'Decadence' and asked whether the British like the Roman Empire was fated to decline – a fact ominously noted by those who wish to emphasize national anxiety in these years. But it is less frequently noted that he answered his own question in the negative, pointing out that 'the modern alliance between pure science and industry' ensured that history need no longer be cyclical. He also, incidentally, returned to an old Conservative theme – the insignificance of national character, arguing that only 'a due succession of men above the average in original capacity [is] necessary to maintain social progress . . . Democracy is an excellent thing; but, though quite consistent with progress, it is not progressive *per se* . . . Movement may be controlled or checked by the many; it is initiated and made effective by the few.'[44]

Overall, as Aaron Friedberg concluded in his study of economic and military strategy in this period, the keynote British response to the threat of decline was complacency; 'an untended engine' was his useful metaphor.[45] This describes, too, the attitude to national character – not only in the sense that old platitudes lingered, but also in a more specific way, for the one genuine novelty in Edwardian considerations of the national character was the addition of 'complacency' to the list of characteristics. Contemporaries were well aware of the frenzy of national reassessment that rivals, particularly Germany, were engaged in at the time; they were also aware of their own comparative inactivity. The contrast was not necessarily a source of worry, but it was noted. Taking up older psychological stereotypes of English phlegm and pragmatism, Mandell Creighton, for instance, in his 1896 lecture confessed that 'we have something of the hardness which goes from a long period of steady success'. For the first time descriptions of John Bull now feature centrally his resistance to novelty. There was an understanding that with the Continental craze for novelties, English and European conceptions of modernity were diverging. As Creighton observed, 'We do not find it necessary to adopt the most modern methods, to follow the newest fashion of advertising, or to explain our procedure to everybody.'[46] Only time would tell whether English complacency or European innovation would prove to be the correct course.

Right up until the First World War, then, the central discourse of national character stuck to the advanced-liberal pieties. The English were a people, not a race; their 'national character' stemmed from some five centuries (or more) of common governance, manners, social and economic experience, fortified in recent years by a conscious effort by such liberals to cultivate awareness of these national commonalities. The national characteristics were those that had brought the English to world dominance: a combination of stubborn independence, mutual tolerance and free association, in which liberty and democracy could be reconciled; a zeal for material accumulation and a spirit of enterprise which had brought them unparalleled prosperity and spread their spawn across the globe.

There were other characteristics frequently cited that I have shortchanged in my account, principally psychological traits that do not have a direct relevance to the question of progressiveness and modernity – hypocrisy, for instance, or reticence, coldness to strangers, warmth within the family.[47] What is distinctly lacking is much hint of overtly *anti*-modern characteristics, aimed at softening or reining in democratization, urbanization, and economic growth. Themes that will appear later are notably absent: an alleged appetite for social hierarchy, for instance, the ideal of the 'gentleman' as a national role-model, or a national preference for the ease and security of the countryside over the rough challenges of town and trade. To the contrary, Mill, for one, regretted that the English rural population shared the frantic possessiveness of the townfolk; so, at the opposite extreme, did Froude.[48] When Victorian liberals did refer to a national preference for the country over the city, they tended to do so in terms of a liking for a cold, brutal Nature that could be traced back to those misty forests of Germany or the Vikings or the venturesome Elizabethans.[49] The image of a cosy, little, cultivated peasant England was, as I have suggested elsewhere, the property of a smaller, marginal, largely artistic coterie, centred on the Arts and Crafts movement, which self-consciously positioned itself *against* the dominant picture of a grosser, blustery, individualistic and commercial nation.[50] Yet even 'Little England' themes existed in versions closer to Victorian Liberal prototypes, and it would be these insular, yet not anti-modern versions that would thrive in the altered circumstances of the interwar period.[51]

IV

These Little England themes did swell during and after the First World War, but in a greatly changed context for conceptions of the national character. There can be no question that the very idea of 'national character' reached its apogee in the interwar decades, breaking the bounds of the Victorian liberal discourse and flowing along a number of disparate channels. There are several reasons for this apotheosis of national character, not necessarily all linked or having the same effects. First and foremost, of course, there was the impact of the First World War, requiring the mobilization of popular patriotism on a scale not seen in England since the 1790s. To some extent this meant a temporary convergence with Continental – especially German – models of *Staat* and *Volk*, though there was also the countervailing concern that in fighting fire with fire, English patriotism should not lose its distinctive (that is, liberal) temperament.[52] Second, and longer lasting, was the continuing sense of *divergence* between the British and Continental experiences that was felt throughout the interwar years, beginning with the Continental revolutions of 1917–20, accelerating with the rise of fascism in Italy and the disturbing volatility and violence of French politics, and peaking after the Nazi seizure of power in 1933. Attention was naturally focused on the possible peculiarities of the English. As Sir John Neale said in his 1935 Centenary Lecture on Local Government, 'particularly in these times of dictatorship abroad, we may thank God that we are not as other men are'.[53] Third, there was the near-total realization of political democracy in 1918, which now required all political parties – including the Tories – to conceive of the nation in popular terms. As David Jarvis has recently suggested, 1918 came as something of a shock to Tory sensibilities and triggered a rush to the library among Tory leaders to root out textbooks of Liberal sociology, which they had hitherto spurned.[54] It would not be long before the first plainly Tory tracts on the 'English national character' would appear. Finally, the rapidly burgeoning democratization of the culture – especially evident in the growth of leisure time and, most relevant for our purposes, in the domestic tourism boom – unleashed a torrent of popular guidebooks to 'England' of a topographical and historical kind. So the first thing to be said about 'national character' between the wars is how heterogeneous it appeared, in contrast to the relative consensus of the pre-war era.

Some generalizations can, nevertheless, be made. One is that the pre-war liberal discourse hardly petered out, but can to a great extent still be seen as central to the genre. Though Mill and Buckle may have gone into eclipse, Seeley and Green were still the most widely-recognized authorities on the national mission, foreign and domestic.[55] Furthermore, it is striking how many of the most famous interwar commentators on national character came from a Victorian Liberal tradition, often with direct ties to the University Liberals of the previous generation – Ernest Barker, Arthur Mee, H. V. Morton, H. W. Nevinson.[56] And even in work from Tory hands, the main themes of the pre-war discourse stand out clearly enough. The English idea of national character was not a racial one.[57] Its main features were still independence and free association, making possible democracy (here, if not elsewhere) and the spirit of enterprise. Contrasts with Continental despotism if anything reinforced the sense of political distinctiveness, now more smug but no less liberal;[58] as Sir John Neale underscored in his 1935 lecture, it was the tradition of self-government embedded in the common law and local autonomy by the sixteenth century that differentiated England from the Continent, then as now.[59] Similarly, contrasts between English free trade and Continental autarky could be used to underscore the unusual English tradition of enterprise. One of the last works by an economist to explain English economic history by reference to national character was Alfred Marshall's *Industry and Trade* (1919), which Stefan Collini aptly calls 'Marshall's version of Our Island Story', and which made the conventional link between 'more self-reliant habits, more forethought, more deliberateness and free choice' and the spirit of enterprise.[60]

One can detect a new emphasis on interiority and introspection, overlapping with the quality of insularity, and stemming from a quasi-psychoanalytic awareness that the 'inner life' was deeper and murkier than the Victorian language of 'character' recognized. This sense of interiority was reinforced by the growth of 'Little England' sentiment in interwar writing about the 'national character', evincing a desire to put behind one the globe-trotting days of the Victorian meridian and to cultivate instead one's own garden (literally as well as figuratively). Should this inward turn be interpreted as a rebuff to modernity? Raphael Samuel and Alison Light have argued very much to the contrary, seeing it rather as a new statement of 'conservative modernity', and one that, I would add, had precedents in Victorian Liberal and *fin-de-siècle* 'Little England' thought.[61] Turning inward did not necessarily mean turning backward. For example, as Light shows, the 'national characteristic' of domesticity – which had used to imply patriarchy – could now be construed in a more egalitarian way as homeliness.[62] Not all conservative appropriations of 'national character' were consonant with democratic social change, of course; some could indeed be restrictive and disciplinary. In Tory accounts, there was a tendency to re-present old Liberal virtues with an upper-class twist, so that 'individuality' became 'eccentricity', the sense of justice became 'fair play' or 'a talent for games' (especially cricket), and the resistance to abstract thought became 'amateurishness' (very much a post-1914 concept).[63] The idea of the gentleman, a Victorian commonplace when speaking of the elite but not of the nation, was also now employed in many Tory accounts of 'national character', either absorbing older traits or insinuating new ones.[64]

The point I would stress about these more exclusive, anti-modern representations of the 'national character' is that they were part of a widening spectrum; there was no longer a consensus over what defined the English. A survey in 1940 of recent depictions of the English national character reported that it had been found to be both enterprising and hostile to trade, licentious and puritanical, independent and obedient, formal in dress and informal in dress, plainspeaking and reticent, liberty-loving and non-political. And it was not only this straightforward debunking exercise – entitled *The Illusion of National Character* – that came to this conclusion. A surprising number of interwar works purporting to anatomize the national character granted, at the outset, that the task was a hopeless one. The English were simply too various and the times too changeable. The most illiberal Conservatives – the ones most likely to set the English national character against modernity – were those most likely to come to this conclusion. They knew well that the very idea of national character had originated in a period of confident popular Liberalism; and as that confidence ebbed, so, they felt, the comforting notion of a bonding national character must ebb with it. Victorian modernity had created the national character; the flux of interwar modernity had decomposed it. Thus in his widely-read tract on *England* of 1926, Dean Inge quoted ironically the words of the Liberal Ramsay Muir written only a few years before:

> Liberalism has always had a profound belief in the national spirit – a nation being a great body of people who feel that they belong together because they are linked by a multitude of ties, which create a real homogeneity. 'It is only the homogeneity which nationhood creates [wrote Muir] that renders self-government possible among vast masses of men and women.' In other words, Liberalism postulates an underlying loyalty and patriotism in all sections of the population. Where this loyalty and patriotism are absent [Inge concluded], democratic Liberalism, which is government by public opinion, becomes impotent, and the impotence of government leads to anarchy.[65]

Today, Inge thought, 'the country is in a state of chronic civil war'. Not for nothing was he known as the 'Gloomy Dean'.[66]

It is in this light, I think, that the association between 'Englishness' and the countryside, made more widely between the wars, must be read. As I have already suggested, much of the interwar literature about the countryside avoids the question of 'Englishness' altogether: it is concerned to introduce 'the unknown island' to the swelling ranks of motor-coach and motor-car tourists and ramblers.[67] But there is also, undoubtedly, a nostalgic, anti-urban, anti-industrial streak in some of this writing that picks up pre-war concerns about degeneration and argues for the regenerative powers of the countryside in restoring the vitality of the national character. Yet in speaking of restoration, these ruralist voices were acknowledging that the national character had already been shattered, altered beyond recognition. Both romantic conservatives and romantic radicals (and some romantic liberals, like G. M. Trevelyan) employed the relatively new concept of the 'Industrial Revolution' to express their conviction that Englishness before around 1800 and Englishness after that great divide were incommensurable. (The pre-war idea of Englishness – from Mill to Marshall – had stressed continuities from at least the Elizabethan age, and had not employed the concept of an industrial revolution.) If interwar romantics wished to recreate the 'world we have lost' under modern conditions – and they did, passionately – it was a matter of restoring something all but extinguished, rather than calling upon deep, underlying continuities, as

Victorian liberals had done. This realization accounts for much of the anguish and frustration in their tone. 'Most of us to-day are town-dwellers', said Arthur Bryant in a radio broadcast of 1934, 'yet there are few of us whose great-great-great-grandparents were not country folk . . . We are shut off from them as it were by a tunnel of two or three generations – lost in the darkness of the Industrial Revolution – but beyond is the sunlight of the green fields from which we came.'[68]

Though Bryant clung to the hope that 'our subconscious selves' might still recognize those green fields if faced with them, he and others realized that they were essentially starting from scratch. Enough of the old world remained physically intact, in the form of historic monuments and unspoilt landscape, to serve as the basis for a re-education in lost traditions, but the 'national character' could not be relied upon; it would have to be rebuilt from the bare foundations.

If true ruralites like Bryant, or G. M. Trevelyan, or Clough Williams-Ellis despaired of the national character in this respect, how are we to understand the appeal to the essential rurality of the English by a fair-weather countryman like Stanley Baldwin? As Philip Williamson has argued, Baldwin's notorious evocation of rural Englishness in 1924 – 'To me, England is the country, and the country is England' – was an opportunistic party-political point, aimed at distancing himself from his opponents' industrial sectionalism at a time of industrial strife in the mid-1920s. It was not characteristic of his party's interwar rhetoric, or even of Baldwin's career. A more consistent feature of Baldwin's rhetorical armamentarium was the resort to the old Liberal verities – 'the qualities of individuality, initiative, enterprise, thrift . . . honesty, respect for the law, and love of freedom and justice' – that the Conservatives had accepted, somewhat nervously, as those characteristics of the people that made democracy possible. To these Baldwin added grace notes of his own, references to 'common sense, moderation, calmness, kindliness, brotherliness' meant to point up the recession of class conflict. These themes, Williamson shows, then gave way to a more overtly Christian rhetoric of Englishness in Baldwin's speeches of the 1930s. And Neville Chamberlain offered a different version altogether.[69]

Politicians have never ceased using the idea of 'national character', but by the 1930s it no longer had the solid, consensual, binding effect that its most ardent advocates have hoped for it (and its most committed enemies feared). My argument has been that 'national character' had never sunk the deep roots in English political consciousness and language that it could claim in France or Germany. It was the product of a particular moment of late Victorian Liberalism, when for a time it did express, among one comparatively democratic section of the governing classes, the consciousness of modernity. It was not much suited to, nor ever enthusiastically embraced by conservatives, and the predominant interwar revisions of the idea of 'national character', while more domesticated and psychologized, were extensions rather than repudiations of earlier liberal arguments.

As that liberal understanding of modernity fragmented and collapsed in the interwar years, so, too, did any stable or useful concept of the English national character. No doubt, as some commentators have urged, the Nazi example helped in the long term to discredit the strongest (and especially the racial) expressions of nationality in the anti-fascist world. But the English idea of 'national character', which had not been racial to begin with, had by then already begun to decompose. Nor did an inevitable revival of national language during the Second World War make much difference. After the war, an attempt by the BBC to commission a series of radio broadcasts on the 'national character' was abandoned on the grounds that the idea could no longer be taken seriously.[70] Instead of being deployed as a conceptual tool to combat modernity, 'national character' gave way to other idioms better suited to expressing the consciousness of modernity in a world no longer comprehensible in Victorian-liberal terms.[71]

Notes

1 This essay represents a revised version of the 1998 Neale Lecture in British History. I am grateful to Martin Daunton and the Department of History at University College London for the invitation to give the lecture. For very helpful comments on earlier drafts of this essay, I would like to thank Stefan Collini, Martin Daunton, David Feldman, Bernhard Rieger, Julia Stapleton and Miles Taylor.

2 Martin J. Wiener, *English Culture and the Decline of the Industrial Spirit 1850–1950* (Cambridge: Cambridge University Press, 1981); and Robert Colls and Philip Dodd (eds), *Englishness: Politics and Culture 1880–1920* (London: Croom Helm, 1986), esp. the essays by the editors, 'Englishness and the National Culture', pp. 1–28, and 'Englishness and the Political Culture', pp. 29–61; but cf. Dennis Smith, 'Englishness and the Liberal Inheritance after 1886', pp. 254–82.

3 See, further, Peter Mandler, 'Against "Englishness": English Culture and the Limits to Rural Nostalgia, 1850–1940', *Transactions of the Royal Historical Society*, 6th ser., 7 (1997): 155–75.

4 The argument of this section is developed further in Peter Mandler, '"Race" and "Nation" in Mid-Victorian Thought', in *History, Religion and Culture: Essays in British Intellectual History 1750–1950*, ed. Stefan Collini, Richard Whatmore and Brian Young (Cambridge: Cambridge University Press, 2000).

5 Paul Langford is currently engaged in a study of national stereotyping among Europeans in the period immediately before mine; for a start, see 'British Politeness and the Progress of Western Manners: An Eighteenth-Century Enigma', *Transactions of the Royal Historical Society*, 6th ser., 7 (1997): 53–72.

6 For this distinction, see Peter Mandler, '"In the Olden Time": Romantic History and English National Identity, 1820–1850', in *A Union of Multiple Identities: The British Isles, c.1750–c.1850*, ed. Laurence Brockliss and David Eastwood (Manchester: Manchester University Press, 1997), pp. 78–92.

7 J.W. Burrow, *A Liberal Descent: Victorian Historians and the English Past* (Cambridge: Cambridge University Press, 1981), pp. 21–9, 36–8, 48–53, 59–60, 65–70, 78. On the progress from 'virtue' to (individual) 'character', see Stefan Collini, *Public Moralists: Political Thought and Intellectual Life in Britain 1850–1930* (Oxford: Clarendon Press, 1991), Ch. 3. The work of Burrow and Collini, to which I am very greatly indebted, slights 'national character' for a number of reasons: it was shunned as too demotic by the Whig figures on whom they focus; it featured more prominently in the work of less academic figures like Buckle, whom they omit; and it seems to fall more into the category of sociology than of politics, whereas the persistence of the latter against the challenge of the former is one of Burrow's and Collini's leading themes. See their entire corpus, but esp. Stefan Collini, Donald Winch and John Burrow, *That Noble Science of Politics: A Study in Nineteenth-Century Intellectual History* (Cambridge: Cambridge University Press, 1983), pp. 167–73, 191–3, 236–44, 328–31, and Collini, *Public Moralists*, Ch. 9.

8 John Burrow, *Evolution and Society: A Study in Victorian Social Theory* (Cambridge: Cambridge University Press, 1966), esp. pp. 98–100.

9 The shift after 1848 can be detected by comparing the predominantly whiggish, institutional and non-national attitudes of the older generation of advanced liberals discussed in Miles Taylor, *The Decline of British Radicalism* (Oxford: Clarendon Press, 1995), esp. pp. 191–200, with the more positive approach of the younger generation discussed in Christopher Harvie, *The Lights of Liberalism: University Liberals and the Challenge of Democracy, 1860–86* (London: Allen Lane, 1976).

10 *Collected Works of John Stuart Mill* (Toronto: University of Toronto Press, 1981–91), Vols 7-8, *A System of Logic*, pp. 868–70, 905.

11 *Miscellaneous and Posthumous Works of Henry Thomas Buckle*, ed. Helen Taylor, 3 vols (London: Longman, Green & Co., 1872), Vol. 1, xlii–xliii.

12 *Collected Works of Walter Bagehot*, ed. Norman St John-Stevas, 15 vols (London: *The Economist*, 1965–86), Vol. 7, *Physics and Politics*, pp. 22–3, 34–9, 67–9, 80, 134. See also Collini *et al.*, *That Noble Science*, p. 256.

13 W. H. Mallock, *The Limits of Pure Democracy* (London: Chapman and Hall, 1918), pp. 7–8, 18–29.

14 This bias helps to explain, for example, the Tory historian Stubbs's reduced dependence upon national-character arguments, in comparison to his Liberal friends Freeman and Green.

15 Burrow, *Liberal Descent*, pp. 236–40. It might be thought that Disraeli was the exception to this rule, and it is true that Disraeli never entirely shook off

his youthful nationalism during his rise to political prominence; however, generally speaking, the higher he rose, the more muted became his nationalist effusions. Other Conservative leaders – notably Salisbury – were more determinedly hostile.

16 Greta Jones, *Social Darwinism and English Thought: The Interaction between Biological and Social Theory* (Brighton: Harvester Press, 1980); Nancy Stepan, *The Idea of Race in Science: Great Britain, 1800–1960* (London: Macmillan, 1982); Catherine Hall, *White, Male and Middle-Class: Explorations in Feminism and History* (Cambridge: Polity Press, 1992); and Robert J. C. Young, *Colonial Desire: Hybridity in Theory, Culture and Race* (London: Routledge, 1995); but cf. Paul B. Rich's excellent *Race and Empire in British Politics*, 2nd edition (Cambridge: Cambridge University Press, 1990) and cautions in Douglas A. Lorimer, 'Race, Science and Culture: Historical Continuities and Discontinuities, 1850–1914', in *The Victorians and Race*, ed. Shearer West (Aldershot: Scolar, 1996), pp. 12–33.

17 *Collected Works of John Stuart Mill*, Vol. 2, *Principles of Political Economy*, p. 319 (the passage does appear in the first, 1848, edition); see also many parallel references in his work, but particularly on the over-reaction of the nineteenth century against the eighteenth, his letter to Charles Dupont-White, 6 Apr. 1860, ibid., Vol. 15, p.691; Buckle's citation is in *History of Civilization in England* (1857–61), ed. John M. Robertson (London: Routledge, 1904), p. 22.

18 Francis Galton, 'Hereditary Talent and Character' (1865), in *Images of Race*, ed. Michael D. Biddiss (Leicester: Leicester University Press, 1979), pp. 68–9; for another believer in biological race who doubted its significance for national character, see Bagehot, *Physics and Politics*, pp. 65–7, 78–80. See also Stepan's discussion in *Idea of Race*, pp. 78–82.

19 Jones, *Social Darwinism*, pp. 106–7, 172–3.

20 E. A. Freeman, 'Race and Language' (1877), in *Images of Race*, ed. Biddiss, p. 222, and *Comparative Politics* (London: Macmillan, 1873), pp. 45–50, 57–8, 61, 81–2, 333; for Mill's views on the possibility and desirability of anglicizing the Irish, see, e.g., his 1846 *Morning Chronicle* leaders, esp. *Collected Works*, Vol. 24, 955–6 (but cf. p. 958, where he speaks of *Celticizing* the Irish to make them more like the Bretons!), and p. 1004; for Arnold, see Nicholas Murray, *A Life of Matthew Arnold* (London: Hodder & Stoughton, 1996), pp. 167, 170, 229–31. For mid-Victorian Liberal arguments about the desirability of assimilating the Jews, see David Feldman, *Englishmen and Jews: Social Relations and Political Culture, 1840–1914* (New Haven, CT and London: Yale University Press), esp. pp. 37–47, 72–6. The situation of the Jews was complicated by doubts, in part about the assimilability of an Asiatic race, which did not arise so acutely even with the Irish.

21 Geographical determinism was seen as a French speciality: see William McDougall, *The Group Mind* (Cambridge: Cambridge University Press, 1920), pp. 214–41; Ernest Barker, *National Character and the Factors in its Formation* (London: Methuen, 1927), p. 51; both cite Buckle as the signal exception. It returned later in dilute form in the work of the *Annales* school.

22 Buckle, *History of Civilization*, pp. 87–9.

23 Freeman, 'Race and Language', p. 211, and *Comparative Politics*, pp. 81–2; J. R. Seeley, *Introduction to Political Science* (London: Macmillan, 1896), pp. 35–6; similar language in James Bryce's 1915 Creighton Lecture, *Race Sentiment as a Factor in History* (London: University of London Press, 1915), pp. 6–9, 25.

24 *Collected Works of John Stuart Mill*, Vol. 20, 'Guizot's Essays and Lectures on History' (1845), pp. 274, 291–2.

25 Buckle, *History of Civilization*, pp. 352, 354; see also 'England in the Nineteenth Century', *Works of Buckle*, ed. Taylor, pp. 246–7.

26 J. R. Green, *A Short History of the English People* (London: Macmillan, 1874), p. 542.

27 See in particular the essays by R. H. Hutton, Lord Houghton, James Bryce and A. O. Rutson in *Essays on Reform* (London: Macmillan, 1867).

28 Harvie, *Lights of Liberalism*, pp. 144–7, 153–7; Deborah Wormell, *Sir John Seeley and the Uses of History* (Cambridge: Cambridge University Press, 1980), pp. 138–9, 148; Collini *et al.*, *That Noble Science*, pp. 234–44. For a less intellectualized expression of the same point, see T. H. S. Escott, *England: Its People, Polity, and Pursuits*, 2 vols (London: Cassell, 1879), Vol. 1, pp. 239–41.

29 Mill to Gustave D'Eichtal, 15 May 1829, in *Collected Works*, Vol. 12, pp. 31–3; for the later elaboration of this theme, see 'The English National Character', ibid., Vol. 23, pp. 717–22, and *Principles of Political Economy*, ibid., Vols 2–3, pp. 104–6, 171–2.

30 Ibid., *Considerations on Representative Government*, Vol. 19, pp. 408–10.

31 Miles Taylor, 'John Bull and the Iconography of Public Opinion in England c.1712–1929', *Past and Present* 134 (1992): 93–128.

32 Burrow, *Liberal Descent*, p. 143, notes in particular Carlyle's and Stubbs's contempt for the fat and idle Saxons.

33 J. R. Seeley, *The Expansion of England* (London: Macmillan, 1883), pp. 84–7; Mandell Creighton, *The English National Character* (London: Henry Frowde, 1896), pp. 29–31. Mill's views are more elusive: see *Principles of Political Economy*, p. 104, and Mill to Pasquale Villari, 26 Jan. 1862, *Collected Works*, XVI, p. 771. Buckle was the odd man out in cleaving to more traditional Scottish Enlightenment themes, seeing the eighteenth century's application of the physical sciences to manufacturing as a turning-point in the promotion of materialism. 'England – For Introduction', in *Works of Buckle*, ed. Taylor, Vol. 1, pp. 204–5.

34 Seeley, *Expansion*, pp. 179–305; Sir Charles Dilke, *Greater Britain: A Record of Travel in English-Speaking Countries*, 8th edn (1868; London: Macmillan, 1885), pp. 535–52. Similar problems were encountered by Bryce: see his 1902 Romanes lecture, *The Relations of the Advanced and the Backward Races of Mankind* (Oxford: Clarendon Press, 1902).

35 Goldwin Smith, cited by Christine Bolt, *Victorian Attitudes to Race* (London: Routledge & Kegan Paul, 1971), pp. 214–15; see also Lucian Oldershaw (ed.), *England: A Nation* (London: R. Brimley Johnson, 1904) for mostly Liberal statements about insularity, and the discussion in Rich, *Race and Empire*, pp. 13–17, 20–5, about the difficulties of applying liberal ideas of the English national character to the Empire.

36 Charles H. Pearson, *National Life and Character: A Forecast* (London: Macmillan, 1893); and Harvie, *Lights of Liberalism*, pp. 233–5. Harvie also gives reasons to think Pearson was exceptional, and stresses the return to Liberalism of many of his cohort by 1906.

37 See, e.g., W. Macneile Dixon, *Poetry and National Character* (Cambridge: Cambridge University Press, 1915), pp. 8–10; William Ralph Inge, *England* (London: Ernest Benn, 1926), pp. 40–2, 52; and Barker, *National Character*, Ch. 1. See also Julia Stapleton, *Englishness and the Study of Politics: The Social and Political Thought of Ernest Barker* (Cambridge: Cambridge University Press, 1994), pp. 107, 122, on the stimulus Pearson gave to Barker's thought.

38 For a degenerationist perspective on national character after Pearson, see W. M. Flinders Petrie, *Janus in Modern Life* (London: Archibald Constable, 1907); but against this, see Ford Madox Hueffer, *The Spirit of the People: An Analysis of the English Mind* (London: Alston Rivers, 1907).

39 J. H. Grainger, *Patriotisms: Britain 1900–1939* (London: Routledge & Kegan Paul, 1986).

40 E. H. H. Green, *The Crisis of Conservatism: The Politics, Economics and Ideology of the British Conservative Party, 1880–1914* (London and New York: Routledge, 1995), esp. pp. 159–83, 331–2.

41 On the weakness of 'crowd psychology' in Britain, see Reba N. Soffer, *Ethics and Society in England: The Revolution in the Social Sciences, 1870–1914* (Berkeley, CA: University of California Press, 1978). Earlier Liberal thinking about the reliability of the English national character helped to cushion the impact of Graham Wallas and others who pondered the irrationality of human nature at this time, a point that seems to be acknowledged by Collini *et al.*, *That Noble Science*, p. 242.

42 G. R. Searle, *Eugenics and Politics in Britain 1900–1914* (Leiden: Noordhoff, 1976); Stepan, *Idea of Race*, pp. 124–39; also Rich, *Race and Empire*, pp. 94–101, on the weak purchase of eugenics on British sociology.

43 This was the conclusion of G. R. Searle in *The Quest for National Efficiency: A Study in British Politics and Political Thought, 1899–1914* (Oxford: Basil Blackwell, 1971) and of the only genuinely comparative study to date, Andrew Lees, *Cities Perceived: Urban Society in European and American Thought, 1820-1940* (Manchester: Manchester University Press, 1985).

44 Arthur James Balfour, *Decadence* (Cambridge: Cambridge University Press, 1908), pp. 40, 48–50, 59–60. He also cast doubt on the salience of race.

45 Aaron L. Friedberg, *The Weary Titan: Britain and the Experience of Relative Decline, 1895–1905* (Princeton, NJ: Princeton University Press, 1988), p. 295, and Chs. 6–7 *passim*; see also Grainger, *Patriotisms*, esp. pp. 56–7.

46 Creighton, *English National Character*, pp. 17–18; T. W. H. Crosland ['Angus McNeill'], *The Egregious English* (London: Grant Richards, 1903), Ch. 21; Spencer Leigh Hughes, *The English Character* (London: T. N. Foulis, 1912), Ch. 26; J. S. Mackenzie, *Arrows of Desire: Essays on Our National Character and Outlook* (London: George Allen & Unwin, 1920), pp. 95–7; Frank Fox, *The English, 1909–1922: A Gossip* (London: John Murray, 1923), p. 97.

47 Most of these psychological traits appear in Mill and Creighton.

48 John Stuart Mill, 'De Tocqueville on Democracy in America (II)' (1840) and 'The Condition of Ireland [24]' (1846), in *Collected Works*, Vol. 23, pp. 199–200, Vol. 24, pp. 969–71; James Anthony Froude, *Oceana, or England and Her Colonies* (London: Longman, Green, 1886), pp. 8–10, 385–7, and see Burrow, *Liberal Descent*, pp. 281–5.

49 Charles Kingsley, 'Froude's History of England', in *Miscellanies*, 2 vols (London: John W. Parker, 1859), pp. 70–1; Revd James Byrne, 'The Influence of National Character on English Literature', in *The Afternoon Lectures on English Literature* (London: Bell and Daldy, 1863), pp. 16–17, 25–6. See also Avner Offer's suggestive comments on the difference between Liberal transcendentalism and Tory hierarchicalism in *Property and Politics 1870–1914* (Cambridge: Cambridge University Press, 1981), pp. 332–49.

50 See Mandler, 'Against "Englishness"'. This view was also developed by some of the 'Little England' thinkers writing against the imperial consensus *c.*1900.

51 For some examples, see Grainger's discussion of Little Englandism in *Patriotisms*, pp. 142–59.

52 Ibid., pp. 329–30.

53 J. E. Neale, *Essays in Elizabethan History* (London: Jonathan Cape, 1958), pp. 202–3.

54 David Jarvis, 'The Shaping of Conservative Electoral Hegemony, 1918–39', in *Party, State and Society: Electoral Behaviour in Britain since 1820*, ed. Jon Lawrence and Miles Taylor (Aldershot: Scolar Press, 1997), pp. 135–7, 142.

55 Raphael Samuel suggests Green even more than Seeley after 1918: *Island Stories: Unravelling Britain* (London: Verso, 1998), pp. 81–2.

56 This point is usefully brought out in Stapleton, *Englishness and the Study of Politics*, the subtlest work on the subject yet written.

57 For admissions of the defects of racial theory from roughly Tory viewpoints, see Mackenzie, *Arrows of Desire*, p. 64; Inge, *England*, pp. 10–17, 39–40; Esme Wingfield-Stratford, *The History of British Civilization* (London: Routledge, 1928), p. 89; W. Macneile Dixon, *The Englishman* (London: Edward Arnold, 1931), pp. 18–28, 105–14.

58 Dixon, *Poetry and National Character*, pp. 8–10; Inge, *England*, pp. 42–32, 223, 227; Barker, *National Character*, Ch. 6; Dixon, *Englishman*, pp. 65–71, 77–86; Sir Stephen Tallents, *The Projection of England* (London: Faber & Faber, 1932), pp. 14–15; Arthur Bryant, *The National Character* (London: Longman, Green, 1934), pp. 32–3.

59 Neale, *Essays*, pp. 204–5. Neale pursued the same line of argument after 1945, in a Cold War context, contrasting Anglo-American liberty to Russian despotism.

60 Collini *et al.*, *That Noble Science*, pp. 328–331. See also Harold Nicolson, *National Character and National Policy* (Nottingham: University College, 1938), pp. 7–8.

61 Alison Light, *Forever England: Femininity, Literature and Conservatism Between the Wars* (London: Routledge, 1991); Raphael Samuel, 'Introduction: Exciting to be English', in *Patriotism: The Making and Unmaking of British National Identity*, ed. Samuel, Vol. 1, *History and Politics* (London: Routledge, 1989), esp. pp. xviii–xxv; Samuel, *Island Stories*, *passim*.

62 Light, *Forever England*, pp. 8, 47.

63 Mackenzie, *Arrows of Desire*, pp. 76–8. As Julia Stapleton shows, Ernest Barker harped on the themes of 'amateurishness' and 'gentlemanliness' only late in his life, after the Second World War, at which point he attracted charges of fogeyishness: Stapleton, *Englishness*, pp. 161–9, 173–4.

64 Mackenzie, *Arrows of Desire*, pp. 101–3; Inge, *England*, pp. 52–6. The idea of the gentleman as central to Englishness was more a Continental import than a native English growth: the most influential statements of the idea appear in George Santayana, *Soliloquies in England* (London: Constable, 1922) and Salvador de Madariaga, *Englishmen, Frenchmen, Spaniards* (1928; London: Pitman Publishing, 1970). Weber had it in 1917: see Max Weber, 'National Character and the Junkers', in *From Max Weber: Essays in Sociology*, ed. H.H. Gerth and C. Wright Mills (London: Kegan Paul, Trench, Trubner, 1947), p. 391.

65 Inge, *England,* p. 247. The quote is from Muir's *Politics and Progress: A Survey of the Problems of To-Day* (London: Methuen, 1923), p. 21.

66 Inge, *England*, p. 261.

67 'The unknown island' was the title of a series of 17 broadcasts made by S. P. B. Mais in 1932, and published as *This Unknown Island* (London: Putnam,

1932); see also the similar and even more popular *In Search of England* (London: Methuen, 1927) by H. V. Morton, which went through 23 editions by 1936.

68 Bryant, *The National Character*, pp. 22–3. The same language was employed by socialists like Clough Williams-Ellis and liberals like G. M. Trevelyan.

69 Philip Williamson, 'The Doctrinal Politics of Stanley Baldwin', in *Public and Private Doctrine: Essays in British History Presented to Maurice Cowling*, ed. Michael Bentley (Cambridge: Cambridge University Press, 1993), esp. pp. 184–5, 190–4.

70 The idea for the 'Heritage of Britain' series, despite its title devoted to an investigation of the national character, was mooted and abandoned in 1950; there is a file on it in the BBC Written Archives Centre, Caversham.

71 For some of these new idioms, see Becky Conekin, Frank Mort and Chris Waters (eds), *Moments of Modernity: Reconstructing Britain, 1945–64* (London: Rivers Oram, 1999).

7

Envisioning the Future: British and German Reactions to the Paris World Fair in 1900

Bernhard Rieger

One of the most striking features of historical narratives of the 'modern' is the profound sense of rupture that informs them. David Harvey refers to the 'ruthless break with any or all preceding historical conditions' that created the foundation for an awareness of modernity.[1] Jose Harris, writing of late Victorian and Edwardian Britain, identifies a 'marked decline in a popular sense of continuity with past history' that left contemporaries with the sensation of undertaking 'a quantum leap into a new era of human existence'.[2] Similarly, a maelstrom of perpetual disintegration and renewal that left no stone unturned figures prominently in Marshall Berman's classic account, aptly entitled *All That Is Solid Melts Into Air*.[3] 'Rupture' has thus become the inseparable twin of 'modern' sensibility. According to Reinhart Koselleck, expectations of what lay ahead 'distanced themselves ever more from all previous experience'. In his terms, the 'spaces of experience' and the 'horizons of expectations' to which people resorted to imagine the flow of time became separated when observers considered their own times as 'modern' and novel.[4]

While Koselleck thoughtfully conceptualizes how 'spaces of experience' and 'horizons of expectations' help individuals negotiate the relationships between the past, the present, and the future, he stops short of considering the possibility that narratives of continuity might also inform visions of a 'modern' future. In this respect his work resembles other projects that emphasize that a sense of historical dislocation necessarily defines the consciousness of modernity. Although these inquiries have greatly enhanced our understanding of how contemporaries conceived of modernity, the dominance of such approaches among historians also risks obscuring alternative notions of modernity that did *not* primarily hinge on ideas of disruption. Scholars still need to address whether – and if so, how – continuity informed assessments of the modern. This chapter examines visions of the future put forward by visitors to the Paris World Fair in 1900 to determine how Britons and Germans narrated rupture and continuity in conceptions of modernity.

Taking articles about the 1900 Paris World Fair published in German and British review journals, this chapter compares how notions of the future constructed meanings of the 'modern' at a particular historical juncture.[5] As we shall see, these scenarios of the future envisioned modernity and simultaneously passed normative judgements on it. The *exposition universelle* invited visitors to reflect on the future not only because the show exhibited imminent changes by displaying the most advanced artistic and technological artefacts of the day, but also because, being staged in 1900, the Fair invited observers to contemplate what the twentieth century might hold in store.[6] British reviews and their German equivalents, the *Rundschauzeitschriften*, provide an excellent source for a comparative investigation of the ways members of the British and German educated elites discussed the Fair in Paris. Reviews and *Rundschauzeitschriften* provided forums for leading opinion-makers of the German and British middle classes and are therefore rich in material conveying debates over conceptions of the future as well as of the character of modernity.[7] In order to determine how British 'public moralists' and German *Bildungsbürger* envisioned the future, this analysis will ask the following questions.[8] Did positive or negative appraisals of the 'modern' underlie narratives of the future in these journals? Did commentators argue that the 'modern age' had reached a watershed in 1900, and if so, for what reasons? Finally, which factors account for the differences between the German and the British concepts of the future presented in the periodicals?

* * *

In the nineteenth century world fairs functioned quite literally, rather than metaphorically, as spaces of experience with a pronounced orientation towards the future. They provided opportunities to document present trends and enabled observers to cast tentative glances into the future. Thus, universal expositions documented 'change', and linked the past, the present, and the future. Of course, this was by no means the sole objective of world fairs. They simultaneously acted as urban entertainment spectacles, arenas of industrial competition and educational institutions aiming to spread social discipline through education. In addition, international fairs popularized, legitimized and formed colonial policies.[9] Only their character as colourful spectacles serving a variety of purposes can account for their exceptional crowd-pulling abilities. The Paris Fair in 1900 sold 50 million tickets. With an average daily attendance of 150,000, the number of people at the fair could rise to 400,000 on holidays.[10]

No matter how multidimensional the Paris universal exhibition was, its orientation towards the future represented one of its defining aspects. First, the *exposition universelle* situated itself in the contemporary discourse of 'progress'. In his opening speech on Easter Sunday in 1900, the French president Emile Loubet was convinced that, thanks to the affirmation of certain generous thoughts which the dying century has echoed, the twentieth century will see the glow of a little more fraternity and less misery of all kinds, and that, soon perhaps, we shall have passed an important stage in the slow work of evolution of work towards happiness and of men towards humanity.[11]

On the same occasion, French socialist trade minister Alexandre Millerand shared this optimism about the future when he welcomed an increase in altruism. He expected improved social and international relations to result from progress in Europe. The cautious tone of Loubet's speech and Millerand's choice of topic indicate that such rhetorics of progress implicitly reacted to contemporary scepticism and fear of revolution. In this context, world fairs can be understood as institutional mechanisms of self-reassurance against the fears of the future permeating contemporary European and North American societies.

Unlike many other exhibitionary projects, they did not devote their primary attention to the supposedly unchanging conditions of the past. Instead, world fairs staged the present as a time of transition or a glamorous yet provisional arrangement whose full potential would be developed in the later future. International exhibitions normally lasted for about half a year, and were subsequently demolished. Since they institutionalized transitoriness, universal exhibitions facilitated the document-ation of progress. Growing in size and splendour, their succession created a chronology from show to show, and thus underlined the transformation of the world. International fairs were aimed at demonstrating, through their provisional arrangements, world development towards a better, if not a clearly defined, future. In 1900 this provisional character was particularly striking, since the grounds presented themselves as a huge unfinished building site after the opening. While a British visitor encountered 'the whole area . . . [as] one vast confusion, in which scaffold poles were more conspicuous than anything else', a German colleague compared the unfinished façade of the main building on *Champs de Mars* with a 'face eaten away by cancer'.[12] Others bemoaned the fact that the impressive, lavishly decorated and lighted exteriors made of plaster would not last: The 'palaces' resembled 'soap bubbles in vividly coloured splendour [which] disappear tracelessly after a short time'.[13] It was therefore expected that the fair would live on in visitors' memories in the future once its 'beautiful evanescent buildings' had become 'matters of history'.[14]

The atmosphere of transitoriness and transition that universal exhibitions radiated permitted glimpses of the future. At the same time, the provisional char-acter of the shows betrayed an insecurity about the different paths that might lead toward that future. This problem of orientation was not rooted merely in the general perception of change as it gained intensity with industrialization alone; for by exhibiting an ever-changing world of artefacts in breathtakingly new ways, these very international exhibitions themselves added to the dilemma faced by contemporary forecasters. Change generated a continual demand for fresh prognoses while simultaneously undermining their reliability. The commentators cast this problem in the language of the 'modern'.

Contemporary perception of the 'moving pavement' or *trottoir roulant* that facilitated transit between sites on the grounds provides a case in point. The reporter for *Blackwood's Edinburgh Magazine*, uninhibited in his criticism of the show on other grounds, expected the moving boardwalk to remain 'the liveliest memory. For this admirable invention has never ceased to amuse the crowd.' He considered it 'the last word of modern ingenuity'.[15] While some observers loathed the confusion on the *trottoir roulant*, others found it a 'sight to refresh one indescribably after the serious business of sightseeing'. It literally swept people off their feet. This 'marvellous attraction' brought together 'rich and poor, young and old, Parisians and provincials, Americans and Orientals, Arabs and Esquimaux jostling, walking, falling, laughing'.[16] Visitors could not resist the urge to ascribe future significance to this recent modern wonder: 'For who can tell? – may not this venture, shown for the first time in Paris in 1900, revolutionize the future appearance of our cities, and that even in the lifetime of those visiting Paris this year?'[17]

In more general terms, writers referred to the fair as a 'giant spectacle of modern genius' which built a 'wonderland of delights' or a 'realm of magic', leaving visitors with impressions of a world under an enchanting and lyrical spell of progress.[18] In this context the languages of wonder and magic served to underline enthusiastically and proudly the unparalleled character of recent achievements. The universal exposition thus promoted an exhibitionism of progress and paraded the results of 'madly concentrated work, gigantic speculation, of genius and knowledge'.[19]

Yet the fetishization of the world of objects that resulted directly from dazzling modes of exhibiting could transform the grounds into 'phantasmagorias'.[20] Thus, the *exposition universelle* also became a cause for concern and confusion. Commentators related on several occasions how they wandered through the 'labyrinth of labyrinths' devoid of orientation.[21] Visitors left the fair accidentally and had to purchase new tickets for readmittance because boundaries blurred between the fair's grounds and the surrounding urban environment.[22] The world fair was therefore by no means an unproblematic field of experience. The rhetoric of modern wonder voiced not only admiration but also surprised incomprehension, as well as a sense of being intellectually overwhelmed. Such moments rendered it difficult to arrive at precise interpretations of the future by going to the fair. At best, the universal exposition served as an 'augury' or as a contemporary equivalent of the classical oracle.[23] 'Have we not, in our modern exhibition, with all its limitations, a reproduction of Delphi, all the more real because unconscious?'[24]

Commentators thus endowed world fairs with meanings that might, however, remain entirely inaccessible to visitors. When contemporaries addressed the *exposition universelle* as an unreadable quasi-mythological cipher, a detailed anticipation of the future reached its limits, and the temporal continuum ended in a present that was only partially understood. Resorting to the supposedly timeless languages of ancient mythology and religion provided one way of compensating for this loss of the future. In this context commentators constructed the universal exhibition as a 'modern Babel', a combination of Leviathan, Behemoth and Mammon; or, alternatively, as a prescience of a Golden Age.[25] No matter whether these interpreters harboured positive or negative expectations, they only succeeded in conceptualizing the future as a state *beyond* temporality, and thus effectively in the realm of mythology.

The ability to anticipate or construct the future in detailed ways arrived at its limits on the occasion of the fair in 1900. Commentators employed the language of the 'modern' when writing about the ways in which the exhibition staged the transitoriness of the present, thus providing views of the future. At the same time they were confused by dazzling modes of display that rendered concrete conceptualizations of times to come impossible. Instead, commentators resorted to supposedly timeless rhetorics of mythology and religion to imagine the future.

* * *

Contemporaries had to find their bearings in a maze of modern time. Rather than providing a clear and straightforward vision of the future in itself, the *exposition universelle* represented an intellectual challenge to those aiming to make sense of coming times. The problematics of envisioning the future at the universal exhibition only rarely led to full-scale rejections of modernity's consequences in British and German review periodicals. Still, an examination of the themes covered in the journals brings out clear national differences. British debate about the world fair reveal a less problematic relationship with modernity than German discourse.

Some British sceptics of progress chose aesthetics to denounce the world fair as an exercise in vanity. *Blackwood's Edinburgh Magazine*, a bastion of traditionalism in the arts, pointed out rather conventionally that 'the triumph of the modern world is purely mechanical'. Formally, the modern period had not yet come to terms with itself, because 'in the modern style there is no growth, there is no character . . . The style is of no place, of no time – it is merely modern.' This was not even the worst aspect of contemporary design, 'though that should be sufficient to condemn it. Its lack of sincerity is a more heinous sin, because that sin not only ruins the present but makes the future appear hopeless.'[26] Timelessness here equalled undesired stylistic arbitrariness that turned the present into an aesthetic desert beyond which there seemed to lie no territory at all. In short, the universal exhibition represented the final episode in a history of aesthetics that ought not to continue.

Others sharpened their quills to expose as hollow the liberal rhetorics that surrounded the opening ceremony. Alluding to the origins of world fairs in the industrial exhibitions of the period of the French Revolution, a contribution in *The Fortnightly Review* reminded readers that 'the movement had its rise in a feast of blood'. The author added that the supposed pacifistic impact of international fairs had not prevented wars in the past, and that future expectations to that effect were unrealistic.[27] Set against the background of the Boer War and its concomitant demonstrations of nationalism, this relatively pessimistic conception of the future could not easily be brushed aside.

Such interventions provoked dissent. Several visitors hailed the exhibition as an 'outbreak of sheer originality' and paid homage to its high aesthetic standards.[28] British observers were especially taken by a new steel bridge over the Seine named after Czar Alexander III:

> All the metallic decoration, which is very elaborate, is symbolic. It represents the flora and fauna of the sea, in order to typify the part which the French and Russian Navies played . . . at bringing about the *rapprochement* of the Powers. In the centre of the bridge, on the one side there are the Russian Arms, supported by the Nymphs of the Neva, while on the other are the Arms of the City of Paris, supported by the Nymphs of the Seine. It is a very pretty idea, very ingeniously carried out. No such ornate bridge has been built in our time . . . no modern builder has lavished all the resources of sculpture and art in order to beautify a city and symbolise a political alliance.[29]

The architect Heathcote Statham also considered the bridge exemplary, since it combined recent technological advances with a historicist stylistic vocabulary. It was 'one of the most remarkable erections in modern times'.[30] Similarly the *Edinburgh Review* sided with the proponents of artistic progress: with 'moral and intellectual elevation . . . abundantly present' the exhibition celebrated 'a cult of beauty'.[31] The majority of commentators writing for the British periodical press considered the World Fair in 1900 a successful demonstration of 'modern', i.e. contemporary, aesthetics.

When treating political and social trends British commentators also underlined optimistic signals through which the *exposition universelle* supported liberal optimism about the future. Articles stressed that the show addressed European social problems and singled out its scientific approach. A host of international conferences bore witness to this concern. As a 'University of the Present' the world fair was also 'a school of social science' and 'a school of social duty'.[32] Moreover, the exhibition demonstrated an international will to preserve peace. While the 'appliances of destruction, as befits the times, are indeed naturally much in evidence [and] war has its palace on the largest scale . . . a still vaster exposition of the possibilities of peace' dwarfed the military section.[33] The *Review of Reviews* welcomed the world fair as 'a great security for peace' and 'a great monument of peace'.[34] The Socialist journal *New Age* agreed, and considered the show as 'Labour's Hope'.[35]

British periodicals confronted sceptics of progress with a fundamental critique, too. Supporters of the 'modern' alleged that their opponents maintained a simplistic notion of progress. Several authors considered it unrealistic to expect progress without setbacks and to take too literally the hyperbolic oratory of the opening ceremony. *The New Age* argued that 'often we are too sanguine, and take too little into account the forces that have to be overcome in the march of Progress'.[36] Setbacks were therefore inevitable. Patrick Geddes conceded the pompousness of claims by organizers that the exhibition provided a synthesis of the nineteenth century alongside a philosophy for the twentieth. 'It savours strongly of after-dinner eloquence, no doubt, that gorgeous promise of M. Picard,' Patrick Geddes admitted in reference to the chief administrator of the fair. Yet he also asked: 'Is there not in each of these exaggerated phrases a clear grain of truth?'[37] The *Edinburgh Review* was less affected by such modesty. After a survey of the fair it maintained that 'the days may dawn when man shall really live in the whole, the true, the good'.[38] The liberal future appeared bright.

British analysts of the Paris fair disagreed about its messages concerning the future. Casting their interpretations in rhetorics of the 'modern', they addressed political, social and aesthetic issues without prioritizing any of these themes. A minority remained unimpressed by the liberal rhetorics of the exhibition concerning international understanding. Sceptics of progress also elaborated on the stylistic deficiencies of the show. Yet those intoning a swan song for the 'modern' future competed with a larger chorus striking a more optimistic note. Subscribing to languages of progress, the latter considered the show an aesthetic, political and social success. While British commentators contested the futures inherent in the 1900 world fair, they shared one assumption. No matter whether promoters or sceptics of progress, they did *not* stipulate that modernity had reached a fund-amental turning-point at the beginning of the twentieth century. British discourse about political and social issues remained within the paradigms of liberalism. How do these British narratives compare with the interpretations in German *Rundschauzeitschriften*?

* * *

German contributors chose to address the world fair in different ways. Some voices argued that universal exhibitions had had their day. To substantiate this claim they did not criticize official liberal rhetorics. Instead, they maintained that an overcrowding of the grounds with objects rendered it impossible for visitors to ascribe meaning to the exhibition. Wilhelm Hasbach found 'the arbitrary and confusing character of this exhibition' particularly repelling.[39] He therefore posed the question if it 'was not best if the last world fair of the nineteenth century would also be the last one altogether'. His colleague August Schricker concurred that 'the time of universal exhibitions is over. The epoch of specialised fairs begins, and we return to a path which should not have been left in the first place.'[40] Hasbach and Schricker thus stated that, as far as universal exhibitions were concerned as institutions, the beginning of the twentieth century amounted to the end of an era. They did not reflect on the wider implications of this diagnosis for the future course of modern times.

The majority of German analysts, however, considered the *exposition universelle* a meaningful event. Unlike British narratives, German reports rarely approached the world fair from the perspective of liberalism in a British sense. Rather German observers visited the exhibition to learn primarily about *Kultur*.[41] Extending beyond aesthetic and stylistic concerns, *Kultur* commanded the characteristics of a totalizing category. No matter whether German commentators approached artistic, economic, social, military or political issues, their intention frequently consisted in identifying contemporary *Kultur*. Friedrich Naumann's explicit conceptualization provides a case in point. He wrote that the fair exhibited 'the dominant industrial capitalistic *Kultur*, the *Kultur* of triumphant white man'. It, therefore, charted the 'genuine movement of modern *Kultur*'.[42] This agenda produced concepts of the future that differed from British interpretations of the fair.

One line of thought argued that the country's prime responsibility consisted in continuing those traditions that had provided the basis for imperial national identity over the past hundred years. Launching an implicit attack on liberal tenets, the official German catalogue expressed the view that 'industrial and political prosperity does not depend on the accidental development of arbitrary forces but on the earnest endeavours of a conscious purpose based on a well regulated and many sided system of education and culture'. To guarantee progress in times to come and to maintain national identity, it was necessary to add to a national gallery of venerable ancestors. The twentieth century was expected to follow the footsteps of Kant, Schiller, Goethe, Beethoven, Stein, Scharnhorst, the Humboldts, Gauss, Liebig, Semper, Bismarck, Moltke, Helmholtz, Bunsen, Virchow, Krupp, Siemens, Wagner, Brahms, Menzel and Lenbach. Rather than considering this cast in its heterogeneity, the catalogue ultimately viewed the group as homogeneous. They represented 'the embodiment of the most varied expression of German intellectual power [in the German original: *deutsche Geisteskraft*]'. The challenge was 'to emulate and be true to them, as the guardian of internal and external peace, as the promoter of the great civilising [in the German original: *kulturell*], social and moral objects of the age'.[43] The official German catalogue thus put forward a concept of the future stressing the need to preserve continuity between the nineteenth and the twentieth centuries for the sake of *Kultur* and national identity.

Next to the supporters of continuity existed a politically diffuse camp of reformers proclaiming as their main concern an aesthetic inconsistency characterizing the world of objects displayed at the fair. Writing for the Socialist periodical *Die neue Zeit* Felicie Nossig surveyed the universal exhibition from 'the aesthetic vantage point'. The new bridge over the Seine in the name of Alexander III provided her with an example of dominant 'banality'. Technologically, she hailed the construction as 'a wonderful monument of modern progress'. Yet 'the shiny golden pillar figures which are dwarfed by the gigantic construction' created only an 'embarassing impression'.[44] A fundamental split ran through the entire fair. While its technological artefacts symbolized the future of a 'morally healthy and socially rising working class', the exhibitionary architecture testified to the death of the bourgeoisie. The palaces, avenues and bridges on the ground represented the products of 'the exhausted brain of a degenerate class hurrying towards its decay'.[45] Only the transition to socialism would solve this fundamental aesthetic problem and harmonize form and contents. In Nossig's view, modernity had arrived at a turning-point.

While Henry van de Velde and Julius Meier-Graefe, who wrote for *Die Zukunft*, belonged to different political camps they shared Nossig's diagnosis of contemporary historicist aesthetics. Meier-Graefe did not hide his disgust at the Seine bridge, which had been 'built by intelligent engineers but became subsequently defaced by decorators'.[46] On the whole, the show was 'the victory of a demonstration *ad absurdum*': 'Many will be enlightened who, up to now, have thoughtlessly managed machinery and have lived in old-fashioned houses at the same time, who never had the idea of protesting against the fact . . . that our strong present is looking for its forms in times to which we have no connection at all.'[47] Henry van de Velde also protested against the 'unorganic' 'patchwork of decorations' on display in Paris.[48] How was this much-lamented inconsistency of contemporary *Kultur* to be overcome?

German commentators were not at a loss to provide a solution. It lay in the promotion of a modernist aesthetic reconstruction of the world of objects that would re-invest the man-made environment with a consistency between form and contents. In agreement with van de Velde and Meier-Graefe, Friedrich Naumann pointed towards the products of recent technological innovation for stylistic guidance. All of them still singled out the 'incomparable' Eiffel Tower as a model for the future, even though it had been built in 1889: 'An object of daily pleasure, a work which I would wish to have created if I were an engineer. This is modern! No superfluous girder, completely made of iron, a heroic poem cast in metal, an artwork without artistry. Thus comes the new age . . . Here is the style which we need and want.'[49]

Naumann took such reasoning one step further by linking it to the issue of national identity. An electrical generator designed in Germany embodied his ideal:

'The whole construction commands a fabulous unity. It is an entity in itself like the system of a great philosopher.' It was no coincidence that the machine had been assembled in Germany: 'Our engineers are born into the same intellectual nest [in the German original: *geistiges Nest*], which Melanchthon, Leibniz, Kant and Hegel built. Even if they don't know anything about the prehistory of German thought, it is still their foundation.'[50] Thus, for Naumann an aesthetic reconstruction along modernist lines was both a national necessity and an opportunity. It aimed at a rejuvenation of the foundations of German national identity in order to safeguard the future of the nation and strengthen its link with the past.

Like the British commentators, the majority of the writers for German periodicals did not reject modernity. In fact, one of the main criticisms of the universal exhibition in Paris alleged that it was not modern enough and therefore lacked orientation to the future. German analysts operated with two opposite notions of the future of modern times. The imperial political establishment promoted the idea of building the future seamlessly in line with traditions developed in the nineteenth century. Many German commentators disagreed with this traditionalist approach and called for a vigorous and radical modernism that would re-invest the world of objects with aesthetic consistency through stylistic reform. In their view, change had pushed the 'modern' era to a turning-point at which it became necessary to recast the material world along the lines of an aesthetic that took account of change. As Naumann's articles bear out, aesthetic reformers did not necessarily intend to tear all links with the past. Rather he perceived himself as reforging them in novel and 'modern' ways. No matter whether German analysts belonged to the traditionalists or the modernists, they shared the concept of *Kultur* when interrogating the universal exhibition. Additionally, German articles displayed a tendency to link considerations of contemporary *Kultur* with examinations of the best ways to construct national identity in the future.

* * *

The overwhelming majority of both British and German commentators displayed a positive evaluation of modernity. Rejections of the fair in a spirit of anti-modernity were extremely rare. Yet German and British responses to the *exposition universelle* differed in three major respects.

First, German and British commentators cast their analyses in different categorical frameworks. British reports covered political, social and aesthetic aspects of the show. They did not privilege any of these categories, but located them loosely within established paradigms of liberalism. In contrast, German reports covered similar aspects and sometimes identical objects; but they subsumed the political, the social and the aesthetic under the universalizing category of *Kultur*. As a result, German narratives tended to construct their comments within a normative framework implicitly demanding the consistency of *Kultur*.

Second, German contributions often linked their invocation of *Kultur* with the issue of national identity – a topic rather absent from British articles. German commentators scrutinized the universal exposition to determine its potential implications for what they considered as the foundation of national identity: the *Kultur* of a nation.

A third difference between German and British discourse concerns the ways in which they conceived of adequate future responses to the perceived pressures of modernity. Practically all British writers and a significant number of their German colleagues argued in favour of an uninterrupted continuation of 'modern' traditions that had emerged during the nineteenth century. In this view, it was not necessary to initiate fundamental reforms to cope with the perceived results of change. Rather, change itself was seen to generate the solutions to problems.

These German and British interpretations affirming modernity *and* its established traditions contrast with a second strand of German discourse about the Paris exhibition that had no British equivalent. A highly articulate and politically diverse minority of German cultural critics proclaimed the need for a fundamental aesthetic reconstruction in order to come to terms with the condition of modernity. They were concerned with the creation and promotion of a modernist aesthetics lending expression to purportedly novel qualities of 'modern' life that could not be captured in the historicist vocabularies so popular throughout the nineteenth century.[51]

Three related questions emerge, which have to be separated for analytical purposes. Why did German commentators stress the universal category of *Kultur* when their British colleagues did not employ a similar term? Why did the German debate about the exhibition turn into a debate about national identity? – a concern absent from the British discussion. Why did some German commentators formulate demands for modernism when the silence of their British colleagues on the subject suggests that the latter did not perceive a need for it?

As members of the educated elite, the majority of German commentators were *Bildungsbürger* attempting to assert their traditional claims to national moral authority. Their self-identity rested on idealist notions of *Bildung* that prescribed an open-ended process of self-formation through the intellectual study of *Kultur* embodied in topics such as literature, philosophy, history or ancient languages. For them, the universal category of *Kultur* represented the main referent for the interpretation of aesthetics, politics, social and economic life.[52] *Kultur* thus implied that a metaphysical unity or consistency underlay the diverse universe of phenomena. For the German educated elites, the intellectual appropriation of the world was synonymous with the appropriation of its *Kultur*. Around 1900, the overwhelming majority among the German educated elite subscribed to this style of thought, irrespective of political orientation. In the context of the interpretation of the Paris world fair, it emerged among Liberals and Conservatives as well as among the Social Democrats.

British commentators did not operate with a similar universal interpretational category. This resulted not only from British empiricist traditions, but also from the dominant educational ideal fostered in the public school and Oxbridge systems. While these institutions had taken up elements of the German ideology of *Bildung*, they also emphasized character formation through sports and striving towards individual 'independence'. The ideal of self-identity among the elites stressed the intellectual, moral and physical development of the male individual towards the role model of the 'gentleman'. This diversity built into English and British educational regimes worked against the exclusivist privileging of the intellectual aspects of character formation that characterized German educational ideology.[53] Moreover, it blocked the emergence and internalization of an interpretational master category such as *Kultur* among those who constituted the educated elite in Britain writing about the Paris exhibition.

The dimension of metaphysical unity inscribed into the concept of *Kultur* had far-reaching consequences for the construction of national identity in Germany. Since one of the most frequent ways of conceptualizing German national identity consisted in stressing the 'cultural' foundations of the *Reich*, German narratives of nationhood tended to be modelled around notions of a harmonious unity of *Kultur*.[54] Around 1900, locating constructions of German national identity within a normative framework of cultural homogeneity created more problems than it solved. While an imperial national culture arose in the form of monuments, public buildings and popular festivals, no contemporary could assert that the *Reich* provided the national home for all German-speakers.[55] In addition to the essential role that the exclusion of Austria had played in the foundation of the *Reich*, intense political conflict between the Left and the Right about the definition of national *Kultur* added another fundamental problem.[56] Even though the idea of homogeneity in principle aimed at rallying traditions, it simultaneously aggravated arguments about claims for inclusion into, and exclusion from, the stock of national culture. The theory that national identity was rooted in a homogeneous culture was fundamentally at odds with the pressures and tensions expressed in discourses about the 'modern', which tended to promote political, social or aesthetic conflict.[57] Thus articles about the exhibition in Paris can be read as interventions in a wider, highly contentious debate about the cultural foundations of German identity under the condition of modernity.

In contrast, 'Britishness' discouraged attempts to found national identities on narratives of cultural homogeneity. Concepts of Britishness accommodated several national identities within a framework of Protestantism and Empire. This contrast explains the silence of British commentators on the potential implications of perceived trends at the Paris fair for British national identities. While German notions of nationality were constructed around the idea of a homogeneous national culture that potentially aggravated conflicts over claims to inclusion or for exclusion, Britishness had to grant space to various national cultures. Indeed, British writers were remarkably uninterested in the issue of national identity in the first place.[58] Considering the heated domestic debate about the Boer War in 1900, this British silence about issues of national identity may come as a surprise. Yet political conflict over the war in South Africa stopped short of fundamentally questioning Britain's imperial activities in general. Thus, British national identities continued to derive strong legitimization from the allegedly civilizing mission of imperial enterprise.[59] Unlike their German colleagues, British writers on the Paris exhibition did not consider national identity a problematic topic requiring specific attention.

Moreover, the justification that British national identities gained from imperialism may have inoculated the metropolitan culture against radical demands for modernist aesthetic reform. German imperialistic ideology did not possess claims to a civilizing motivation underlying overseas expansion. As a consequence, German domestic cultural presuppositions lacked this concomitant effect and were therefore liable to be questioned more fundamentally.[60]

Yet the contrasting political cultures in which German and British commentators wrote probably also have a further importance in accounting for the different strengths of modernist narratives in Britain and Germany. German modernist reform movements either formed in opposition to state-sponsored cultural establishments or were quickly driven on to the defensive by them. Given the alliance between anti-modernists in the establishment and Wilhelm II, modernist creeds could serve to voice diffuse political discontent indirectly.[61] This is particularly true of the clamorous interventions by the reformist Liberal Friedrich Naumann, who found it difficult to rise from political marginality.

In contrast, 'the English tradition of *laissez-faire*, especially in cultural matters' – partly a function of as well as a prerequisite for a multinational sense of Britishness – rendered it difficult to express political discontent with the state or its artistic establishment in a language of aesthetic reform.[62] In this sense, one of the prime targets at which German modernists directed their charges simply did not exist in Britain. At the same time, cultural *laissez-faire* was embedded in a wider political culture that liberalism shaped in a more fundamental way in Britain than in Germany. The prominence of the liberal paradigm in British evaluations of the fair bears witness to this difference in comparison with Germany.

In conclusion, it appears that in 1900 writings in British review periodicals perceived the future of modernity as less problematic than contributions in similar German journals. While the majority of analysts in both countries affirmed what they considered as the defining characteristics of the 'modern', British narratives conceptualized the future within a framework of continuity. Imperialistic legitimations of domestic cultures and the multinationality of British identities, in addition to the strength of liberalism, contributed to maintaining a sense of relatively uninterrupted progression towards times to come. By contrast, German commentators engaged in a contestation over the periodization of modernity in 1900. With members of the establishment arguing in favour of continuity, critics disagreed and stressed that modern times had arrived at a turning-point. The prominence of *Kultur* as a universal interpretational category and constructions of national identities in normative frameworks of cultural consistency, in addition to the illiberalism of the imperial political establishment, contributed to the conviction that a new age was about to begin in 1900. For a long time, scholars have tried to trace a sense of modernity through contemporary debates about the advantages and disadvantages of modernism. In 1900, one peculiarity of the British upper middle-class may well have consisted in the absence of a prominent discourse about modernism. At that time, British public moralists appear to have been more at ease with the flow of modern time than their German colleagues. In Koselleck's terms, British intellectuals managed to maintain a unity between their 'spaces of experience' and 'horizons of expectations' while pronouncing their belief in modernity in 1900.

Notes

I would like to thank Elizabeth Buettner, Rebecca Spang, Martin Daunton, Peter Mandler and Johannes Paulmann for challenging discussions of this article. I have also profited from debates initiated by the participants in the Neale Colloquium in British History at University College London in 1998 and in the workshop on *Jahrhundertwende-Zeitenwende: Modernitätserfahrung um 1900* at the University of Erlangen in 1997.

1 David Harvey, *The Condition of Postmodernity: An Enquiry into the Origins of Cultural Change* (Oxford: Basil Blackwell, 1989), p. 12.

2 Jose Harris, *Private Lives, Public Spirit: Britain 1870–1914* (Harmondsworth: Penguin, 1994), p. 33.

3 Marshall Berman, *All That Is Solid Melts Into Air: The Experience Of Modernity* (London: Verso, 1983), p. 15.

4 Reinhart Koselleck, '"Space of Experience" and "Horizon of Expectation": Two Historical Categories', in *Futures Past: On the Semantics of Historical Time* (Cambridge, MA: MIT Press, 1985), pp. 267–88, here 276. The German original, first published in 1976, draws heavily on a linguistic similarity that cannot be readily rendered into English. *Neuzeit* denotes the 'modern age' as an epoch starting around 1500; but it also plays directly on '*neue Zeit*', which translates as 'novel age'. See Reinhart Koselleck, '"Erfahrungsraum" und "Erwartung-shorizont" – zwei historische Kategorien,' in *Vergangene Zukunft: Zur historischen Semantik geschichtlicher Zeiten* (Frankfurt/M.: Suhrkamp, 1989), pp. 349–75, here 359.

5 I am here following a recent suggestion by Diane Hughes to think of concepts of time as sources of knowledge. See Diane Owen Hughes, 'Introduction', in *Time: Histories and Ethnologies*, ed. Diane Owen Hughes and Thomas R. Trautmann (Ann Arbor, MI: University of Michigan Press, 1995), pp. 1–18, here 9.

6 Richard D. Mandell, *Paris 1900: The Great World's Fair* (Toronto: University of Toronto Press, 1967).

7 For reasons of spatial constraint, these methodological remarks have to be kept to a minimum. The German source body comprises the following journals: *Deutsche Rundschau, Die neue Rundschau, Die Neue Zeit, Die Zukunft, Die Hilfe, Die Gartenlaube*. The British source sample includes *Contemporary Review, Fortnightly Review, Blackwood's Edinburgh Magazine, The Speaker, The New Age, Edinburgh Review, Art Journal, Review of Reviews*. While many articles, particularly in British journals, were released anonymously, personal information was available for: F. G. Aflalo, H. Butler, Patrick Geddes, and H. Heathcote Statham as well as Julius Meier-Graefe, J. C. Heer, Friedrich Naumann and August Schricker. Biographical compendia consulted are the volumes making up both the *Dictionary of National Biography* (Oxford: Oxford University Press) and the *Neue Deutsche Biographie* (Berlin: Duncker und Humblot). Also *Who Was Who: A Companion to Who's Who 1916–1928* (London: A. C. Black, 1929) and *Deutsches Biographisches Archiv*, ed. Willy Gorzny (Munich: K. G. Saur) (microfiche).

8 For the definition and roles of public moralists see Stefan Collini, *Public Moralists: Political Thought and Intellectual Life in Britain, 1850–1930* (Oxford: Clarendon Press, 1993).

9 See Paul Greenhalgh, *Ephemeral Vistas: The Expositions Universelles, Great Exhibitions and World's Fairs, 1851–1939* (Manchester: Manchester University Press, 1988); Evelyn Kroker, *Die Weltausstellungen im 19. Jahrhundert: Industrieller Leistungsnachweis, Konkurrenzverhalten und Kommunikationsfunktion unter Berücksichtigung der Montanindustrie des Ruhrgebietes zwischen 1851 und 1880* (Göttingen: Vandenhoeck und Rupprecht, 1975); Tony Bennett, 'The Exhibitionary Complex', in *Culture/Power/History: A Reader in Contemporary Social Theory*, ed. Nicholas B. Dirks, Geoff Eley and Sherry B. Ortner (Princeton, NJ: Princeton University Press, 1994), pp. 123–54; and Timothy Mitchell, 'Orientalism and the Exhibitionary Order', in *Colonialism and Culture*, ed. Nicholas B. Dirks (Ann Arbor, MI: University of Michigan Press, 1992), pp. 289–317.

10 Mandell, *Paris 1900*, p. xi; 'Is the Exhibition a Failure?', *The Speaker*, n. s., 2 (1900): 585.

11 Quoted from 'Outlook', *The New Age*, 19 April 1900: 241.

12 'The Opening of the Paris Exhibition', *Review of Reviews* 21 (1900): 335; and Wilhelm Hasbach, 'Weltausstellungseindrücke', *Die Zukunft* 31 (1900): 429.

13 Felicie Nossig, 'Pariser Weltausstellung 1900', *Die Neue Zeit* 18:2 (1900): 119.

14 'Opening of the Paris Exhibition', p. 343; Herbert E. Butler, 'The Rue des Nations', in *The Paris Exhibition 1900*, ed. D. Croal Thomson (London: H. Virtue and Co., 1901): 110. The last work assembles articles from the *Art Journal*.

15 'Musings without Method', *Blackwood's Edinburgh Magazine* 168 (1900): 115.

16 Herbert Butler, 'The Moving Pavement', *The Paris Exhibition 1900*, ed. D. Croal Thomson (London: H. Virtue and Co., 1901), p. 272. For a critical view of the moving platform see Heer, 'Spaziergänge durch die Weltausstellung in Paris', p. 544.

17 Butler, 'The Moving Pavement', pp. 271–2.

18 Nossig, 'Pariser Weltausstellung', p. 118; Heer, 'Spaziergänge durch die Weltausstellung in Paris', *Die Gartenlaube* 49 (1900), pp. 702, 703.

19 Julius Meier-Graefe, 'Die Architektur auf der Weltausstellung', *Die Zukunft* 31 (1900): 570.

20 Walter Benjamin, 'Paris, die Hauptstadt des XIX. Jahrhunderts', in *Gesammelte Schriften*, Vol. i, ed. Rolf Tiedemann (Frankfurt/M., Suhrkamp, 1982), p. 51. The term 'phantasmagoria' was employed by contemporaries to describe the show. See Patrick Geddes, 'The Closing Exhibition', *Contemporary Review* 78 (1900): 660. On spectacular modes of staging the world fair in 1900 see Robert Brain, 'Going to the Exhibition', in *The Physics of Empire: Public Lectures*, ed. Richard Staley (Cambridge: Whipple Museum of the History of Science, 1994), pp. 113–42.

21 Geddes, 'The Closing Exhibition', p. 655. Schricker and Heer ran into similar trouble. See Schricker, 'Die Pariser Weltausstellung', p. 295; Heer, 'Spaziergänge durch die Weltausstellung in Paris', p. 706.

22 H. Heathcote Statham, 'The Paris Exhibition', *The Fortnightly Review* 68 (1900): 132. Travel guides to Paris also warned of this risk. See *Anglo-Saxon Guide to the Paris Exhibition 1900*, ed. B. Bernard (London: Boot and Son, 1900), p. 7.

23 'Musings Without Method', p. 108.

24 Geddes, 'The Closing Exhibition', p. 664.

25 Geddes, 'The Closing Exhibition', p. 661; 'Opening of the Paris Exhibition', p. 338; 'Paris in 1900', *Edinburgh Review* 393 (1900): 139.

26 'Musings Without Method', pp. 109–10.

27 F. G. Aflalo, 'The Promise of International Exhibitions', *Fortnightly Review* 67 (1900): 832–3.

28 'Paris in 1900', p. 134.

29 'Opening of the Paris Exhibition', p. 339.

30 H. Heathcote Statham, 'The Paris Exhibition', p. 131.

31 'Paris in 1900', p. 134.

32 Geddes, 'The Closing Exhibition', p. 658; 'Paris in 1900', pp. 134, 138.

33 Geddes, 'The Closing Exhibition', p. 664.

34 'Opening of the Paris Exhibition', p. 341.

35 'Outlook', p. 242.

36 Ibid., p. 242.

37 Geddes, 'The Closing Exhibition', p. 664.

38 'Paris in 1900', p. 139.

39 Wilhelm Hasbach, 'Weltausstellungs-Eindrücke', *Die Zukunft* 31 (1900): 432.

40 Schricker, 'Die Pariser Weltausstellung', p. 295.

41 To avoid terminological confusion the English translation of *Kultur* or *kulturell* appears in inverted commas: 'culture' or 'cultural.' When the word culture is used without inverted commas it denotes the analytical category.

42 Frierich Naumann, 'Pariser Briefe', *Die Hilfe*, 24 June 1900: 4.

43 *International Exposition Paris 1900: Official German Catalogue of the German Empire*, ed. Otto N. Witt (Berlin: Imperial Commission, 1900), pp. 57–8. For the German original see: *Weltausstellung in Paris 1900: Amtlicher Katalog der Ausstellung des Deutschen Reichs* (Berlin: J. A. Stargardt, 1900), pp. 57–8.

44 Felicie Nossig, 'Pariser Weltausstellung 1900', *Die Neue Zeit* 18:2 (1900): 121.

45 Ibid., p. 121.

46 Meier-Graefe, 'Architektur auf der Weltaustellung', p. 572.

47 Ibid., pp. 573–4.

48 Henry van de Velde, 'Pariser Eindrücke', *Die Zukunft* 31 (1900): 14–23.

49 Friedrich Naumann, 'Pariser Briefe', *Die Hilfe*, 1 July 1900: 3. For Meier-Graefe's and van de Velde's praise of the Eiffel Tower, see Meier-Graefe, 'Architektur der Weltausstellung', p. 570; van de Velde, 'Pariser Eindrücke', p. 18.

50 Friedrich Naumann, 'Pariser Briefe', *Die Hilfe*, 8 August 1900: 10.

51 The German *Werkbund* was to develop a literal mass following. Its exhibition in Cologne in 1914 – cut short by the outbreak of the First World War – attracted over one million visitors in one month. On the *Werkbund*, see Joan Campbell, *The German Werkbund: The Politics of Reform in the Applied Arts* (Princeton, NJ: Princeton University Press, 1978); Wolfgang Hardtwig, 'Kunst, liberaler Nationalismus und Weltpolitik: Der deutsche Werkbund 1907–1914', in *Nationalismus und Bürgerkultur in Deutschland, 1500–1914* (Göttingen: Vandenhoeck und Rupprecht, 1994), pp. 246–73, here 250.

In comparison with Germany, similar English/British movements look pale. See Stella K. Tillyard, *The Impact of Modernism, 1900–1920: Early Modernism and the Arts and Crafts Movement in Edwardian England* (London: Routledge, 1988).

52 On *Bildung*, see: Rudolf Vierhaus, 'Bildung', in *Geschichtliche Grundbegriffe: Historisches Lexikon zur politisch-sozialen Sprache in Deutschland*, Vol. 1 (Stuttgart: Klett Verlag, 1972), pp. 508–51; and Reinhart Koselleck, 'Einleitung: Zur anthropologischen und semantischen Struktur der Bildung', in *Bildungsbürgertum im 19. Jahrhundert. Teil III: Bildungsgüter und Bildungswissen*, ed. Reinhart Koselleck (Stuttgart: Klett-Cotta, 1990), pp. 11–46.

53 On English/British educational ideals, see: John Honey, 'The Sinews of Society: The Public School as a System', in *The Rise of the Modern Educational System: Structural Change and Social Reproduction, 1870–1920*, ed. Detlev K. Müller, Fritz Ringer and Brian Simon (Cambridge: Cambridge University Press, 1987), pp. 151–62, esp. 152–3; J. A. Mangan, *Athleticism in the Victorian and Edwardian Public School: The Emergence and Consolidation of an Educational Ideology* (Cambridge: Cambridge University Press, 1981); and J. A. Mangan, 'Social Darwinism and Upper-Class Education in Late Victorian and Edwardian England', in *Manliness and Morality: Middle-Class Masculinity in Britain and America, 1800–1940*, ed. J. A. Mangan and James Walvin (Manchester: Manchester University Press, 1987), pp. 135–59.

54 For overviews of German models of national identity, see Otto Dann, 'Nationale Fragen in Deutschland: Kulturnation, Volksnation, Reichsnation', in *Nation und Emotion: Deutschland und Frankreich im Vergleich im 19. und 20. Jahrhundert*, ed. Etienne François, Hannes Siegrist and Jakob Vogel (Göttingen: Vandenhoeck und Rupprecht, 1995), pp. 66–82; James J. Sheehan, 'Nation und Staat: Deutschland als "imaginierte Gemeinschaft"', in *Nation und Gesellschaft in Deutschland. Historische Essays*, ed. Manfred Hettling and Paul Nolte (Munich: C. H. Beck, 1996), pp. 33–45; and Dieter Langewiesche, 'Reich, Nation und Staat in der jüngeren deutschen Geschichte', *Historische Zeitschrift*, 254 (1992): 340–81.

      The term *Kulturnation* was, of course, first analytically developed by Friedrich Meinecke. It needs to be stressed that Meinecke's model allows for considerable contestation within the *Kulturnation*: see Friedrich Meinecke, *Weltbürgertum und Nationalstaat: Studien zur Genesis des deutschen Nationalstaates*, 2nd edn (Munich: Oldenbourg, 1912), pp. 11–12.

55 On the nationalization of culture between 1871 and 1914, see Wolfgang Hardtwig, 'Bürgertum, Staatssymbolik und Staatsbewußtsein im Deutschen Kaiserreich, 1871–1914', *Geschichte und Gesellschaft* 16 (1990): pp. 269–95.

56 For an excellent analysis of a concept of national identity on the far Right, see Roger Chickering, *We Men Who Feel Most German: A Cultural Study of the Pan-German League, 1886–1914* (Boston: George Allen & Unwin, 1984), esp.

pp. 74–101. Social Democratic concepts of *Nationalkultur* have hardly been studied. For an overview of negotiations of loyalty to the nation on the Left at the time see: Dieter Groh and Peter Brandt, *'Vaterlandslose Gesellen': Sozialdemokratie und Nation, 1860–1990* (Munich: C. H. Beck, 1992), pp. 65–111.

57 This proved particularly irritating for those members of the educated elite adhering to Liberal political creeds in the 1890s and 1900s. See Dieter Langewiesche, 'Bildungsbürgertum und Liberalismus im 19. Jahrhundert', in *Bildungsbürgertum im 19. Jahrhundert: Teil IV: Politischer Einfluß und gesellschaftliche Formation*, ed. Jürgen Kocka (Stuttgart: Klett-Cotta, 1989), pp. 95–121, esp. 104–13; Gangolf Hübinger, 'Hochindustrialisierung und die Kulturwerte des deutschen Liberalismus', in *Liberalismus im 19. Jahrhundert: Deutschland im europäischen Vergleich*, ed. Dieter Langewiesche (Göttingen: Vandenhoeck und Rupprecht, 1988), pp. 193–208; and Gangolf Hübinger, *Kulturprotestantismus und Politik: Zum Verhältnis von Liberalismus und Protestantismus im wilhelminischen Deutschland* (Tübingen: J. C. B. Mohr, 1994), pp. 28–41, 303–13.

58 Good systematic examinations of Britishness at the end of the nineteenth century are rare. The best work focuses on the eighteenth century. See Linda Colley, *Britons: Forging the Nation, 1707-1837* (London and New Haven: Yale University Press, 1992). On Scottishness, Englishness and Britishness, see Keith Robbins, *Nineteenth-Century Britain: Integration and Diversity* (Oxford: Oxford University Press, 1988), pp. 6-8. For reflections on current scholarship see James Vernon, 'Englishness: The Narration of the Nation', *Journal of British Studies* 36 (1997): 243-9.

59 Debates about the implications of the Boer War have been most recently examined in Andrew S. Thompson, 'The Language of Imperialism and the Meanings of Empire: Imperial Discourse in British Politics, 1895–1914', *Journal of British Studies* 36 (1997): 147–77. On the relationships between British identities and imperial ideology see Antoinette Burton, *Burdens of History: British Feminists, Indian Women, and Imperial Culture, 1865–1915* (Chapel Hill, NC: University of North Carolina Press, 1994), pp. 33–41.

60 On the absence of a civilizing mission in German imperialistic ideology see Heinz Gollwitzer, *Geschichte des weltpolitischen Denkens: Band II: Zeitalter des Imperialismus und der Weltkriege* (Göttingen: Vandenhoeck und Rupprecht, 1982), esp. pp. 78–82, 229–31.

61 Irrespective of political orientation, historians of Germany agree on the importance of 'Wilhelmian' opposition to the rise of modernism around 1900. See Wolfgang J. Mommsen, 'Kultur und Politik im deutschen Kaiserreich', in *Der autoritäre Nationalstaat: Verfassung, Gesellschaft und Kultur im deutschen Kaiserreich* (Frankfurt/M.: Fischer Taschenbuch, 1990), pp. 257–86; Wolfgang

J. Mommsen, 'Die Kultur der Moderne im Deutschen Kaiserreich', in *Deutschlands Weg in die Moderne: Politik, Gesellschaft und Kultur im 19. Jahrhundert*, ed. Wolfgang Hardtwig and Harm-Hinrich Brandt (Munich: C. H. Beck, 1993), pp. 254–74; Thomas Nipperdey, *Wie das Bürgertum die Moderne fand* (Berlin: Siedler, 1988), pp. 63–88; and Peter Paret, *The Berlin Secession: Modernism and Its Enemies in Imperial Germany* (Cambridge, MA: Belknap Press, 1980).

62 Peter Mandler, 'Against "Englishness": English Culture and the Limits to Rural Nostalgia, 1850-1940,' *Transactions of the Royal Historical Society*, 6th ser., 7 (1997): 155–75, esp. 161.

8

Modernity, Community and History: Narratives of Innovation in the British Coal Industry

Michael Dintenfass

On 24 May 1928, *The Times* chronicled the life of the first Baron Buckland of Bwlch, who had been 'killed in a riding accident' the previous day. The opening paragraphs of its memorial sketched the route Lord Buckland had taken from Merthyr Tydfil to 'public notice' and the Palace of Westminster. Born Henry Seymour Berry, the eldest son of an estate agent, valuer, auctioneer and alderman, he had been 'trained for a scholastic career, but', according to *The Times*, 'his father's business prospered to such an extent that he found it necessary to take into it his son, then in the early twenties. Immediately . . . [the future peer's] business acumen showed itself, and till the day of his death he had gone steadily forward to increasing success.' He had done so, *The Times* continued, in the company of 'Lord Rhondda, a shrewd judge of business capacity, [who] took a deep personal interest in him, and in association with Lord Rhondda and the present Lady Rhondda he . . . [had become] connected with numerous commercial and industrial undertakings.' In the Birthday Honors List of 1926 Berry had been raised to a barony.[1]

The Lord Buckland who emerged from the thick description that followed this précis combined extensive business responsibility, civic exertion and philanthropic largess. Portraying him as the chairman of Guest, Keen, and Nettlefolds, 'with iron, steel, coal and allied trade interests, not only in this country, but in Australia, South Africa, and elsewhere', and of John Lysaght, Limited and the Meiros Collieries and as a director of North's Navigation Collieries, the Consolidated Cambrian Colliery Group and the Western Mail, Limited, *The Times* also pictured Lord Buckland as the joint proprietor, with Sir David Llewellyn, of the Vale of Neath Colliery Company and as 'associated with' the Celtic Collieries, the Imperial Navigation Coal Company and 'a number of other colliery and shipping concerns'.

In addition, the paper identified Lord Buckland as a magistrate for Merthyr and Breconshire, a member of the Usk Board of Conservators and a high sheriff of Breconshire, and it recalled that in 1923, as 'a tribute to his wide popularity', this titan of industry and trade had been 'presented with the freedom of . . . his native town, at a time when Labour was in the majority on the Council.' Though a knight of grace of the order of the Hospital of St John of Jerusalem in England, a governor of the National Museum of Wales and 'a member of the governing bodies of a number of hospitals and nursing associations in South Wales', *The Times*'s Lord Buckland was very much a Merthyr man. He had married a local girl, who bore him five daughters, and his charitable gifts included £30,000 to establish a technical institute in the town in memory of his father, £12,000 for a new wing for Merthyr General Hospital and £10,000 for swimming baths.[2]

In the eyes of *The Times*, Lord Buckland's story 'was one of the romances of modern industrial and commercial life'. Where, though, did the modern reside in the biography the paper scripted for him? Was it perhaps in the 'numerous commercial and industrial undertakings', some with interests throughout the empire, to which he had progressed from his father's prosperous estate agency? Did it inhere in the aristocratic patronage thanks to which he had become associated with these concerns? Did the modernity of the Buckland romance have to do with the peerage that followed on from its hero's success in business or with the paternalism that his captaincy of industry had allowed him to exercise as an official and benefactor of his native place? Or was it the bond between master and men, symbolized by Lord Buckland's election as a freeman of Merthyr, that *The Times* construed as the authentically modern dimension of his industrial and commercial life? [3]

The industries to which *The Times* connected Lord Buckland – iron, coal and steel, shipping and newspaper publishing – were not in any sense self-evidently modern, and the account the paper provided of his involvement in them did not place him at either their establishment or their reformation along new lines. Indeed, *The Times*'s brief life of Baron Buckland of Bwlch positively resounded with traditional motifs: the ascent from commoner to noble, the dispensation of aristocratic favour to the humble but worthy, the harmony of rich and poor, the assumption of imperial burdens and the obligation of the newly arrived to those from among whom he had come. In this context, modern reads very much like a synonym for recent, and as such, it suggests an understanding of the modern as entirely of a piece with the past.

The Times's life of Lord Buckland poses the problem of what modernity meant to those Britons whose business it was to comprehend their nation's commercial and industrial life. Did the modern signify in the language of enterprise and trade continuity with what had come before or a radical break in time? Were its connotations essentially civic or primarily economic? Was modernity within the discourse of British business a domestic plant or a foreign growth?

I

This chapter explores the meaning of modernity in the British coal industry during the first half of the twentieth century. It does so through a close reading of the life histories that contemporaries composed in tribute to the 155 individuals the *Colliery Guardian*, the leading journalistic voice of the mining business, designated as 'Men of Note in the British Coal Industry' in an illustrated series that ran through the 1920s. The tales I examine include those written for the edification of coal-mining men – the profiles the *Colliery Guardian* itself published and the memoirs carried in the *Transactions of the Institution of Mining Engineers* – as well as stories aimed at a more general audience, such as the obituary of Lord Buckland in *The Times*. As the *Colliery Guardian* only honoured the living in its Men of Note series, the earliest of the documents on which this study is based dates from 1923, and the latest dates from 1974, the great majority having been printed between 1925 and 1945. Needless to say, these brief biographies were not conceived as objective 'warts and all' portrayals of their subjects. Each was written to commemorate an eminent mining career.

The discourse of industrial distinction that these texts make audible was by no means the private speech of British coal owners and managers. If we can hear it in their trade press and technical journals, we can also hear it outside mining in organs such as *Who's Who* and *The Times*, whose business was the recognition of distinction and not the raising and selling of coal. Nor was this discourse of industrial prominence specific to a single moment in the economic and political history of British coal-mining. Its characteristic catchwords and cadences are as evident in the celebrations of the *Colliery Guardian*'s Men of Note published in the 1940s, 1950s and 1960s as in those from the 1920s and 1930s. The contemporary construction of distinction in mining, then, bespeaks a culture that endured long after the crises that immediately followed the First World War had passed and that extended well beyond the confines of the coal business proper.

My concern in these pages is with the play of the modern in the conversation of contemporaries about the best and brightest of British coal. I begin in Section II with the different languages of the new discernible in the life stories of mining's leading figures. Here I locate the invocation of the modern in relation to the idioms of primacy and exploration, and I scrutinize the terms in which these other discourses narrated change. I then turn in Section III to the uses of modernity in the celebration of industrial distinction. Was the modern a referent for materiality and method or for spirit and state of mind? Did its salience derive from an association with profit and production? What did the turn to modernity mean for memories of the past?

The chapter concludes with a discussion of what contemporary conceptions of the modern disclose about the construction of the economic in the British coal industry in the first half of the twentieth century. My argument is that as one of the languages of the new the language of modernity constituted the realm of business as a co-operative commonwealth rather than a competitive marketplace. History, in the form of narratives of the industrial past, played an integral part in the imagining of this economic *civitas*, naturalizing innovation and making it available as a source of prestige at home and abroad. The comprehension of the modern in mining thus drew on a vocabulary that had deep roots in the culture of nineteenth-century Britain and that was deployed concurrently in representations of the new in domains far removed from the business of coal.

II

The principal languages for representing the new in the life stories of the Men of Note in the British coal industry were those of temporal priority and pathfinding. For the *Colliery Guardian*, the South Staffordshire mining engineer H. W. Hughes was 'one of the pioneers of underground photography', Percival Muschamp, agent for the New Hucknall Colliery Company, 'a pioneer in the use of electric lamps below ground' and Finlay Gibson of the Monmouthshire and South Wales Coal Owners' Association 'the pioneer of statistical methods in relation to the coal industry', while the consulting engineer A. Dury Mitton had 'introduced the first system of [mechanical] coal cutting, and by-product coke making in Lancashire' and Percy Lee Wood, general manager of the Clifton and Kersley Coal Company, had been 'the first to introduce the "drop shaft" method of sinking [pits] into this country'. W. C. Blackett, the managing director of the Charlaw and Sacriston Collieries, appeared in the *Transactions of the Institution of Mining Engineers* as 'the first in the North of England to use inert dust to render harmless the coal-dust on mine roads' and in the *Colliery Guardian* as 'the first to introduce . . . [coal-face conveyors] into British mining'. According to his coal-trade biographer, A. M. Henshaw, managing director of the Talk o'-th'-Hill Collieries, had been 'one of the first to adopt rescue apparatus, using the original Meyer oxygen apparatus for exploration work at the Talk o'-th'-Hill explosion in 1901, and was one of the pioneers of "Safety First" in mines, instituting the movement at Talk o'-th' Hill in 1913'.[4]

Modernity and its cognates appeared only occasionally amidst this profusion of pioneers and firsts in the narratives of change the authors of exemplary mining lives scripted for their heroes. Conscious though they were of the new, those whose business it was to sing the praises of Britain's leading coal men did not as a matter of course characterize change in terms of the modern. For that matter, they hardly employed the languages of primacy and pioneering to signal discontinuity.

The tales contemporaries of the Men of Note told of change in mining failed to mark any break with the past simply because they did not site the new in relation to what had been before. In its life of A. Dury Mitton, the *Colliery Guardian* said nothing at all about the practice of coke production in Lancashire before the advent of by-product procedures, and the paper's tribute to Percy Lee Wood was no more revealing about how pits had been sunk prior to the employment of the drop shaft technique. W. C. Blackett's memoirist at the *Transactions* neglected to say by what means mine managers had attempted to neutralize coal dust on the roadways of northern collieries before Blackett turned to inert dust, and the author of his entry in the *Colliery Guardian*'s honours list was equally indifferent to how coal had been removed from the faces prior to the introduction of conveyors. Lacking connection or contrast with the previous, these narratives of change had no comparative character. Consequently, the representation of the new in the languages of primacy and pathbreaking proceeded independently of any talk of improvement.

This is not to say that the emplotment of change within the discourse of distinction in coal was invariably indifferent to results, although this was commonly the case. Just as the readers of the Men of Note series could only have wondered in vain about the difference A. Dury Mitton's introduction of mechanical coal-cutting and by-product coke-making had made to the Lancashire coal industry, so the *Colliery Guardian*'s story of how the regenerative coking plant that Sir William Johnson installed at the Ffaldau Collieries had been 'about the first of its type in South Wales' did not proceed to an account of the benefits the firm or the region had derived from Johnson's innovation. Nor did *The Times* suggest that 'the Rheolaveur system of washing coal' that H. E. Mitton, a 'director of several colliery companies', had 'introduced . . . into this country' had any importance beyond the fact that Mitton had been the first to make use of it.[5]

The *Colliery Guardian* did, on the other hand, write in praise of A. M. Henshaw that the establishment of the Safety First movement at Talk o'-th'-Hill had been a 'signal success', even if it was not terribly forthcoming about what this amounted to. Had a large proportion of the workforce been schooled in the most up-to-date ways of safely working coal? Had the safest practices been made routine below and above ground? Had injuries and fatalities at the firm declined? The same organ's description of the success Percy Lee Wood had enjoyed thanks to the drop shaft method 'in negotiating the difficulties of sinking through the quicksand and gravel met with in [the] Astley Green shafts' was equally opaque. Had Wood's success been in driving a functional shaft to the desired depth or in sinking a pit whose proceeds of production exceeded the costs of construction? *The Times*, at least, was much more direct in its tribute to Sir William Galloway, the one-time mines inspector, professor of mining and consulting engineer. Remembering this member of the British coal-trade elite for his contribution 'to the pioneer observations and experiments . . . in this country that [led to] the coal-dust theory of great colliery explosions', Galloway's obituarist stressed that his 'pioneer researches . . . were among those which led to the saving of many lives'.[6]

Not one of these tales of success set the significance of the new in an economic light, and the absence of the language of production and profit is one of the most striking features of the narratives of change contemporaries wove into their biographies of the best and brightest of British mining. There is but one text in the entire annals of the Men of Note that insinuates notions of the enterprise, the market, and the competition into a story of the new: the profile with which the *Colliery Guardian* inducted the Scottish mechanical engineer and equipment manufacturer Sam Mavor into its gallery of eminent coal-mining men. Let us look at it closely.

The history the journalistic voice of coal ascribed to this member of its mining-industry honour roll was written almost entirely in the idioms of exploration and temporal priority. While still an apprentice with Messrs Crompton and Company, it began, Mavor had 'carried out the first introduction of electric light in many towns in the United Kingdom and Ireland'. Joining his brother's engineering practice, he became 'actively associated with much pioneer electrical work, including the establishment of the first public electric supply station in Glasgow'. As the business branched out into the manufacture of electrical appliances, Mavor became 'identified with many progressive steps in the design and application of electrical machinery, notably in connection with mining'. The firm whose leadership the Man of Note now shared became 'the first to produce motors of the type . . . known as "Ironclad"'. It also originated 'the tube-cooled type of motor', and it was 'the first to put on the market a completely enclosed coal-cutter'. In a rather different sphere, Mavor and company 'pioneered marine electric propulsion with alternating current and in 1908 and 1913 equipped two experimental vessels to demonstrate the equipment'.[7]

Since 1897, the *Colliery Guardian* continued, Mavor had 'devoted himself chiefly to the development of coal-face machinery'. He had 'been very influential at home and abroad in promoting machine mining [and] for a number of years prior to the war he [had] spent much time on the Continent exploiting the application of coal-cutting machinery'. By '1914 there were very few coal cutters (apart from percussive tools) in Europe that had not been supplied by his firm'.[8]

The singularity of this story of near-monopoly among the hundreds of contemporary texts portraying the industrial lives of Mavor's fellow Men of Note speaks volumes by itself about how alien the economic was to the discourse of distinction within the coal business. The fine points of the *Colliery Guardian*'s narrative, though, articulate just as eloquently the foreignness of the new. The stage on which the paper located Mavor's pioneering, after all, was not that of mining proper but the ancillary theatre of mine-machinery production and distribution. The site where his innovatory efforts were shown to have borne fruit was quite literally abroad, with the coal companies of the Continent, and not those of Mavor's native Scotland, the East Midlands or South Wales.

The configuration of the new as external to British mining in the *Colliery Guardian*'s tale of Sam Mavor did not derive from the representation of his marketplace success, for change appeared as equally foreign in texts that excluded the economic. The coal-trade biography of Samuel Hare depicted the distinction of the chief mining engineer of Messrs Bolckow, Vaughan and Company without recourse to the language of outputs and sales, and yet characterized the coal-face appliances Hare had been 'the first to introduce . . . into this country' as 'the American "Sullivan" coal-cutting machines'. That the author of Hare's life history employed precisely the same terms – 'the first to introduce . . . into this country'– to describe the part his subject had played with respect to 'Still benzol recovery and refining plants' suggests that the new could readily figure as alien even in the absence of any reference to another land. Indeed, the very frequency with which the phrases 'into this country' and 'into British mining' echo through the published lives of Percy Lee Wood, W. C. Blackett and H. E. Mitton, as well as their repetition in Samuel Hare's Man of Note profile, indicates the extent to which the talk of 'first' and 'pioneering' was a discourse of importation.[9]

If change was intrinsically foreign for the authors of these eminent mining lives, embedding innovation in narratives of former times performed the work of domesticating it. The histories to which they resorted to naturalize the new were of several varieties, but in each case they grounded the individual whom they associated with change solidly within the past of British mining. Percy Lee Wood's history was a personal one, the point of which was that the pioneer of the drop shaft method of sinking mines had been a constant servant of the Clifton and Kersley Coal Company, having 'spent the whole of his life with this firm, being appointed manager of their Newtown pits on completion of his apprenticeship, and becoming general manager in 1898'. Recommending W. C. Blackett to his colleagues in the coal business as one of the most notable figures of the trade, the *Colliery Guardian* invested the pioneer of coal conveying with a lifetime of mining experience, beginning with his apprenticeship 'in the workshops and drawing office of the Grange Iron Co.,' an articled pupillage to John Daglish, and work 'as a stoneman, deputy, surveyor, back overman, engineer, manager, and mining agent' in 'various coal fields' and proceeding to his occupation of 'many public posts' in connection with 'several Government and Department Committees', the investigation of 'the circumstances of many colliery explosions and other accidents' and testimony 'before Royal Commissions on varied subjects'. Casting Blackett as the pioneer of the stone dusting of underground roadways in Durham and Northumberland, the *Transactions of the Institution of Mining Engineers* fitted him with an industrial genealogy that 'through his mother' traced back to a 'fourth generation interested in the mining of coal in the Northern Coalfield'.[10]

Family was likewise the narrative context for the emplotment of change in the coal-trade biographies of A. M. Henshaw and Sir William Johnson. By the lights of the *Colliery Guardian*, the pioneer of Safety First instruction and mine rescue apparatus had been born into mining, having been the 'eldest son of the late John Henshaw of the Kingswood and Parkfield Collieries'. A pioneer of regenerative coke ovens in South Wales, Johnson took his place among the Men of Note as the most recent in a line of mining innovators. His father was 'the late Mr. George Johnson who put in the first tip at Maryport', and earlier generations of Johnsons had 'been associated with mining since its inception in Cumberland'. Here, we might say, the representation of distinction in coal familiarized the new by rendering it familial.[11]

While personal and family histories were essential components of the mining life stories that narrated change, the language of the corporation had no meaningful place in the representation of the new. Consider the case of William O'Connor, a colliery manager and engineer who, in the words of the *Colliery Guardian*, had 'always [been] keen in [*sic*] improvements in practical mining'. In the course of a long career in the Rhondda Valley, in the coalfields of Monmouthshire and in the Welsh anthracite district, O'Connor had 'introduced and persevered with the successful use of mechanical coal-cutters at a time when these were generally considered to be unsuited to South Wales conditions'. He had also been 'one of the earliest to carry mechanical haulage right up to the coalface, thus entirely eliminating horses from the pit', and he had 'arranged one of the first instances of electrical shotfiring from the surface in sinking pits'. In addition, O'Connor had carried out 'some of the earliest tests of electric safety lamps', and he had 'introduced the Barry system of working in thin seams with heavy sandstone roofs with conspicuous success'. Just as there is no suggestion in these passages that O'Connor's successes were those of profit or production, so there is no association of the Man of Note's innovations with the firms at which they had been introduced. The author of O'Connor's industrial biography freely recorded the mines his subject had managed – the Gelli and Tydraw collieries of Messrs Cory Bros and Company, the Ponthenry collieries and the Abernaunt and Llandover Collieries of the Messrs Bargoed Coal Company – but these undertakings found no place in his construction of O'Connor as the agent of new departures in coal.[12]

Where particular enterprises entered into the narratives of change depicting the lives of mining's most prominent participants, they did so as the locations of events whose significance lay elsewhere. In the *Colliery Guardian*'s account of Sir William Johnson's career, the Ffaldau Collieries Company just happened to be the firm at which this member of the paper's coal-trade elite introduced regenerative coking plant into South Wales, and Astley Green just happened to be the colliery at which the journal placed Percy Lee Wood's introduction of drop shaft sinking into British mining. For the author of Samuel Hare's life in coal, the collieries of Messrs Bolckow, Vaughan and Company were merely the platform from which his protagonist had launched the American Sullivan coal-cutting machines and the Still benzol recovery and refining plants 'into this country'.

The *Colliery Guardian*'s celebration of A. Dury Mitton carefully tracked his progress from the Hetton Colliery to the Acklam Iron Company's Gordon House Colliery, the Shipley Collieries, the Trust of the Duke of Bridgewater and Messrs Stanley Brothers, but when it reached the Man of Note's pioneering deployment of by-product coke-making and a system of mechanical coal-cutting, the individual undertaking disappeared, and Lancashire replaced it as the centre of the action. H. E. Mitton's biographers at both *Who's Who* and *The Times* displaced the Rheolaveur system of coal-washing that was his glory from the the Butterly Company, where they had had Mitton employed, to 'this country', while the location of the new in the mining life of W. C. Blackett was the region, according to the *Transactions*, and the nation, for the *Colliery Guardian*. Within the discourse of distinction in British mining, then, the locus of change, whether the north of England, South Wales or Britain itself, was a scene of shared allegiances rather than a site of competitive rivalries. Situated thus, tales of the new were very much narratives of civic virtue in which the enactment of change was a service to the community.[13]

Preferring the idioms of primacy and pathbreaking for the representation of change, the authors of exemplary mining lives in the first half of the twentieth century configured the new as a foreign phenomenon with no association to previous practice, which consequently could constitute a success but not an improvement. Though change as such had no history to those who told tales of distinction in coal, the men responsible for it most certainly did, and it was their personal and familial links to the past of British mining that rendered the new safely importable. The harbours most suitable for the arrival of the new in contemporary narratives of industrial change were the country and the county, but not the company, and to the extent that the biographers of the *Colliery Guardian*'s coal-trade elite read success into the new, theirs was not an economic notion of achievement. Again, the predominant languages of the new in the British coal industry gave voice to a civic discourse. Did the language of the modern function any differently?

III

The portraits of John Gregory, chairman and general manager of the Sneyd Collieries, and the pitman-turned-palaeobotanist James Lomax that the *Colliery Guardian* presented to the business world of coal both employed the language of the modern in conjunction with the language of pathbreaking. Lomax could 'be accredited', said the journalistic voice of British mining, 'as the pioneer of the modern methods of microscopical examination of coals', on the subject of which he had 'written many papers, including contributions on "The Microscopical Examination in Relation to Inflammable Dust" and "The Various Kinds of Pyritiferous Matters in Coal Seams"'. The work Gregory's biographer highlighted in delineating his subject's distinction had 'mainly consisted in the enlargement and modernisation of an old colliery. He . . . [had been] a pioneer in the application of three-phase power transmission underground and the utilisation of exhaust steam in turbo-generation.'[14]

Both these profiles of Men of Note in the British coal industry tied the modern directly to the past. The methods of studying coal Lomax pioneered had led to the discovery of 'a large number of new species of petrified plants' and permitted the identification of 'the origins and nature of various structures and ingredients in coal'. Gregory's claim to the attention of the trade lay in having made an old mining works anew. Both of these tributes to members of the *Colliery Guardian*'s coal-industry elite fitted their modernizing protagonists with mining histories. Gregory, like Percy Lee Wood, appeared before his compatriots in coal as the loyal servant of a single enterprise. Joining the Sneyd Collieries as a surveyor in 1892 after the completion of his apprenticeship, he had advanced to manager in 1901, general manager in 1912 and chairman in 1923.[15]

The *Colliery Guardian* wrapped the story of the transformations Lomax had wrought in the techniques of natural history in three different accounts of his mining past. First, there was the family history that cast this eminent member of the industry, as Sir William Johnson and A. M. Henshaw were also cast, as a child of the trade – his father, Joseph Lomax, having been the manager of the Eldon Collieries – and also as a father to mining in his own right, for, according to his biographer, his son Joseph R. Lomax had followed him in the study of 'the petrifications of coal'. Then there was the Lomax whose occupational history resembled the curriculum vitae the *Colliery Guardian* compiled for W. C. Blackett in the suggestion it gave of extensive personal experience in the business. This was the Man of Note who had commenced work in the pit at the age of ten, become an engineer and winder at the Clifton and Kersley Collieries at nineteen and spent more than a decade as a colliery engineman at the Radcliffe Collieries of Messrs A. Knowles and Sons.[16]

Lastly, the author of this exemplary industrial life represented Lomax's pioneering work in the modernizing of palaeobotanical methods as an enterprise with a history of its own. Originating in the 'collecting [of] specimens from the roof shales of various seams and sinking pits in the collieries in the Bolton, Radcliffe, and Worsley districts' that Lomax had pursued 'from an early age', his efforts advanced to a higher plane in 1885 when he became 'associated with . . . Dr W. C. Williamson, the founder of the English School of Palaeobotany.' Ten fruitful years of collaboration followed, and after Williamson's death, Lomax renewed this co-operative approach to the modern investigation of coal by founding 'with a few well-known and eminent botanists' the Lomax Palaeobotanical Company, the object of which was 'the collection and preparation of fossil plants, both impressions and petrifications, and their distribution for studying and teaching purposes'. Fourteen years later, the story went, the Lomax laboratories passed into the hands of the Lancashire and Cheshire Coal Research Association, and the 67-year-old Lomax continued to work actively at 'microscopical research'.[17]

The narratives of the new in the mining life histories of John Gregory and James Lomax defined the modern in terms of techniques and technologies. In Lomax's case, the pioneering practices the author of his Man of Note profile identified were of scientific and educational import. The *Transactions of the Institution of Mining Engineers* likewise placed the modern squarely in the scholarly domain in its memoir of Professor I. C. F. Statham, and here too the material connotations of the term were unmistakable. 'During his tenure in the Chair of Mining at the University' of Sheffield, Statham's biographer recalled, he had 'developed an excellent Mining Department . . . excellent lecture rooms, well-equipped laboratories and other services.' Statham's distinction in this account, however, resided as much in his transcendence of the materiality of the modern through the perspective he brought to it as in his realization of it:

> Modern facilities . . . albeit important [continued the text] do not alone constitute a first-class University Department. For its real completion is needed a capable staff, ably led by a man not only eminent in his profession but also with the necessary administrative ability and sympathetic understanding of staff and students. It is in the latter sense, as much as in the planning and execution of the material aspects of the Mining Department at Sheffield, that Statham excelled.[18]

The sketch *The Times* drew of the physician Sir Josiah Court was also about scientific inquiry and modern appliances, but the emphasis lay, as it did in the biographies of A. M. Henshaw and Sir William Galloway, on innovations beneficial to men employed underground. 'When working as an ordinary doctor,' Court's obituarist recollected, the Man of Note had 'found that great numbers of miners who came to him had been lying on their sides all day using the old-fashioned miners' lamp. After research underground and study overhead' Court had determined that poor illumination was the cause of the 'total or partial blindness' to which his patients were prone. Thereafter he had been 'instrumental in obtaining the installation of better lighting and [had] had not a little influence in securing the adoption of the modern electric safety lamp' – in the campaign for which the *Colliery Guardian* had recognized Percival Muschamp as a pioneer.[19]

The place of new methods in the *Colliery Guardian*'s tribute to John Gregory approximated to that which they occupied in the coal-mining biographies of A. Dury Mitton and Sir William Johnson. The appeal each man's industrial life story made to the admiration and respect of the world of British coal involved the adoption of new technologies for the satisfaction of long-standing colliery requirements. New practices were also the essence of the modern in *The Times*'s portrait of the Scottish coal master J. A. Hood, but its record of his career in the industry failed to identify the 'modern mining methods' he had promoted. The memoir with which the *Transactions* honoured Robert Clive of the South Yorkshire Coal Owners' Association and the *Colliery Guardian*'s feature about Ernest Hart, agent and general manager of the Abram Coal Company, gestured similarly toward the affinity of modernity and technique. In both tales, though, a technological construction of the modern remained undeveloped.[20]

The Ernest Hart who arrived in the ranks of the *Colliery Guardian*'s mining elite had 'carried through the design and construction of several large and important schemes of modernisation in the coal industry' and demonstrated 'expert experience in the design and construction of winding engines, power plants, mine ventilation fans, high speed air compressors, jet surface and barometric condensing sets, haulage gears, bridges, headgears, pulp and paper making plants, [and] evaporating and oil distilling installations'. What had it been about the Man of Note's proficiency with these machineries that made his modernizing work so noteworthy in the judgement of the journalistic voice of the coal trade? The Robert Clive the *Transactions* depicted had spent sixteen years 'in charge of the sinking, surface lay-out, underground lay-out and development' of Messrs Barber, Walker and Company's Bentley Colliery, 'the first of the modern collieries of the Doncaster coalfield, and the technical developments [he had] carried out at Bentley [had] attracted considerable attention'. Where in the eye-catching technological departures Clive had overseen was the modernity his mining biography attributed to the Bentley Colliery?[21]

The *Colliery Guardian*'s portrayal of W. Newton Drew's industrial responsibilities explicitly aligned the modern with the material. It did so, though, not with respect to coal-mining proper but in relation to metal-making, an allied trade. The story the paper presented of its honouree's authority over the manufacture of pig iron 'in the most efficient and modern plant' appeared in a narrative of the facilities and activities of the enterprises over which Drew presided, and the keynote of this recitation was familiarity. In addition to the mining of coal, tar distillation and iron production, these concerns manufactured the 'well-known Izal disinfectant' and operated 'the well-known Hurst–Bell centrifugal process for the manufacture of cast iron pipes, cylinders, etc.'. 'The Thorncliffe iron house, of which many thousands . . . [had] recently been erected, . . . [was] also one of their branches.' These invocations of the new and the known were in turn elements of a mining family romance. The Drew whom the leading journal of British coal first presented to the business world of mining was not the chairman of Newton, Chambers and Company and its sister firms, the Hoyland Silkstone Coal Company and Thorncliffe Coal Distillation Limited, but the great-great-grandson of Thomas Chambers and the great-grandson of George Newton, co-founders of Newton, Chambers in 1793. When in the course of its profile the *Colliery Guardian* had the Man of Note ascend to the leadership of the firm of his forebears, it was into the shoes of his uncle, Thomas Chambers Newton, that he stepped. As in the exemplary industrial lives contemporaries composed of James Lomax and John Gregory, so too in this tribute to W. Newton Drew's merits as a mining man did historical narrative serve as the site for representing the materiality of the modern.[22]

At first sight, the language of the *Colliery Guardian*'s brief life of Mungo Mackay, manager and subsequently agent and general manager of the Lothian Coal Company's Newbattle Colliery, suggests a decidedly immaterial conception of modernity. At Newbattle, the paper's columnist wrote, 'all the most modern ideas' could be appreciated, and it was the Man of Note who had 'been the moving spirit' in bringing this about. Mackay's achievement, however, was that he had 'worked [all the most modern ideas] out on a practical basis', and his biographer left no doubt that this had meant making them mechanical – in the shape of 'coal cutters and conveyors' – and material – in the shape of 'steel arches and props'.[23]

The means by which Mungo Mackay had rendered the modern material at Newbattle had included importation. Like the picture of Samuel Hare that appeared in the *Colliery Guardian*'s gallery of prominent mining men, the published portrayal of Mackay's coal-industry distinction had him turn to the United States in pursuit of the new, 'one of . . . [his] latest experiments . . . [having been] the adoption of the American type of mechanical loader'. The exoticism contemporaries attributed to change in their lives of H. C. Mitton and W. C. Blackett coloured the *Colliery Guardian*'s construction of Mackay as well, embodied this time by the 'mining engineers from all parts of the world' who had flocked to Newbattle to behold modernity in practice.[24]

The foreignness of Mackay's modernizing, of course, was but one thread in a narrative fabric that was predominantly historical. Indeed the *Colliery Guardian*'s short chronicle of this noteworthy career in coal managed to weave together a story of lifetime service that was also a family history with an archaeology of the site at which its hero had demonstrated his distinction. In the beginning, Mackay had been apprenticed at the Ballochmyle Colliery of W. W. Hood, and 'the whole of his subsequent service . . . [had] been devoted to the Hood family'. He had finished his articles at the Whitehill Colliery of Hood's father, Archibald Hood, and when the Hoods formed the Lothian Coal Company in 1890, they appointed him manager of the Polton Colliery. Five years later Mackay commenced a tenure at Newbattle that was to extend over the next thirty-two years.[25]

According to the *Colliery Guardian*, Newbattle had a 'remarkable' history of its own, and Mackay's biographer interrupted his paean to the Man of Note to share it with the coal trade at large. At the very spot where Mackay had made the modern materialize, there had been coal-getting, under 'ecclesiastical' auspices, as far back as 1140. Moreover, the quarries at Newbattle constituted 'the earliest recorded instance of coal mining in Scotland'. Inserted into the tale immediately after Mackay's arrival at the mine in 1895 and just before its development on a modern basis, these fragments of history grounded the innovative equipment Mackay had installed in a sacral and medieval past.[26]

There was, by contrast, no intimation of the economic in the *Colliery Guardian*'s celebration of Mungo Mackay. Apparently, the significance of 'the extensive use' he had made of American loaders, mechanical coal-cutters and steel props and arches was unrelated to the output and profitability of the pit where he had employed them. Evidently, measures of business performance had no part to play in confirming his stature in the coal trade. Nor was the economic much more visible in *The Times*'s memorial to J. A. Hood, managing director and chairman of the Lothian Coal Company for most of Mackay's time at Newbattle. The author of Hood's obituary wrote of the 'world-wide reputation for efficiency' the firm had earned under the guidance of this pioneer of modern mining, but he was no more forthcoming about what efficiency meant in this context than he was about the modern methods he associated with Hood. The *Colliery Guardian* attributed annual outputs of 1.5 million tons of coal and 250,000 tons of coke to the companies W. Newton Drew chaired, but yardsticks of this type were conspicuously absent from its characterization of the Newton, Chambers blast furnaces as 'the most modern and efficient'. For the rest, the language of modernity in the contemporary life histories of the British coal-trade elite was innocent of business categories, and the economic meaning of the modern remained faint and indistinct.[27]

The reckoning of the modern in the coinage of public notice, on the other hand, possessed a certain palpability. The *Colliery Guardian*, after all, registered the magnitude of Mungo Mackay's modern machine-mining by reference to the great interest – the visits from mining engineers from the four corners of the globe – that it had generated. *The Times* took the international prestige of the Lothian Coal Company as the proof of J. A. Hood's industrial eminence, and the value for the *Transactions of the Institution of Mining Engineers* of the developments Robert Clive had directed at the first modern colliery in South Yorkshire inhered in the considerable attention they had attracted. It was, then, the recognition of the community, rather than profit or production, that established the worth of the modern in the discourse of distinction in British mining.

IV

The language of modernity was just one of the languages the biographers of the best and brightest of British coal employed to represent change, and they by no means preferred it to the languages of temporal priority and pathbreaking. There were, though, no fundamental differences between the narratives of the new that invoked the modern and those that spoke of firsts and pioneers. Each rendered innovation as alien. Whether in the form of an association with another land or through the depiction of change as importation, the new was of foreign provenance in the discourse of industrial distinction.

The narratives of the new in the life histories of the coal-trade's most eminent personages were very much about the past and not at all about the future. In one vein, they told of novel solutions to long-standing mining problems having to do with sinking pits, colliery explosions, cutting and hauling coal and the health of the workforce. In another, they were stories of resurrection and recovery, be it of old workings or plants from the Carboniferous age. Whatever their theme, the representations of change that the authors of exemplary mining lives offered to contemporaries reached back decades in the lives of their protagonists, across generations and to centuries long gone. Read in this light, the traditional motifs that informed the romance *The Times* made of Lord Buckland's career in industry and commerce were just one instance of how the historical naturalized the modern by making it continuous with the British past.

If the discourse of innovation in mining in the first half of the twentieth century emplotted modernity in historical terms, the delineation of the new configured the economic as a non-competitive realm. The changes in methods, materials and machines that reference to the first, the pioneer and the modern signalled were changes that belonged to the community – the county, the region and the country as a whole – and not to individual enterprises. The touchstone that determined the value of these innovations was public opinion, and not the marketplace of profit and loss. Indeed, in the published life of a Mungo Mackay the regard of the international mining community could valorize changes that, though foreign in origin, history had made securely British. Free of rivalries for custom and the discipline of the bottom line, the economic in the discourse of distinction in coal was a commonwealth where the innovation of one was the property of all and collective judgement the arbiter of worth. The languages of the new, then, were part of a civic discourse that paid homage to the leading lights of the British coal industry as model citizens rather than exemplary businessmen.

In representing the *Colliery Guardian*'s Men of Note as patriots rather than profit-seekers, the narrators of their life stories paid handsome tribute to the culture Victorian and Edwardian Britain had bequeathed. The inscription of civic virtue in the vocabulary of British politics, after all, had been a singular contribution of Millite liberalism, and Nonconformity and liberal Anglicanism had performed a similar service in the religious realm. A classically-inspired idealism had breathed new intellectual life into the idea of citizenship at the ancient universities, and Smilesian self-help had broadcast the doctrine of public responsibility into popular culture. The celebration of industrial eminence in coal after the First World War was but a further descant of this wide-ranging conversation about the co-operative commonwealth.[28]

The discourse of civic responsibility, moreover, was the language with which Britons gave expression to innovations unrelated to those in coal-mining but concurrent with them in time. The development of history as an academic discipline at Oxford and Cambridge proceeded under the sign of the *civitas* and the citizen. The elaboration of centralized state social-service provision was represented in the same terms. In both cases, the civic construction of the new made sense of change within the flow of history and not as a decisive break with it. The meaning of the modern to which the discourse of industrial distinction in mining bears witness thus testifies to how deeply embedded the coal trade was in the larger British culture – and to how pervasive were the discursive resources with which that culture comprehended modernity.[29]

Notes

1 *The Times*, 24 May 1928, pp. 18e and 20.
2 Ibid., p. 18e.
3 Ibid.
4 *Colliery Guardian*, 20 March 1925, p. 703 (Hughes), 19 February 1926, p. 433 (Muschamp), 24 August 1924, p. 483 (Gibson), 30 July 1926, p. 241 (Mitton), 28 October 1927, p. 831 (Wood), 19 September 1924, p. 743 (Henshaw) and 7 March 1924, p. 617 (Blackett) and the *Transactions of the Institution of Mining Engineers* (hereafter *Transactions*) LXXXIX (1934–5): 339–41.
5 *Colliery Guardian*, 20 January 1928, p. 243 (Johnson) and *The Times*, 9 September 1946, p. 7e (Mitton).
6 *Colliery Guardian*, 19 September 1924, p. 743 (Henshaw) and 28 October 1927, p. 831 (Wood) and *The Times*, 4 November 1927, p. 17d (Galloway).
7 *Colliery Guardian*, 31 August 1928, p. 835.
8 Ibid.
9 Ibid., 20 July 1928, p. 249.
10 Ibid., 28 October 1927, p. 831 (Wood) and 7 March 1924, p. 617 (Blackett) and the *Transactions* LXXXIX (1934–5): 339–41.
11 *Colliery Guardian*, 19 September 1924, p. 743 (Henshaw) and 20 January 1928, p. 243 (Johnson).
12 Ibid., 25 May 1928, p. 2053. It may not occasion much surprise at this point to note that, despite the language of improvement, the narrative of change in the story of O'Connor's mining eminence identified only one of the practices his innovations superseded – the use of ponies to remove coal from the faces – and there is no indication in the text of what kind of improvement this represented.

13 *The Times*, 9 September 1946, p. 7e and *Who Was Who, 1941–50* (H. E. Mitton).

14 *Colliery Guardian*, 24 December 1925, p. 1523 (Lomax) and 13 November 1925, p. 1155 (Gregory).

15 Ibid., 24 December 1925, p. 1523 (Lomax).

16 Ibid.

17 Ibid.

18 *Transactions* 127 (January 1968): 257.

19 *The Times*, 9 February 1938, p. 14c.

20 Ibid., 21 November 1941, p. 7e (Hood).

21 *Colliery Guardian*, 27 May 1927, p. 1231 (Hart) and the *Transactions* 104 (1944–5), p. 172 (Clive).

22 *Colliery Guardian*, 11 May 1928, p. 1849.

23 Ibid., 21 December 1928, p. 2474.

24 Ibid.

25 Ibid.

26 Ibid.

27 Ibid., 21 December 1928, p. 2474 (Mackay) and 11 May 1928, p. 1849 (Drew) and *The Times*, 21 November 1941, p. 7e (Hood).

28 Stefan Collini, *Public Moralists: Political Thought and Intellectual Life in Britain 1850–1930* (Oxford: Clarendon Press, 1991), pp. 67–74, 79–80, 86, 100–1 and 186–7; R. J. Morris, *Class, Sect, and Party: The Making of the British Middle Class, Leeds 1820–1850* (Manchester and New York: Manchester University Press, 1990), p. 330; Frank M. Turner, *The Greek Heritage in Victorian Britain* (New Haven, CT: Yale University Press, 1981), pp. 358–68; Craig Jenks, 'T. H. Green, the Oxford Philosophy of Duty and the English Middle Class', *British Journal of Sociology* XXVII (December 1971): 481–97; Jose Harris, 'Political Thought and the Welfare State 1870–1940: An Intellectual Framework for British Social Policy', *Past and Present* 135 (May 1992): 116–41; and Kenneth Fielden, 'Samuel Smiles and Self-Help', *Journal of British Studies* XII (December 1968): 155–76.

29 Reba N. Soffer, *Discipline and Power: The University, History, and the Making of an English Elite, 1870–1930* (Stanford, CA: Stanford University Press, 1994), especially Chapter 3; and Harris, 'Political Thought'.

Part III
Empire and British Notions of Modernity

–9–

Modern Mountains: The Performative Consciousness of Modernity in Britain, 1870–1940[1]

Peter H. Hansen

'Antiquity meets modernity.' Thus reads the *Daily Chronicle*'s caption of a photograph of three Tibetan Buddhist monks standing before a radio microphone in London. The monks were visiting the metropolis in a troupe of 'dancing lamas' who performed before the screening of *The Epic of Everest*, the film of the 1924 Mount Everest expedition. The caption renders the microphone as modernity and the monks as incongruous artefacts of antiquity. Likewise, the *Leeds Mercury* labelled this image 'White Man's Magic'. The *Liverpool Post*, however, gave the scene the less pejorative label, 'Native Music'.[2] Indeed, the scene may be interpreted otherwise, in ways that do not fix the monks in an Orientalist gaze or represent them as befuddled by modern technology. One might ask, for example, what the monks themselves thought of the microphone. While what they made of it remains unclear, what they made with it may still be heard on sound recordings from similar events. A phonograph record made by the same monks in Germany, for example, preserves for posterity the euphonious tones of their Buddhist chants. From this evidence, the monks appear to have interpreted radio and sound recordings – as they also interpreted film – not as white magic or the technology of an inscrutable modernity, but as a new medium for the transmission of their own missionary message to all sentient beings.[3]

Yet the caption's binary opposition of modernity and antiquity has implications for understanding the British consciousness of modernity in the late nineteenth and early twentieth centuries that need to be further explored. Jose Harris has suggested the 'unique dominance of the present time' in Britain in this period, and some of the fluid meanings of what it meant to be 'modern'.[4] Such newspaper headlines, which mixed metaphors of race and religion, time and the other, represented the monks in opposition to the British in familiar ways. 'Antiquity meets modernity' placed the monks in a primitive and primeval 'space-time' that, as Johannes Fabian has noted, established a temporal distance with the monks and denied their 'co-evalness'.[5] In phrases such as 'White Man's Magic', Edward

Said and other scholars have discerned discursive strategies for 'dominating, restructuring, and having authority over the Orient'.[6] Moreover, scholars of British history have for some time examined the ways in which British identities have been constituted in relation to a variety of 'others'.[7] In some less sophisticated works of this kind, however, there is a tendency to restrict the boundaries of Britain too rigidly, and to define identities in a process that is too oppositional.[8] A more fruitful approach considers the boundaries of Britain as porous and diasporic, extending well beyond the British Isles, and the process of constructing identities as reciprocal. As Paul Gilroy has argued, this 'inside/outside relationship should be recognised as a more powerful, more complex, and more contested element in the historical, social, and cultural memory' of British 'modernity' than is often recognized.[9]

The British consciousness of modernity was sometimes defined in contrast to 'others' who, like the dancing lamas, were considered non-modern, ancient, backward, primitive, traditional or superstitious. While there were many ways of being 'modern,' one of the particular ways the British expressed their modernity was through mountaineering. British mountaineers defined themselves as 'modern' in relation to the peasants with whom they climbed as well as the urban, industrial society that they were escaping. Similar movements have been described by Jackson Lears and others as 'anti-modern'.[10] But mountaineering was not so much 'anti-modern' as emblematic of the multiplicity of modernity, containing within it a range of meanings that do not fall easily on to a dichotomous modern/anti-modern axis. Indeed, the practices of mountaineering suggest the limitations of the Weberian view of modernity as the triumph of instrumental rationality, secularization, disenchantment, and so forth. As Anthony Appiah rightly suggests, 'to understand our – our human – modernity we must first understand why the rationalization of the world can no longer be seen as the tendency either of the West or of history; why, simply put, the modernist characterization of modernity needs to be challenged'.[11]

In this regard, it may be useful to consider the British 'consciousness of modernity' as performative. While this term could suggest several avenues of inquiry, from the theatrical practices of public performances to speech acts that 'do things with words', I would like to explore the ways in which British modernity was performed through mountaineering. To be 'modern' is not something that can be established once and for all; it has to be continually demonstrated and performed. Mountaineers may have been escaping one kind of modernity in Britain, but they intended to demonstrate their distinctive modernity through climbing mountains. By understanding mountaineering as performative, I want to suggest not merely that it was the expression of some underlying condition – of modernity or anti-modernism – but that the languages, gestures, and symbols of mountaineering actually constituted the 'modernity' they were said to describe.[12] Such an approach may clear the space in which to locate the agency of the 'others' on whom these images of modernity were dependent, and whose presence rendered these images themselves ambivalent. Indeed, the more profound ambivalence of this particular form of modernity stemmed from mountaineering's combination of the 'traditional' veneration of mountains with the more 'modern' impulse to conquer them.

When Leslie Stephen brought Melchior Anderegg, his Swiss guide, to London by train, the man of letters remarked that the view of the London suburbs from their railway carriage 'is not so fine a view as we have seen together from the top of Mont Blanc'. Melchior Anderegg replied, 'Ah sir, it is far finer.' Stephen, who considered the scene a 'dreary expanse of chimney-pots' on the edge of 'this dingy metropolis,' was shocked at the discrepancy between his views and those of his guide.[13] He later used this exchange to begin his discussion of the change in attitudes towards mountains since the eighteenth century in *The Playground of Europe* (1871). Stephen noted that in previous centuries, many people who lived in or visited the Alps feared that devils, dragons, elves, fairies, goblins or gnomes haunted the mountains. 'These picturesque beings', Stephen wrote, 'disappeared before the early dawn of science, much as the natives of Tasmania have disappeared before the English immigrants.'[14]

Before the mid-1850s, Switzerland was still visited rarely and the Alps were almost never climbed. Within a decade, however, Albert Smith's West End performances about his ascent of Mont Blanc popularized mountain climbing among the British middle classes. By adopting the discourse of discovery from explorers in the rest of the world, the members of the Alpine Club represented the Alps as a *terra incognita* to be explored and conquered.[15] When these climbers visited the Alps, they considered the local population to be primitive peasants or superstitious seigneurs who would rather live at the foot of a mountain than plant their feet on its summit. By systematically climbing the Alps, Stephen and other British mountaineers represented themselves as agents of a progressive modernity, in which their imperial masculinity conquered the space that indigenous superstition had left undisturbed for centuries. When they extended their reach into other parts of the world, these mountaineers took these sentiments with them. In the mid-1930s, for example, General C. G. Bruce wrote: 'For the Himalayas at the present time, as far as its indigenous inhabitants are concerned, are far and away behind what a Swiss or a Northern Italian population was like 200 years ago, and further, the scale of life, clothing, food, etc., still remains far beneath European standards.'[16]

The backwardness of the Alps or the Himalayas or other ranges appealed to British tourists and climbers for yet another reason. They wanted to escape from contemporary British society. Leslie Stephen, for example, was attracted to mountains as a refuge from modernity: 'Mountain scenery is the antithesis not so much of the plains as of the commonplace. Its charm lies in its vigorous originality;

and if political philosophers speak the truth, which I admit to be an exceedingly doubtful proposition, the danger of modern times consists in our loss of that quality.'[17] Stephen noted that people in Britain wore the same clothes, read the same papers, 'talk the same twaddle', and submit to the same conventions of propriety and respectability. The Alps remained 'places of refuge where we may escape from ourselves and from our neighbours'.[18] Paradoxically, British mountaineers were escaping themselves to become themselves, escaping one form of modernity in Britain in order to represent or perform another modernity in Switzerland. Mountaineering was not 'anti-modern', but represented an ambivalent modernity that combined mountain conquest with mountain worship.

Mountain conquest was often expressed in the search for first ascents. The so-called 'golden age' of mountaineering in the 1850s and 1860s had witnessed the first ascent of nearly all the major peaks of the Alps. Once these feats had been achieved, however, climbers did not put themselves out to pasture. Instead, they developed novel ways to demonstrate their modernity. In the late nineteenth century, climbers sought to achieve first ascents of the *same* mountains in the Alps in winter, or without guides, or by a woman, or by many new routes. This last variation, especially, seemed to create a vast array of possibilities. Each innovation elicited at least mild derision from the old guard, who had assumed that mountaineering was synonymous with the 'exploration' of new ground. In 1878, for example, Clinton Dent bemoaned the 'ascents of old mountains from "new sides" – to use a thoroughly Alpine phrase, for which I am almost tempted to substitute "wrong sides"'. Within a decade, 'guideless' climbing was so well developed that by 1886 Dent had to acknowledge its validity.[19] Dent himself climbed with guides in the Caucasus, and other climbers went to the Himalayas as well as the Andes, Africa, Canada, Norway, and New Zealand. Once again, inasmuch as these peaks had not been climbed by the people who lived among them, these British ascents were seen by the climbers as evidence of the modernity of those men who could summon the nerve to climb them.

Alongside mountain conquest, another dimension of the ambivalent modernity of mountaineering derived from what might be called, for lack of a better term, mountain worship. While there were precedents for veneration and awe of nature in Britain and elsewhere, it is not easy to assign mountaineers to one 'tradition' or the other. For example, some of the later Alpine writings of Leslie Stephen, a noted agnostic, were more mystical in their appreciation of mountains than his earlier works.[20] While his attitudes have sometimes been interpreted as 'Wordsworthian', it may be equally plausible to see them as 'Melchior-Anderreggian'. Stephen and the other climbers who spent long periods with guides in the Alps appear to have engaged in a mutual mimesis with their guides. Such exchange became somewhat less common in the Alps in later generations, as contact between guides and climbers became more formal and distant.[21] From the late nineteenth century onwards, many climbers travelled outside Europe to recover the experience that earlier climbers had enjoyed with 'primitive' peasants in the Alps.

The particular modernity represented by mountaineering frequently combined mountain conquest and mountain worship in some degree. Consider the writings of the Revd Walter Weston, an Anglican missionary in Japan, a country with a venerable 'tradition' of mountain worship. Weston began climbing in Japan while serving as a missionary in Kobe and Yokohama for extended periods between 1888 and 1915. While nearly all the mountains he climbed had already been ascended, often innumerable times over hundreds of years by Japanese as the destination for local pilgrimages, he did make many first ascents by a foreigner. Beginning in the 1890s, Weston wrote frequently about his ascents and was fascinated by the Japanese mountain cults.[22] The 'modernizing' Japan of the Meiji restoration, however, is absent from his account. In the *Playground of the Far East* (1918), Weston reassured the 'traveller bound for Japan in search of the primitive and the picturesque' that these were 'combined to a degree unknown in any other country'. They could be found two days' journey from Tokyo in 'lonely valleys whose old-world ways, quaint superstitions, and primitive institutions' suggested 'a leap backward from the twentieth century to the tenth.'[23]

Weston's only mountain conquest that was his alone was the first ascent of Ho-wo-zan. Even Kôbô Daishi, a renowned figure who had climbed many of the highest Japanese peaks a hundred years earlier, had failed to climb it. Weston was joined by three local hunters, two of whom quickly deserted him to hunt a large chamois. The third hunter continued with him, but stopped 150 feet below the summit, where Weston managed, by heaving a rope up a steep ledge, to pull himself alone up the final ridge. 'I found myself standing, for the first time in my life, on a hitherto untrodden, though famous peak, the top of Ho-wo-zan.'[24] On their descent, they met the hunters carrying their massive chamois, which they ceremoniously cut open, offering to Weston its raw liver, in honour of his ascent, so that he could partake of the chamois' agility, strength, and speed. Several days later, another guide proposed that Weston erect at the foot of the mountain a shrine in honour of the summit deity, and that Weston become the first *Kannushi*, or guardian priest, of the mountain god.[25] He declined both the liver and patronage of a shrine, though after his retirement he referred to the post of *Kannushi* as the highest preferment ever offered in his ecclesiastical career.

Each of these incidents reinforced the ambiguous 'modernity' that Weston found in Japan. In language that suggests the central theme of his books, he wrote that on one occasion he 'fell to meditating upon the strange contrasts suggested by this combination of the ancient and the modern – the science of today side by side with the quaint nature-worship of a thousand years of yesterday' symbolized by a surveyor's stone and the ruins of a shrine.[26] On other occasions, he made this same contrast using meteorological instruments and shrines where peasants prayed for rain. At the summit of Fuji, he observed next to weather-forecasting instruments 'some white-robed pilgrim take his stand to pay his devotions to the rising sun before he goes off to the post office, recently erected a few yards away, to dispatch to some 40 friends in far-off provinces the latest forms of picture postcards in which a licensed vendor on the summit drives a "roaring trade"!' Although he notes that these scenes took place 'without apparent objection or incongruity in native eyes', in Weston's account they are crucial in performing his awareness of his own modernity.[27] In other words, just as the presence of the pilgrims affirmed the modernity of the meteorology, so too the mountain cults were necessary to demonstrate Weston's own sense of being modern, even as he shared their sense of wonder in the mountains. At his death in 1940, Weston became known in British mountaineering circles as the 'father of Japanese mountaineering'.

Given the very long tradition of mountain worship in Japan, this claim would sound even more hyperbolic and absurd than it does if it did not fit a wider pattern. Similar claims were made for William Cecil Slingsby, whose climbs in Norway beginning in the 1870s led other British mountaineers to consider him the 'father of Norwegian mountaineering'. The title of Slingsby's book, *Norway, the Northern Playground* (1904), also had a familiar ring. In addition, by the turn of the century British alpinists retrospectively claimed Alfred Wills's ascent of the Wetterhorn in 1854 as inaugurating the 'golden age' of mountaineering in the Alps.[28] Each of these foundation myths was a performative representation of British modernity. The claims for alpine paternity suggested that indigenous populations had learned to climb from the British; whereas local guides had almost invariably showed them the way. Moreover, the phrase 'the playground of_____' depopulated the landscape and redefined the complex societies that they had invaded for their pleasure into mere 'playgrounds'.

While the mountains of Japan and Norway never became 'British' playgrounds, some parts of the Alps apparently did, and the rapid development of the Alps changed the ways in which mountaineers could demonstrate their modernity among them. In 1879, over one million tourists visited Switzerland, with British tourists accounting for more than a quarter of the total and almost one-third of all tourist expenditures.[29] So many British climbers and tourists came to the Alps that many parts of Switzerland briefly became British enclaves if not British colonies. In 1886, James Bryce reported to a friend in America that 'Switzerland has become quite English – at least in these health resorts. One changes the scenery but not the conversation, so there is little mental refreshment. When you come over it will be nice to tell you to which places to go to get real foreign life and natural beauty combined – they are few and growing fewer.'[30] The throngs of British tourists created a range of services, ranging from hotels to English churches. Dorothy Pilley Richards recalled that the Swiss resort was still very 'English' in the 1920s. 'There too, the English Church and the four-square hotels, institutional, dominant, already mature instruments of an invasion. New visitors now will find it hard to imagine how "English" they could be . . . Entering one of them, you felt you were joining something. You realized it most of all when you sat down in your appointed place at the long table. Ritual had you in its velvet paw.'[31] In this environment, it became even more difficult to escape the conventions of British society in Switzerland, at least in the way that earlier British mountaineers had done.

The very 'Englishness' of the Alps has implications for the British consciousness of modernity. Peter Mandler has rightly argued that the nostalgic vision of rural 'Englishness' was neither as dominant nor as 'anti-modern' as has often been supposed. Rural nostalgia was less well developed in Britain than elsewhere in Europe by the early twentieth century.[32] It should be emphasized that these two conditions were related. Put another way, this kind of rural nostalgia was not well developed in Britain *because* it was well developed elsewhere in Europe. Mandler astutely notes that there is no equivalent in Britain to the *Heimatschutz* movement. In much of German-speaking Europe, the *Heimatschutz* movement advocated the preservation of the countryside and of the peasantry in a nostalgic vision of 'homeland'.[33] Britain developed no equivalent to the *Heimatschutz* movement because that movement itself extended into Britain. British mountaineers founded the English branch of the *Schweizerische Vereinigung für Heimatschutz*, or in francophone Switzerland, *Ligue pour la Conservation de la Suisse Pittoresque*, in 1905, barely a year after the organization took root in Switzerland. The British professional classes that vacationed in Europe idealized the peasantry, but not a 'British' peasantry, since the peasantry by then had all but disappeared in Britain. The English branch attracted strong support in the press before the First World War, much of it in response to proposals to build a railway to the summit of the Matterhorn.[34]

The English branch of the Swiss *Heimatschutz* is indicative of the extent to which the British consciousness of modernity was often defined in relation to people and places outside Britain, whether in Europe, the empire, or elsewhere. Many developments that in other countries would have taken place domestically were thus imported/exported by the British. Characteristically, when Henry Lunn, a Nonconformist travel agent, organized an oecumenical conference on the model of the American Chautauqua movement, he held the event not in Britain but in Grindelwald, Switzerland. As a travel agent, Lunn was able to mix business and pleasure, turning the prophets into profits. He made the travel arrangements to Grindelwald and organized excursions for the *conférenciers* to Mont Blanc, the Matterhorn, the St Gotthard pass, the Italian lakes, the Engadine, and the falls of the Rhine.[35] Lunn also led the development of winter sports in the Alps. In 1902, he organized winter tours exclusively for Eton and Harrow old boys. After expanding eligibility to wider range of schools, Lunn formed the Public Schools Alpine Sports Club in 1905. By the winter of 1906, the Club had 5,000 clients, completely occupying thirty hotels, which temporarily became English colonies.[36] William Martin Conway admired their efforts as 'through the agency of the club the members formed part of an assemblage which seemed to produce the old kind of comradeship which formerly existed in Switzerland'.[37]

If the Alps were the most popular destination for British climbers before 1914, during the period between the wars a few climbers looked upward to the Himalayas while many more turned inward to Britain for places to demonstrate their modernity. After the war, returning servicemen yearned for forms of domesticity removed from military models.[38] Alison Light has also identified a 'conservative modernity' between the wars that moved away from a masculine rhetoric of heroism and national destiny 'to an Englishness at once less imperial and more inward looking, more domestic and more private'.[39] One sign of these trends was the increasing popularity of outdoor recreations in Britain, including rambling, hosteling, scouting, orienteering, and climbing. These activities drew on traditions of liberal middle-class culture, working-class respectability, rational recreations, self-improvement and natural history in new ways that appealed to men and, significantly, to women, from a variety of social groups.[40] Several factors pushed and pulled in this direction. Outdoor recreations in the English landscape became important ways for men and women to assert their citizenship and modernity through the 'arts of right living'.[41] In Britain, such activities were readily accessible and easily affordable. By contrast, the cost of a Swiss holiday rose after the war (after falling throughout the nineteenth century), and the 1931 devaluation of the pound put the price even further out of reach for many people in Britain.[42]

In their place, alpine climbers from Germany, Austria, and Italy thought themselves the most up-to-date and 'modern' mountaineers between the wars. After the German and Austrian Alpine Clubs effected their own *Anschluss* in 1924, they moved from advocating the anti-cog-railway and anti-tourist positions that had been common before 1914 to anti-Semitism and later National Socialism.[43] The British mountaineers who had joined them in opposing mountain railways with the Swiss *Heimatschutz* did not follow the same political trajectory. The 'Bavarian school' of German and Austrian climbers risked their lives and achieved nationalist acclaim by using pitons and other mechanical aids to make first ascents of treacherous north faces. British climbers considered the nationalism unseemly, the methods unsporting and the north faces simply too dangerous. Indeed, fanatical fascists soon replaced alpine peasants as the British 'other' in the Alps in the 1930s.

Yet British mountaineers recognized in the practices of German climbing enough of their own 'modernity' to make them uncomfortable.[44] In a philippic on 'the perversion of mountaineering', C. F. Meade defined British mountaineering in opposition to the foolhardy risk-taking, nationalism and 'modern spirit of competition' that classified mountaineering as a sport. Meade conceded that by excluding foreigners from the Everest expeditions, Britain was not entirely free from nationalist chauvinism. He also ridiculed British advocates of 'safety first' in climbing and, writing in the conservative *Quarterly Review* in 1936, in politics as well. Meade believed that mountaineering blended 'a longing for adventure, a love of nature and a sentiment that can only be called mystical'. Yet he did not oppose mountain worship to mountain conquest so much as advocate the position that climbers had to love nature to conquer it: 'The mountaineer is matching himself against the forces of nature, not vying with other men.'[45]

This combination of modernity and mysticism was also evident in the British Everest expeditions. Since the 1850s, the Survey of India had mapped and named the world's highest peaks and British hill stations had colonized parts of the Himalayas as British resorts; and Lord Curzon, as Viceroy, proposed the ascent of Everest in order to represent British authority on the boundaries of India.[46] In 1921 Francis Younghusband, an explorer and mystic and then President of the Royal Geographical Society, launched the first Everest expedition to advance scientific knowledge, to elevate the 'human spirit' and to inspire man's conquest of nature. Once the Everest expeditions reached the mountain, however, they encountered the Tibetan Buddhist worship of Everest as a sacred place, and began to describe their own ascent as a 'pilgrimage'.[47] The traditions of British mysticism and religion also influenced how they interpreted Everest. The disappearance of George Mallory and Andrew Irvine on Everest in 1924, for example, briefly revived cults ranging from chivalry and the Christian gentleman, to psychical research and spiritualist seances with Mallory's ghost.

Many British observers argued that Mallory and the other Everest climbers embodied the 'spirit of man' against the material forces of nature. This language was redolent with previous associations from the 'spirit of adventure' of nineteenth-century imperial explorers and the 'spirit of man' that had fortified British morale during the war against Germany. On the one hand, the 'spirit of man' could inspire an emphasis on spirituality and humanism. On Everest, for example, George Mallory had read to other climbers extracts from *The Spirit of Man* (1916), Robert Bridges' wartime anthology of uplifting verse. On the other hand, such rhetoric could shroud the brutality of the very colonial conquest that it justified. Younghusband, who popularized the view of Everest as an epochal struggle between man and nature, considered the Tibetans and Sherpas deficient in 'spirit' and thus as much to be conquered as the rest of the mountain: 'The faint-hearted peoples around [Everest] fear to approach it. They have the capacity of body to reach the summit any year they liked. But they are lacking in spirit.'[48] While Younghusband generously praised the porters, he believed that the British supplied the 'spirit' – the modernity – of the Everest expeditions, just as they had elsewhere in the empire. As David Matless has suggested, Younghusband's emphasis on spirituality, and his imperialism allied with hints of fascism, should be understood as central to the modernity of geography (and, we should add, mountaineering), not as an escape from it.[49]

In the 1930s, similar large-scale, quasi-military expeditions to Everest, Kangchenjunga, and Nanga Parbat met with frustration, futility, and fatalities. On Nanga Parbat, many German climbers and Sherpa porters died on expeditions that were actively promoted by the Nazi government. Partly in reaction to these deaths, and partly in reaction to the imperial excesses of their own Everest expeditions, some British mountaineers began to organize small expeditions to the Himalayas. In 1931, Frank Smythe's ascent of Kamet pioneered the more intimate, small-scale expeditions that Eric Shipton and H. W. Tilman used on expeditions to Nanda Devi and other peaks. This shift to smaller-scale expeditions in the Himalayas was similar to the increasing emphasis on domestic climbing in Britain between the wars. Each signalled novel ways to represent British 'modernity' in a less overtly imperial style. The climbers on the smaller expeditions experienced closer friendships with one another and with their Sherpa porters in ways that highlighted tensions between British attitudes towards mountain worship and mountain conquest.

The contrast between these two approaches – the small scale and large-scale expeditions – may be seen in two films from the early 1930s, *Kamet Conquered* and *Wings Over Everest*. By this period, even small-scale British expeditions to the Himalayas described themselves as performative of Britain's imperial power. *Kamet Conquered* (1932) opens with Frank Smythe, the narrator, recapitulating an imperial theme. He hoped to answer the question his audience must be wondering: 'Why do men do these things? Why are they prepared to undergo difficulties, hardships, even dangers just for the sake of climbing to the top of a mountain? The answer to that question is for adventure. The same spirit of adventure that carried our ancestors across uncharted oceans to new lands. The spirit of adventure upon which the very foundation of our empire rests.'[50] Although Smythe appealed to the spirit of 'ancestors,' climbing mountains to represent adventure had been a mid-Victorian invention. Moreover, even if the film proclaimed Kamet 'conquered', the conquest incorporated 'mystical' attitudes of mountain worship. For example, Smythe's film portrayed the climbers as pilgrims visiting a Hindu temple, and dwelt at length on a shot of the source of the Ganges gushing out of a glacier.

The conclusion of their conquest was also ambivalent. As they reach the summit of Kamet gasping for breath, the film concludes: 'We seized hold of our Sirdar, Lewa [a Sherpa], and shoved him on ahead of us, so that he should be the first on top. It was, I think, the least compliment we could pay to those splendid men, our porters, to whom we owed the whole success of our expedition.'[51] In his book, Smythe adds that when they pushed Lewa on top, 'I do not think that he quite understood what we were doing'; and Lewa almost certainly did not consider this gesture a compliment. The scant evidence suggests he may have thought the British were using him to test the vengeance of the summit deities. Smythe recalled that none of the porters would climb a short distance to retrieve equipment jettisoned on the descent from the summit: 'Superstition was rife among them, and they would not stir . . . Nima Dorje had returned to camp in a hysterical condition and babbling of gods and devils whom [*sic*] he affirmed had taken all the air away. And now the all-powerful god of Kamet had burnt Lewa's feet.' Even though the film's opening narration had extolled the discourses of adventure and empire, its closing sequence includes striking images of Sherpas and Sahibs caressing each other's frostbitten feet. The climbers' conquest of Kamet is tempered by the Sherpas' worship of the mountain and by the reciprocal obligations they owe one another.

Wings Over Everest (1934) depicts the first aeroplane flight over Everest in 1933. As the repeated attempts to climb Everest met with failure, the British flight over the mountain served as its only 'conquest' until 1953. As two pilots look at the snow-capped Himalayas from the hills of Darjeeling, they resolve to look down from above on the mysteries of the mountains. The film then jumps to the dome of St Paul's in London, representing the mysteries of the 'west' to those of Everest in the 'east'. After the flight organizers and pilots, including the Marquis of Douglas and Clydesdale, express grave concern over their lack of funds, the scene shifts to the Scottish estate of Lady Houston, a right-wing millionaire, whom they ask to underwrite the expedition. As she listens to their sales pitch, Lady Houston sits nestled under bedcovers. She then says: 'What appears to me is that the people of India, if it is a success – and it's going to be a success – well, they'll know that we're not the decadents that their leaders try to make us out to be. That's what appeals to me. I agree. I'll help.' Cue the roar of British technology – engines, turbines, power plants, casting equipment and moulding machines. After the RAF assembles the Westland aeroplanes in Karachi, and after training flights in India, crowds of Indians watch them take off for Everest. Several bare-chested Indian peasants briefly look up from their harvest to watch the planes. After they fly over the summit and return safely to India, someone asks the crew 'Did you get there? What was it like?' One of the pilots replies 'All right.'[52]

Kamet Conquered and *Wings over Everest* differed in significant ways. The Everest flight was organized by aristocrats, powered by British technology, and, between take-off and landing, there was no contact between the pilots and the local population. On Kamet (and Everest), the British climbers were almost all middle-class in background and reluctant to use technological aids, including supplemental oxygen, and remained in close quarters for months on end with porters, guides and translators. This long period of association changed the way the climbers interpreted their ascents, incorporating elements of mountain worship alongside mountain conquest. At the summit of Kamet, Smythe gave what he considered the honour of stepping first on the summit to Lewa, the head porter. Their ascent becomes a collaborative endeavour in Smythe's account, rather than merely a demonstration of their spirit of adventure. During the Everest flight, the fleeting glimpse of peasants toiling in the fields is the closest that Indians or Nepalis or Tibetans come to contact with the aeroplane or its pilots.

Both films represented British modernity in relation to the 'other', and the encounter between climbers and porters on Kamet makes clear the ambivalence inherent in both situations. While there is some evidence that Lewa did not consider stepping first on the summit an honour, there is precious little evidence to indicate what the film's Indian peasants thought of the Everest flight. Yet this very lacuna rendered Lady Houston's intentions ambivalent, since the flight almost certainly did not have the effects in India that she intended. Indeed, its impact in Britain is also uncertain. British mountaineers were embarrassed at the pilot's success where climbers had failed, and uncomfortable with the distinctly fascist overtones that accompanied Lady Houston's vocal support of right-wing causes, including Oswald Mosley's British fascists, as well as aviation. Although the contrast between politically motivated, large-scale British or German expeditions of conquest and the more intimate, small-scale expeditions that blended elements of mountain worship should not be overdrawn, the differences between them posed dilemmas for British mountaineers by the 1930s.

These dilemmas were widely recognized. W. H. Auden and Christopher Isherwood's play, *The Ascent of F 6* (1936–7), satirized the imperial context of mountaineering and portrayed the conquest of the mountain as an interior, psychological tragedy. In Auden and Isherwood's play, officials from the Foreign Office and the tabloid press propose the ascent of F 6, the highest mountain on the border between British Sudoland and Ostnian Sudoland, to quell a native insurrection. The natives of Sudoland believe the mountain haunted by a guardian demon and refuse to set foot on it. However, Ostnian agents have propagated the rumour that 'the white man who first reaches the summit of F 6 will be lord over *both* Sudolands, with his descendants, for a thousand years', and launched a secret expedition to climb F 6. The British turn to Michael Ransom, an introspective scholar based on Mallory and Lawrence of Arabia, to lead their expedition. Though eager to climb F 6, Ransom is repulsed by their political motives, and refuses to go until asked by his mother, whose approval he craves.

At a monastery on F 6, Ransom looks into a crystal ball and hears voices of the public calling him to inspire, lead and save them. The Abbot of the monastery warns Ransom against his desire to conquer the mountain demon and save mankind, and urges him to retire to a life of abnegation and contemplation. Ransom considers the offer, but passively accepts the messianic role when the climbers tell him the Ostnians are already hammering the south face full of pitons: 'Very well then, since you wish it. I obey you. The summit will be reached, the Ostnians defeated, the Empire saved. And I have failed.' Ransom fails because he has been corrupted by power. As they ascend, the other climbers are each sacrificed to Ransom's tormented ambition. On reaching the top, he confronts the mountain demon, which appears to him in the shape of his mother, and collapses on the summit. The British public and government pay tribute to his glorious death.[53]

The particular consciousness of modernity represented by British mountaineering was defined and performed in relation to a variety of others, including Alpine peasants, Japanese pilgrims, German climbers, Buddhist lamas, and Hindu saddhus, and their fictional equivalents, the Abbot and the Ostnians on F 6. Sometimes British ascents conquered the superstitions of mountain worship as well as the 'material forces of nature' on the mountain, but on other occasions their modernity was constituted by their very incorporation of mountain worship with mountain conquest. Before 1914, British dominance was so generalized that these performances could take place in Switzerland or Norway or Japan as much as in the 'formal' empire. In areas outside British control, the political impact of the climbers' conquest of superstition was muted and implicit, though by no means absent. In the empire, the same ascents had an explicit political resonance that was celebrated by some (Francis Younghusband or Lady Houston) but ambivalently accommodated by others (Frank Smythe or Michael Ransom). Whether they liked it or not, the very modernity that mountaineers performed in their ascents could also be appropriated. In 1937, for example, the Japanese imperial government awarded Walter Weston the Order of the Sacred Treasure and erected a plaque in his honour in the Japanese Alps, co-opting his climbing as a sign of their own modernity. British attempts on Everest in the 1930s emphasized similar themes, which were revived in 1953 when news of the conquest of Everest was reported on the day of Queen Elizabeth II's coronation as a symbol of British modernity.[54]

The performative 'consciousness of modernity' in mountaineering forged by the 1930s continues to circulate at the end of the twentieth century. When C. G. Crawford gave a lecture on the ascent of Everest to the YMCA at the Stewart Hall, Norwich in November 1933 he appeared to make fun of the Tibetans. 'The Tibetan Government have refused us permission to try again, because they say we bring bad weather and spoil their crops. (Laughter.) They say the gods of the Himalayas are displeased with us, and send bad weather to overwhelm us. But we hope to try again in 1935, if we can get permission. (Applause.)'[55] Gordon Stewart recently cited this passage, and particularly the audience's laughter, to support the view that there was an unchallenged British master narrative of Everest and empire in the early twentieth century.[56] But such a conclusion is a form of imperial nostalgia, a yearning for the time when British narratives were apparently unchallenged and autonomous. Crawford's lecture incorporated within it the Tibetan point of view and thus acknowledged the counter-narrative that he was challenging. Moreover, if the Tibetans did not read the provincial British press, the mandarins of the India

Office did, and they reprimanded the Everest expedition for Crawford's comments. The India Office feared Crawford's remarks would reach the Tibetans (who did read the English papers), and that Tibet would again cancel the expeditions to Everest.[57] In consequence, the climbers were severely restrained from making any similar comments, and Crawford was excluded from future expeditions.

It is also worth reflecting further on the audience reaction to Crawford's lecture. For in their laughter is another performative consciousness of modernity. If one accepts the modernist characterization of modernity, it is easy to assume that Crawford's YMCA audience was laughing at the Tibetans. This is all too easy to assume. Amid the chortles of derision and sniggers of the louts, was there also a nervous laugh, or a chuckle of recognition? Did some members of the audience recognize in his Tibetan tales their own superstitions or the continuing presence of the divine and supernatural in their lives?[58] Their laughter should be located at the margins of the modern, a momentary manifestation of subaltern agency that was soon displaced by the patriotic applause. Perhaps this Norwich audience saw in the Everest expeditions in Tibet elements of both mountain worship and mountain conquest. Like the British climbers who went to the Alps or the Himalayas or other ranges, their reaction was not so much modern or anti-modern as negotiating the instability of 'modernity'. Some of the performances that mountaineers used to accommodate this ambivalence, such as the myths of themselves as the 'fathers' of mountaineering, have also proved to be as transitory as the laughter was ephemeral. Yet even this should not have surprised some of the climbers. As Walter Weston read on the wall of a Japanese inn, 'Though life, like the entrails of a sheep, be many thousands of miles long, yet fame is ever as short as the horns of a snail.'[59]

Notes

1 The author is grateful for comments from the editors and from audiences at the Australian National University and the Neale Colloquium at University College London.

2 See *Daily Chronicle*, *Leeds Mercury*, *Liverpool Post*, on 16 Dec. 1924, in a book of Everest newsclippings, EE 41(b), Royal Geographical Society Archives, London.

3 Peter H. Hansen, 'Der tibetische Horizont: Tibet im Kino des frühen 20. Jahrhunderts', in *Mythos Tibet: Wahrnehmungen, Projektionen, Phantasien*, ed. Thierry Dodin and Heinz Räther, (Cologne: Dumont Verlag, 1997), pp. 87–103.

4 Jose Harris, *Private Lives and Public Spirit: Britain, 1870–1914* (London: Penguin, 1993), pp. 32–6.

5 Johannes Fabian, *Time and the Other: How Anthropology Makes its Object* (New York: Columbia University Press, 1983). See also Marianna Torgovnick, *Gone Primitive: Savage Intellect, Modern Lives* (Chicago: Chicago University Press, 1990).

6 Edward W. Said, *Orientalism* (New York: Pantheon, 1979), p. 3. See also Peter H. Hansen, 'The Dancing Lamas of Everest: Cinema, Orientalism, and Anglo-Tibetan Relations in the 1920s', *American Historical Review* 101 (1996): 712–47.

7 See Linda Colley, 'Britishness and Otherness: an Argument', *Journal of British Studies* 31 (1992): 309–29.

8 Gordon Stewart, 'Tenzing's Two Wrist-Watches: The Conquest of Everest and Late Imperial Culture, 1921–1953', *Past and Present* 149 (1995): 170–97. See also Peter H. Hansen, 'Debate: Tenzing's Two Wrist-Watches: The Conquest of Everest and Late Imperial Culture, 1921–1953, Comment,' *Past and Present* 157 (1997): 159–78.

9 Paul Gilroy, *The Black Atlantic: Modernity and the Double Consciousness* (London: Verso, 1993), p. 11.

10 T. J. Jackson Lears, *No Place of Grace: Anti-modernism and the Transformation of American Culture, 1880–1920* (New York: Pantheon, 1981). See also Frank Trentmann, 'Civilization and its Discontents: English Neo-Romanticism and the Transformation of Anti-Modernism in Twentieth-Century Western Culture', *Journal of Contemporary History* 29 (1994): 583–625.

11 Kwame Anthony Appiah, *In My Father's House: Africa in the Philosophy of Culture* (Oxford: Oxford University Press, 1992), pp. 144–5.

12 Compare Judith Butler's account of the performativity of gender: Judith Butler, *Gender Trouble: Feminism and the Subversion of Identity* (New York: Routledge, 1990), p. 141.

13 Leslie Stephen, *The Playground of Europe* (London: Longman, 1871), p. 1.

14 Stephen, *Playground*, pp. 17–20.

15 Peter H. Hansen, 'Albert Smith, the Alpine Club, and the Invention of Mountaineering in Mid-Victorian Britain', *Journal of British Studies* 34 (1995): 300–24.

16 C. G. Bruce, *Himalayan Wanderer* (London: Maclehose, 1934), p. 277.

17 Stephen, *Playground*, p. 66.

18 Stephen, *Playground*, p. 67.

19 C. T. Dent, 'Alpine Climbing – Past, Present, and Future', *Alpine Journal* 9 (1878): 65–72; and C. T. Dent, 'Amateur and Professional Guides of the Present Day', *Alpine Journal* 12 (1886): 289–300.

20 See Leslie Stephen, 'Sunset on Mont Blanc,' and 'The Alps in Winter,' in *Playground of Europe* (1894 and later editions).

21 Peter H. Hansen, 'Partners: Guides and Sherpas in the Alps and Himalayas, 1850s–1950s', in *Voyages and Visions: Towards a Cultural History of Travel*, ed. Jas Elsner and Joan-Pau Rubiés, (London: Reaktion, 1999), pp. 210–31.

22 See Walter Weston, 'Mountaineering and Mountain Superstitions in the Japanese Alps', *Alpine Journal* 17 (1894–5): 493–510, and Walter Weston, *Mountaineering and Exploration in the Japanese Alps* (London: Murray, 1896).

23 Walter Weston, *Playground of the Far East* (London: Murray, 1918).

24 Weston, *Playground*, p. 120. Weston, 'My Swiss and Japanese Mountaineering,' *Sangaku* 5 (1910): 13.

25 Weston, *Playground*, p. 123.

26 Weston, *Playground*, p. 114.

27 Weston, *Sangaku* (1910): 15–16; Weston, *Playground*, p. 64.

28 See C. D. Cunningham and W. de W. Abney, *Pioneers of the Alps* (London: Low, Marston, 1887).

29 Michael G. Mullhall, *Mullhall's Dictionary of Statistics* (London: Routledge, 1884), p. 453. Of these 350,000 were German, 227,500 were British ('English, &c.'), 210,000 were Americans, and 160,000 were Russian.

30 James Bryce to Mrs S. Whitman, 22 Sept. 1886; MS Bryce, Bodleian Library, Oxford.

31 Dorothy Pilley Richards, 'Old Times in Familiar Places', *Ladies Alpine Club Yearbook* (1957): 18–19.

32 Peter Mandler, 'Against "Englishness": English Culture and the Limits to Rural Nostalgia, 1850–1940', in *Transactions of the Royal Historical Society*, 6th ser., 7 (1997): 155–75.

33 See William H. Rollins, *A Greener Vision of Home: Cultural Politics and Environmental Reform in the German Heimatschutz Movement, 1904–1918* (Ann Arbor, MI: University of Michigan Press, 1997), and Diana Le Dinh, 'Le Heimatschutz, une ligue pour la beauté: esthétique et conscience culturelle au début du siècle en Suisse', *Histoire et société contemporaines* 12 (1992): 1–152.

34 See reports on the meetings of the English Branch in *Alpine Journal* 23 (1907): 630–2; *Alpine Journal* 24 (1909): 451–3, and in the *Times* and *Morning Post* during 1905–1911.

35 See Revd Henry S. Lunn, *The Grindelwald Conference, 1894* (London: Lunn, 1894).

36 Sir Henry Lunn, *Nearing Harbour* (London: Nicholson and Watson, 1934), p. 68.

37 Public Schools Alpine Sports Club, *Yearbook* (1910): 5.

38 Joanna Bourke, *Dismembering the Male: Men's Bodies, Britain and the Great War* (London: Reaktion, 1996).

39 See Alison Light, *Forever England: Femininity, Literature and Conservatism Between the Wars* (London: Routledge, 1991).

40 See Harvey Taylor, *A Claim on the Countryside: A History of the British Outdoor Movement* (Keele: Keele University Press, 1997); see also Chris Waters, *British Socialists and the Politics of Popular Culture, 1880–1914* (Stanford, CA: Stanford University Press, 1990).

41 David Matless, *Landscape and Englishness* (London: Reaktion, 1998), and David Matless, '"The Art of Right Living:" Landscape and Citizenship, 1918–39', in *Mapping the Subject*, ed. Steve Pile and Nigel Thrift (London: Routledge, 1995), pp. 93–122.

42 See the comments in Association of British Members of the Swiss Alpine Club, *Annual Report* (1953): 3.

43 See Rainer Amstädter, *Der Alpinismus* (Vienna: WUV-Universitatsverlag, 1996).

44 See Matless, *Landscape and Englishness*, pp. 58–61, 94–5, for the ambivalent British admiration for German motorways, national fitness, and so on in the 1930s.

45 C. F. Meade, 'The Perversion of Mountaineering', *Quarterly Review* 267 (1936): 24–5. For related contemporary discussions, see R. L. G. Irving, *The Romance of Mountaineering* (London: Dent, 1935).

46 See Dane Kennedy, *The Magic Mountains: Hill Stations and the British Raj* (Berkeley, CA: University of California Press, 1996); Matthew H. Edney, *Mapping an Empire: The Geographical Construction of British India* (Chicago: University of Chicago Press, 1997); and Peter H. Hansen, 'Vertical Boundaries, National Identities: British Mountaineering on the Frontiers of Europe and the Empire, 1868–1914', *Journal of Imperial and Commonwealth History* 24 (1996): 48–71.

47 Hansen, 'Dancing Lamas of Everest'. See also Patrick French, *Younghusband* (London: Harper Collins, 1994).

48 Francis Younghusband, *Epic of Everest* (London: Longman, 1926), p. 311, and Francis Younghusband, *Everest: The Challenge* (New York: Nelson, 1936).

49 David Matless, 'Nature, the Modern and the Mystic: Tales From Early Twentieth Century Geography', *Transactions of the Institute of British Geographers*, n.s., 16 (1991): 272–86.

50 *Kamet Conquered* (1932), National Film and Television Archive, London.

51 See the film *Kamet Conquered* and F. S. Smythe, *Kamet Conquered* (London: Gollancz, 1932), pp. 96, 205.

52 *Wings over Everest* (1934), National Film and Television Archive, London. See also James Douglas-Hamilton, *Roof of the World: Man's First Flight over Everest* (Edinburgh: Mainstream, 1983).

53 W. H. Auden and Christopher Isherwood, *The Ascent of F 6* (London: Faber, 1937).

54 For this period, see Peter H. Hansen, 'Confetti of Empire: The Conquest of Everest in Nepal, India, Britain, and New Zealand', *Comparative Studies in Society and History* (forthcoming), and Becky Conekin, Frank Mort, and Chris Waters (eds), *Moments of Modernity: Reconstructing Britain, 1945–1964* (London: Rivers Oram, 1999).

55 *Eastern Evening News* (Norwich) 30 Nov. 1933, L/P&S/12/4242, Oriental and India Office Collections, British Library, London (OIOC).

56 See Gordon Stewart, 'Debate: Tenzing's Two Wrist Watches: The Conquest of Everest and Late Imperial Culture in Britain, 1921–1953: Reply', *Past and Present* 157 (1997): 189.

57 See the India Office Minutes in L/P&S/12/4242, OIOC.

58 See Dipesh Chakrabarty, 'Minority Histories, Subaltern Pasts', *Postcolonial Studies* 1 (1998): 15–30.

59 *Alpine Journal* 17 (1894–5): 510.

−10−

Modernity and Trusteeship: Tensions of Empire in Britain Between the Wars
Susan Pedersen

Is imperialism modern? At the most basic level, of course it is, for − Schumpeter notwithstanding − Europe's nation states clung to their colonial possessions well into our own century, liberal and socialist politicians showing themselves quite as alive as any 'atavistic elite' to the ideal as well as the material rewards of empire. But if we ask a narrower and somewhat different question − the question of imperialism's relation to that cast of mind that, around the turn of the century, began to think of itself as 'modern' − the problem becomes more complicated. If the 'revolt against rationalism' and the Great War wrought a shift in elite sensibilities away from engagement to detachment and from moral seriousness to scepticism, would the 'civilizing' framework through which the Victorians viewed their empire not also have come into question? Could modernism have caused problems for imperialism, in other words, less because a younger generation would have found imperial ideals reprehensible than because they found them ridiculous?

This chapter explores this question by examining perceptions of British imperialism within two distinct but overlapping intellectual worlds − the literary world of the avant-garde novelist on the one hand, and the political world of liberal and reform-minded elites on the other. I begin the first investigation by looking at the works of two self-consciously modernist writers, Evelyn Waugh and Winifred Holtby. Both Waugh and Holtby travelled in Africa in the 1920s or 1930s; inspired by the spectacle of Haile Sellassie's coronation in the autumn of 1930, both published novels two years later exploring Europe's changing relationship to Africa. And while the perspectives from which the two wrote could not have been more different − Waugh was a Catholic conservative, Holtby a left-leaning feminist − both writers struck a self-consciously modern note, casting their novels as comedies and skewering the mindset, dear to nineteenth-century moralists, that would see Europe's intervention in Africa as a form of international benevolence − as a White Man's Burden, a civilizing mission, *noblesse oblige*. That these 'comedies' would strike us today as embarrassing at best and racist at worst, and that even many contemporaries found them shocking or offensive, should not blind us to their importance, for they made not only imperialism but also the humanitarian sensibility that had been its quarrelsome travelling companion seem absurd.

But did these novels capture some wider shift in mood? Was their scepticism about the moral purposes of empire ever more than a minority view? If we look at the discourse of empire retailed in Parliament and the press by Britain's liberal establishment in the interwar years, we might at first glance conclude that it was not. Certainly, new voices – among them Labour, organized women, and enthusiasts for League internationalism – did seek to influence colonial policy during these years, but they too framed Britain's objectives overwhelmingly in humanitarian and moral terms. Indeed, in their determination to use imperial administration to 'uplift' native populations, such groups if anything strengthened the dominion of humanitarian rhetoric in colonial debates, forcing officials to rely more openly on a rhetoric of 'trusteeship' when seeking to justify Britain's imperial role.

Yet the language of trusteeship brought its own problems, for it promised the kind of wholesale transformation of indigenous culture that was usually anathema to the 'men on the ground'. To the distress of London-based reformers and critics, colonial officials and governors (and not native elites) often proved most protective of 'primitive' practices – in time leading such humanitarians to wonder whether political devolution and economic modernization might be the precondition, rather than the reward, for any lasting change in cultural forms. By the eve of the Second World War, albeit partially and tentatively, some eminent post-Victorians had moved some distance towards Winifred Holtby's critical and quintessentially modern stance.

I

Abyssinia in 1930 was Christian (albeit Coptic) and independent (albeit threatened): it was, therefore, an anomaly in the parcelized, colonized Africa of the interwar years, and an implicit challenge to any tidy dichotomy between 'civilization' and 'barbarism'. Western interest in the country was piqued by the coronation of Ras Tafari (as Haile Sellassie) that autumn – an event that drew a crowd of international dignitaries and journalists (the hastily accredited Waugh among them) to Addis Ababa. Waugh's dispatches from Addis were published in *The Times* and the *Daily Express*, and may well have been read by Winifred Holtby, who was only thirty-two in 1930 but had already published five novels, and who would soon be diagnosed with the kidney ailment that would kill her five years later. Waugh then travelled on to Kenya, Uganda, Zanzibar and Aden, a journey he detailed in his travelogue, *Remote People*, published in November 1931; back in England, he began work on a novel based on his Ethiopian experiences. Holtby, in a rented cottage near Oxford where she was under orders to rest, had also started a novel inspired by Abyssinia. Waugh's *Black Mischief* was published in October of 1932; Holtby's *Mandoa, Mandoa!* three months later.[1]

In their basic outlines, the two novels are remarkably similar. Both take place in an imaginary African land: in Waugh's case, the island of 'Azania'; in Holtby's the remote, mountain-bound 'Mandoa'. Both chronicle the efforts of the native ruler – in Waugh's case, the Oxford-educated Emperor Seth, in Holtby's the Lord High Chamberlain Talal – to modernize his country. In both, the ruler enters into collaboration with a British man-of-action: in Waugh's case, the cheerfully amoral Basil Seal, who has travelled to Azania on a lark; in Holtby's the embittered ex-war-hero Bill Durrant, sent to Mandoa by 'Prince's Tours' to survey the country's tourism possibilities. In both novels, Western interest is spurred by a particular event (Seth's coronation in Waugh's novel; the marriage of the Mandoan princess in Holtby's); in both, that interest turns sour as internal conflict over Westernization develops and the underlying 'barbarism' of the native people is revealed. Both novels end with civil war, the prospect of League of Nations intervention, and the defeat of the modernizing project.

And both novels, remarkably, cast this depressing plot as a comedy. Both are meant to be funny, drawing their humour from what Waugh thought of as incongruity – from the promiscuous presence of Western trappings in an African setting. Both novels thus imagine their African lands not as the primitive 'darkness' of the nineteenth-century imagination, but rather as vital, polyglot worlds. Waugh's Azania is peopled by a colourful assortment of adventurers and diplomats of all nationalities, happily pursuing their stereotypical pastimes (the French intriguing, the English playing parlour games) amid the novel's mayhem and war. Likewise Holtby's imaginary Mandoa, although only 'discovered' as the novel opens, already bears the traces of earlier inadvertent Western visitations – the first by an evangelical missionary around the turn of the century, who taught the noble class Christianity and justified the subordination of women with references to Tennyson, the second by a Hollywood film crew in 1931, whose stock of 'talkies' left the Mandoans speaking a kind of Hollywood argot and bearing names like Byron Wilberforce Gish. Strained as such humour might seem today, in their determination to avoid the tones of earlier fictions of empire – whether bombastic or earnestly pious – both authors underscore their ironic distance from the framework of the 'civilizing mission'.

But while both authors reject this framework, they ultimately do so in very different ways, allowing us to read these novels as, perhaps, two alternative blueprints for British policy towards Africa in a new age. For while the modernizing project fails in both novels, it does so in Holtby's novel not because African culture is simply helplessly primitive (as Waugh eventually decided), but rather because Western visitors insist upon and invent such primitivism. By revealing its constructed character, *Mandoa, Mandoa!* thus succeeds in blurring any clear hierarchy between African and European values, between 'civilization' and 'barbarism', opening the way for a more purely material definition of 'progress'.

Black Mischief, by contrast, ultimately reinscribes that hierarchical framework – a position that Waugh, in his journalism and travel writings, made explicit. Let me flesh out these points by briefly comparing how the novels treat the Western aspirations of their imagined African rulers and explain those projects' defeat.

And on these points, the two are very different. Waugh's Emperor Seth, certainly, is committed to progress. 'Defeat is impossible', he tells his servant: 'This is not a war of Seth against Seyid but of Progress against Barbarism. And Progress must prevail. I have seen the great tattoo of Aldershot, the Paris Exhibition, the Oxford Union. I have read modern books – Shaw, Arlen, Priestley.'[2] Determined to be modern, he orders boots his troops won't wear and tanks that can't run in the climate; 'tipsy with words', he declares unmodern practices – from infant mortality to native dialects – abolished.[3] Yet his infatuation with the West is always ridiculous, for Seth cannot distinguish between profound and trivial Western products, between form and content, between the banknotes he simply prints when he runs out of cash and a functioning financial system. And this is the case because, in Waugh's view, civilization is not something that can be exported abroad: it is, as Waugh wrote explaining his conversion to Rome, not 'talking cinemas and tinned food, nor even surgery and hygienic houses, but the whole moral and artistic organization of Europe'.[4] Inevitably and for ever outside that system, Seth remains fundamentally a 'young darky', who for all his 'acquired loneliness of civilisation' still lies awake at night, his eyes 'wild with the inherited terror of the jungle'.[5] Small wonder, then, that Seth's fantasies fall victim to African realities – a 'reality' that is, in Waugh's vivid imagination, quite as horrifying as anything Joseph Conrad came up with.

But if Waugh ridicules Seth's Westernizing ambitions and chronicles their inevitable defeat, Holtby turns this plot on its head. Her Lord High Chamberlain also hopes to bring the benefits of the West to his land. Unlike Seth, however, Talal sees these benefits in entirely material terms – as 'streets and baths and gramophones and cocktails'.[6] And this makes sense to Holtby, who uses a series of conversations between Talal and Bill Durrant to relativize Western and African morals and thus to demolish the favourite justification for empire, the claim that Western contact will bring Africans to a higher *moral* 'stage of civilization'. Bill, interrogated about Western customs by Talal, ultimately finds little to choose between London and Mandoa: he cannot explain why prostitution is tolerated in the West while polygamy is not, or reconcile the West's humanitarian attack on slavery with labour taxes in Kenya or his own memories of the thin men in the dole queues in Britain. Crowd festivities in Mandoa remind Bill of a cup tie at Wembley, Mandoan witch doctors of the advertisers of patent medicines. It thus makes sense to Bill that Talal would want to bring the material benefits of the West to Mandoa but abjure its morality, and when Bill is accused of moral weakness he retorts that Mandoans will not listen to lectures from the *Boy Scout Handbook*.

'As a matter of fact,' he says, 'they're extremely proud of their local customs and morale and so on. They think that we're no end barbarians with our unemployment and trade cycles and what not.'[7] What Talal is not proud of is Mandoa's poverty, and he has little patience either with Western humanitarians' propensity to read economic deprivation in moral terms or anthropologists' patronizing belief that indigenous culture should be kept unspoiled. To be primitive, Talal tells these people, in the novel's most compelling speech, 'means to sleep in dirty huts, to ride on donkeys, to do the same things day after day. It means to live in a very little world where nothing changes, to suffer from droughts and diseases and tapeworm and lice. . . . Would you *like* to have no books, no photographs, no motor cars?'[8] The British can best contribute to Mandoa's 'civilization' with machines and medicines and tools, and it is this goal of material development that Bill and Talal take as their task.

And while they too come to grief, it is not for the reasons for which Seth fails. Canny pragmatist that he is, Talal understands what tourism can offer his country and cooks up a scheme with Bill Durrant to exploit the upcoming marriage of the Mandoan Royal Princess as a tourist attraction. Yet just as their plans get under way, humanitarian crusaders raise the disturbing charge that, in promoting Mandoan tourism, Prince's Tours may be encouraging slavery. The Mandoan nobility, it seems, lives essentially on the proceeds of the slave trade, which the League of Nations and an 'International Humanitarian Association' (a thinly-disguised Anti-Slavery Society) are determined to eradicate. An Investigatory Commission is thus quickly dispatched to Mandoa to determine how the Western powers should act. Worse, although the Mandoan wedding does bring a host of artists, diplomats, anthropologists and decadent aesthetes to Mandoa, Talal discovers to his horror that what they want, in exchange for their cash, is not Western comfort but rather an 'authentic' primitivism, a spectacle of barbarity. Talal, in despair, gives them their desire: a genuine atrocity, the revelation that the Investigatory Commission has been captured. Instantly, the charm of Mandoa is restored and the tourists stay to organize search parties; but the capitulation to a model of cultural contact in which superior Europeans come to enjoy, condemn and reform the primitive erodes the authority of both Bill and Talal, the first seeing himself bypassed as British administrators swing into action, the latter ousted by a coup aimed at freeing Mandoa from these contaminating Westerners.

Talal's modernizing programme thus fails not because Africans cannot be 'modern', but rather because the West requires that they be primitive: through the West's ghoulish fascination, 'barbarity' is brought into being as an alien force to be overcome. In *Black Mischief*, by contrast, Seth is destroyed because the sea of primitivism surrounding his fragile enclave of progress finally sweeps over him – an ending in which Seth loses his life and the misnamed Prudence, the silly British Minister's silly daughter, is served up in a cannibal feast. Waugh's cavalier treatment of Prudence caused the Catholic *Tablet* to censure the book, but Waugh, in a response addressed to the Cardinal Archbishop of Westminster, explained this incident as merely the final working out of what was the central theme of the book, 'the conflict of civilisation, with all its attendant and deplorable ills, and barbarism'. He had hoped, he said, 'to keep the darker aspects of barbarism continually and unobtrusively present, a black and mischievous background against which the civilized and semi-civilized characters performed their parts', in order to prepare his readers for 'the sudden tragedy when barbarism at last emerges from the shadows and usurps the stage.'[9] And indeed, an attentive reader should have picked up Waugh's shift in tone, for our last glimpse of Prudence, hitherto a figure of fun, is almost elegiac: 'a swift, gay figure under her red beret . . . an English girl returning to claim her natural inheritance'.[10] Knowing the fate he had planned out for her, Waugh's satirical tone deserted him and Prudence became, briefly, that stock figure of imperial fantasy, the innocent English rose ripe for violation. Likewise, her end becomes the signal for Azania's European take-over, under the humanitarian auspices of the League of Nations. Holtby, certainly, understood this move. As one of the gutter journalists of *Mandoa, Mandoa!* put it: 'What our empire builders would have done without the fear of rape, I hardly know.'[11]

Waugh's decision to end his novel by evoking an essential African barbarism is particularly striking in light of the fact that his Abyssinian diaries show that he too was well aware of the ways in which 'barbarism' was in the eye of the Western beholder. In Addis, he was shocked that his journalistic colleagues filed their reports on the coronation before it happened and described palace interiors of marble and ivory rather than the – to him, infinitely more amusing – portraits of Ramsay MacDonald and Raymond Poincaré that actually adorned its walls.[12] Yet Waugh himself cheerfully partook in this process of deception. On 3 November, for example, his diary records that he too wrote his story of a 'barbarous feast' *before* attending that feast:

> Cashed £25 cheques at bank, visited picture-dealer who had promised collect pictures for me. He had done nothing about it. Returned hotel, drank with airmen. Met Polish attaché whose driver had brought him to wrong address. Lunched. Wrote description barbarous *gebbur* [feast]. Went out to see what I could barbarous *gebbur*. 3:30 no signs barbarity.[13]

I want to stress the gap between Waugh's own experience in Africa and his imaginative rendering of that experience, between his sophisticated awareness of the role played by Europeans in constructing the concept of 'barbarism' and his own reliance on that concept, less to make the boringly obvious point that Waugh was a racist than to highlight the investment that even those (like Waugh) who had already rejected the 'Victorian frame of mind' still had in a conceptual opposition between civilization and barbarism. Faced with what he took to be the crumbling of core Western values in a chaotic, materialist world, Waugh had turned to Roman Catholicism; even in Ethiopia he found the Cathedral to be, as he put it in his diary, 'island sanity in raving town'.[14] In the light of that conversion, many critics have defended *Black Mischief* from charges of racism, arguing that Waugh's main concerns were spiritual, and that he also revealed the barbarism of Basil Seal and of European culture.[15] Yet the final outcome of the novel, and especially the fact that Prudence's horrible end finally leads Basil to 'turn serious', confounds this interpretation, suggesting instead that Waugh fell back on some of the most hackneyed images of primitivism – jungle travels, cannibal feasts – in order to restore his belief in the superiority even of a spiritually enervated West. Waugh thus needs the empire precisely for the reasons that Seamus Deane suggests imperialism was useful in an age of High Modernism: because it was 'awesomely effective in affirming the propriety and order of the West in contrast to the chaos and disorder of all that is non-Western'.[16]

But if Waugh's imperialism rested on his conviction that the West and the non-West were always 'incongruous', it was imperialism of a very different kind, one stripped of missionary impulses or universalist ideals. Travelling around East Africa after covering the coronation, Waugh found he had no admiration for the 'caste of just, soap-loving young men with Public School blazers' who were turning Zanzibar into a hygienic modern colony; he much deplored the fact that Britain's high-minded suppression of the slave trade was destroying its traditional Arab aristocracy ('a hospitable and generous race and . . . "gentlemen" in what seems to me the only definable sense, that they set a high value on leisure') and making way for a new elite of East African Indians ('grubby parasites without roots or piety').[17] Genuine reactionary as he was, he sympathized instead with the Kenya settlers, whom he saw as 'normal, respectable Englishmen' pursuing 'a habit of life traditional to them, which England has ceased to accommodate – the traditional life of the English squirearchy . . .'. Perhaps they were 'Quixotic in their attempt to recreate Barsetshire on the equator, but one cannot represent them as pirates and land grabbers.'[18]

True, Waugh admitted, the settlers were 'rabid' about white superiority, but this was 'just a lack of reasoning – I will not call it a failing – to which our race is prone'. Moreover, he added tellingly, 'they may be right': 'It is just worth considering the possibility that there may be something valuable behind the indefensible and inexplicable assumption of superiority by the Anglo-Saxon race.'[19] Three years later, on the centenary of the abolition of slavery, Waugh made his racist views clearer, asking whether Wilberforce had in fact been 'right to free the slaves'. The abolitionist crusade, he wrote, 'depended on all those fallacies that are being abandoned today: the idea of a perfectible evolutionary man, of a responsible democratic voter, of the beneficial effect of mechanization, and, above all, on sentimental belief in the basic sweetness of human nature'. But the descendants of the slaves had proved themselves 'a thriftless and dissolute lot'; perhaps they would have been better off left in slavery. Having repudiated the moralizing imperialism of Wilberforce and the public school boys, then, Waugh retreated to a straightforwardly racist justification for British rule.

But if Waugh's repudiation of the 'civilizing mission' led him towards racism and nostalgia, Holtby, again, moved in a different direction. Certainly, Holtby was no more utopian about the 'civilizing mission', insisting in *Mandoa, Mandoa!* that the three 'engines' driving European intervention – 'policy, profit and reform' – were always helplessly entangled. Yet these three engines were also unstoppable: their impact 'might be good; it might be evil; but in neither case was it negligible'.[20] Given this, she argued, neither ignorance about nor indifference to empire was possible. As she wrote in *The Nation and Athenaeum*, although many might prefer not to think about their imperial responsibilities, 'the member for Tooting Bec [is] responsible to his constituents for a vote affecting the future of the Kikuyu and Masai . . . However much we like to keep ourselves to ourselves, we find that we are willy-nilly our brothers' keepers.'[21] And therefore, as Jean Stanbury, one of Holtby's more admirable characters, put it, one had to act – to 'work for the world we know as best we can', accepting that 'our motives are never . . . quite pure'.[22]

Holtby thus ended *Mandoa, Mandoa!* on a note of compromise. She made a pragmatic peace with humanitarianism, leaving Jean Stanbury slogging away against the evils of slavery under the auspices of the International Humanitarian Association. Yet she also made clear that her own sympathies lay elsewhere – with Bill Durrant, who remains in Mandoa to keep his runway open for the trade he is sure will come, and with Talal, who – as so many early African nationalists did – plans to go to Europe to learn, plot, and raise the money to try again. Moreover, throughout the late 1920s and early 1930s Holtby herself avoided the humanitarian campaigns against child marriage or female slavery that absorbed so many reform-minded women, instead working to oppose white South African efforts to promote racial segregation as a model for colonial development and assisting in the development of African self-governing institutions, especially trade unions. She recruited and helped to fund a British labour organizer in South Africa and subsidized the work of Clements Kadalie, the General Secretary of the Industrial and Commercial Workers' Union and the man who was the model for the Mandoan Lord High Chamberlain, Talal. This work was not without its problems: South African black trade unionism suffered from the same instability that British trade unionism had in its early stages, and Kadalie in particular proved a difficult ally, being a better publicist than businessman, prone to dramatic gestures and unreliable with accounts. Yet Holtby never saw these as more than temporary setbacks, and devoted much time and a substantial slice of her literary earnings to these African efforts until her death.[23]

II

Black Mischief and *Mandoa, Mandoa!* can be read, I have suggested, as two very different but similarly jaundiced comments on liberal and humanitarian ideals of empire, suggesting that – within such literary circles at least – these ideals were by no means hegemonic. But the problem with literary sources for historians is always one of representativeness and reach. If we move outside the avant-garde and modernist circles inhabited by Holtby and Waugh, how common was such disaffection with the central framework within which Britons had learned to understand their empire? Was humanitarianism politically on the defensive? And how, if at all, did the official classes respond?

This is a large question, and any comprehensive answer is, of course, far beyond the scope of a brief essay of this kind. Nevertheless, a few points are in order. What recent research as well as my own forays into the archives suggests is, first, that humanitarian rhetoric if anything strengthened its hold during the interwar years, as a widening circle of would-be imperial reformers pressed officials to undertake ever more ambitious assaults on 'primitive' practices and to elaborate ever more idealized definitions of 'trusteeship'. Yet as they did so, and particularly as they found themselves combating governors and administrators wedded – like Waugh – to the presumption of ineluctable cultural difference, some at least began to show signs of discomfort. By the late 1930s, some humanitarians were beginning to question not their *end* of cultural transformation but rather whether empire could ever be an effective *means* towards that goal. Like Holtby, albeit for somewhat different reasons, they began to contemplate some more thoroughgoing delegation of political and economic power.

'Trusteeship' was not yet the dominant framework for African colonial administration in the immediate postwar period, the official doctrine being, rather, one of reciprocity. As Lord Lugard admitted in his classic formulation, Europe had not become involved in Africa 'from motives of pure philanthropy'; he did insist, however, 'that Europe is in Africa for the mutual benefit of her own industrial classes, and of the native races in their progress to a higher plane', and that benefit could indeed 'be made reciprocal'.[24] Once the League of Nations mandate system was in place, however, and faced with pressure from a small but well-connected humanitarian lobby, rhetorical reliance on the second part of this 'dual mandate' became stronger. The doctrine of 'native paramountcy' – as the famous Devonshire Declaration put it – was useful to officials eager both to restrain the rapacity of those Kenyan settlers so beloved by Waugh and to justify the empire to domestic critics and less well-endowed foreign states. Beyond a commitment to maintain good order and to suppress slavery, however, the content of trusteeship was unclear. African colonial governors were, after all, hampered by minuscule budgets, the policy of making all colonies pay their own way and the simple lack of prestige associated with African – as opposed to Indian – administration.[25] There were also fundamental disagreements among governors over questions of how their territories should be run, Edward Grigg's supine acquiescence to settler interests in Kenya, for example, contrasting sharply with Tanganyika's Donald Cameron's belief (*à la* Holtby) that the first task of colonial administration must be to improve the African population's material well-being.[26]

Yet colonial officials were increasingly forced to refine the definition of trusteeship, less because of overt criticism than because the changed political landscape of the interwar years gave new groups – Labour, feminists, internationalists, and, in time, even organizations representing Britain's overseas subjects and coloured citizens – a chance to say what *they* thought trusteeship might involve. Little of what the first three groups said could be construed as 'anticolonialism', a movement that Stephen Howe is surely right to see as (at least in relation to Africa) a largely postwar phenomenon;[27] it nevertheless did disrupt imperial business as usual. Thus, while most paternalists associated with the Anti-Slavery Society continued to see the suppression of slave-trading as their primary goal, some also joined those colonial critics associated with the Fabian Colonial Bureau and the Labour Party's Advisory Committee on Imperial Questions to articulate a much more ambitious (and costly) agenda.[28] Britain's colonial policy, one Labour parliamentary motion insisted in 1929, must promote economic development for the benefit of the population as a whole (and not just settler communities) and foster self-governing institutions across racial lines.[29] Modest as such aims might sound, they were some distance from the ideals of indirect rule, and suggested that trusteeship might be a worryingly expensive proposition.

Ambitious proposals emerged in these years from two other directions as well – from newly-enfranchised women and from League of Nations officials headquartered in Geneva. Victorian and Edwardian feminists, as Antoinette Burton has shown, often argued for the vote in order to protect and reform colonized women;[30] once enfranchised, activist women exhibited a good deal of interest in colonial affairs. Galvanized especially by the publication in 1927 of *Mother India*, the American Katherine Mayo's prurient and tendentious account of Indian marriage practices, British women's organizations kept a sharp eye out for 'native practices' in need of reform. An *ad hoc* women's lobby led by Clara Haslewood campaigned to abolish the system of indentured servitude of girl children in Hong Kong and Malaya;[31] a cross-party parliamentary 'Committee for the protection of coloured women in the Crown Colonies' set up by Eleanor Rathbone and the Duchess of Atholl urged colonial governors to suppress clitoridectomy in Kenya and bride price throughout Africa;[32] a small 'Council for the Representation of Women in the League of Nations' pressed the Colonial and Foreign Offices to appoint a woman adviser responsible for the status of women in the empire;[33] and a new British Commonwealth League established 'to secure equality of liberties, status and opportunities between men and women in the British Commonwealth of Nations' met to discuss issues affecting women and, tentatively, to form alliances.[34]

As a rule, these women campaigners were anything but critics of empire; most took the superiority of British cultural ideals almost for granted. In doing so, however, they further expanded the definition of trusteeship, arguing that British colonial administration should not only guarantee public order and impartial justice but also impart that superior culture – and especially British marital and domestic ideals – to peoples under its rule. Feminist campaigners thus often envisaged a far *more* interventionist (if 'improving') style of colonial rule – a vision that local and metropolitan officials, concerned about budgets and the prospect of local resentment, viewed with unease. The India Office found itself deeply embarrassed by the virulent anti-Hindu and pro-British sentiment of *Mother India*, and banned one of Mayo's later works;[35] likewise, the Government of Hong Kong found its close relations with local Chinese businessmen compromised by a metropolitan campaign bent on portraying those allies as sexual predators and slavers. Colonial officials and the officers of the Anti-Slavery Society alike were appalled by the intrepid feminist Nina Boyle's efforts to have bride price declared a form of slavery,[36] and the former at least thought the prospect of a woman adviser within the Colonial Office itself simply 'too awful to contemplate'.[37] Yet feminists, once in parliament, could not simply be ignored. On more than one occasion the Colonial Office was forced to receive deputations from women's organizations or to gather information on the status of native women from its African governors.[38]

For the most part, however, feminist agitation could be kept within careful bounds, for women activists had little political power and were often fairly ignorant about the issues they addressed. Dependent on the Colonial Office for information, they were easily out-argued by the men on the ground or appeased by vague promises. More feared and less easily managed was a second development, the steady encroachment of the League of Nations on colonial affairs. The fact that Britain now administered some of its territories as League mandates legitimated international oversight of colonial issues. But in fact the Colonial Office had always been apprehensive about – if not downright hostile to – the League, worrying that it would hamper operations with high-minded but unworkable principles and regulations. The Office disliked the proposal in 1930 to create a Permanent Slavery Commission at Geneva, for example – although they found themselves unable to oppose a plan backed by the Foreign Office as 'Lord Cecil's special baby'[39] – and throughout the 1930s struggled to restrain the enthusiasm of Sir George Maxwell, Britain's own meddlesome appointee to that body.[40] Worst of all, from the Colonial Office's point of view, was the fact that humanitarian pressure groups and League officials and advisers began to work in concert. With voluntary organizations given the right to appoint assessors to the League's advisory committees on child welfare and on the traffic in women, for example, activist women found themselves able to request information and initiate investigations. Officials responded courteously in public, but privately deplored what they saw as disloyal efforts by British nationals to subject their country's internal business to outside scrutiny. Although convinced that Britain's colonial administration could serve as a model for other states, they balked at the prospect of constant international surveillance.

By the mid-1930s, then, British colonial officials found themselves in a new situation. Having always insisted on the moral character of British rule, they were put on the defensive by new groups that wanted to expand the scope (and price) of those beneficent activities and to hold colonial governments more strictly to account. A perusal of Colonial Office records shows that officials often viewed these pressures with trepidation. Colonial administrations, they feared, could scarcely take on new responsibilities for health, education, and welfare without violating the ideals of financial self-support and indirect rule; nor could they meddle with gender relations or cultural practices (at least explicitly, since in fact they did so all the time) without risking local stability. Yet the language of moral uplift and humanitarian progress proved difficult to resist, and some Colonial Secretaries – Philip Cunliffe Lister, Malcolm MacDonald – appropriated it with enthusiasm. In 1932, when Cunliffe Lister addressed the African Society about the accomplishments of British rule, he did so explicitly in a language of trusteeship and without any reference to that benefit to Britain that Lugard had so openly admitted. Pointing especially to the expansion of medical and educational services, Cunliffe Lister argued that British rule had led to 'a great advance in the moral and material welfare of the people of Africa for whom . . . we are trustees'.[41]

This was the kind of language that liberal and humanitarian elites liked to hear, and certainly it did much to limit the kind of sardonic questioning of imperial ideals that Waugh and Holtby expressed. But if the ideology of trusteeship was developed as much to manage domestic opinion as to reshape administrative practice, this effort was not without its own contradictions and tensions. For whatever they said, officials in London (not to mention in Nairobi or Hong Kong) could never see empire primarily as an exercise in disinterested benevolence, and when rhetoric and reality came into conflict, older concerns about imperial defence or trade could well prevail. And as they did so, they drove some humanitarians at least to question the core assumption of 'trusteeship' – the claim that the empire could serve as a tool of moral reformation.

We can grasp the character of this process of disillusionment and re-evaluation by looking briefly at the ideas and politics of Eleanor Rathbone, a woman who in many ways epitomized the humanitarian conscience of the interwar years. After a long career in the suffrage movement and in progressive politics in Liverpool, Rathbone entered Parliament as an Independent in 1929, where she made colonial issues one of her main concerns. Initially at least, her interventions fell along wellworn lines. Horrified (and possibly fascinated) by the lurid revelations of Katherine

Mayo's *Mother India*, she spearheaded British feminists' efforts to force colonial administrations to combat child marriage in India and bride price in Africa. Her own long involvement in the suffrage movement notwithstanding, she exhibited little interest in prospects for self-government, implying that moral and social reform – and especially improvements in the status of women – must *precede* any political transformation.[42] Indeed, in her concentration on social mores rather than political reform, Rathbone could have served as Holtby's model for those 'International Humanitarians' whose high-minded meddling destabilizes Mandoan politics and triggers League intervention.[43] With Holtby's warning before us, we might expect Rathbone's moral obsessions to have led her to justify – under the aegis of trusteeship – ever more intense forms of direct European rule.

Yet in Rathbone's case, Holtby's prediction proved false: involvement in 'imperial humanitarianism' led Rathbone to question, and ultimately to reject, those very assumptions of Western cultural superiority and disinterestedness upon which trusteeship was based. For having failed in her efforts to get the Government of India to enforce new legislation against child marriage, Rathbone concluded, as she told the Commons, that 'by far the most reactionary' views on women were held *not* by Indians but by the Government of India itself.[44] And if British claims to moral superiority were hollow and the cause of humanitarian progress would be safer in Indian hands, how could one oppose meaningful steps towards self-government? Within two years of her entry into the Commons, Rathbone's views on the Indian question had undergone a 180-degree turn. Having once argued that constitutional reform could be postponed until Indian culture had been 'uplifted' and reformed, she now argued that constitutional questions must be settled in order for the work of social reform to begin.[45] A closer involvement in imperial affairs, remarkably, thus returned Rathbone to those core democratic principles from which the rhetoric of trusteeship had decoyed her. 'There is only one safeguard for any one section of people who are differentiated from others, whether by race or creed or colour or sex,' she told the Commons in 1931, 'and that is the safeguard of their full and real participation in the working of self-governing institutions.'[46]

Of course, views about Indian devolution were not always readily extended to Africa, and Rathbone was only one individual voice – but her scepticism about Britain's fitness as a 'trustee' found some echoes across the liberal intelligentsia. Consider, for example, elite responses to the Italian attack on Abyssinia – a loyal member of the League of Nations – in 1935. In theory, Britain was obliged to come to Abyssinia's defence; in practice, Italy was given a virtually free hand. The Foreign Office initially sought to persuade Sellassie not to appeal to the League at all; when he did so, they colluded with the French to limit League action to the most trivial of sanctions, and urged Abyssinia to appease Mussolini with massive territorial concessions. This less-than-principled stance was driven very largely by Britain's desire to retain Italian friendship and prevent an Italo-German alliance; but it also reflected long-standing Foreign Office scepticism about Abyssinia's status as a stable and civilized state. Britain had, after all, opposed Abyssinia's entry into the League in 1923 in part because of its notorious reputation for slave-trading, and throughout the 1920s and early 1930s the Anti-Slavery Society and the Foreign Office continued to press Abyssinia for stronger efforts at suppression. Given this reputation, the Foreign Office expected little public outcry over Britain's pusillanimous response to the Italian action. As the British Consul in Addis Ababa warned Haile Sellassie in 1934, Britain's Parliament and public thought of Abyssinia 'chiefly as a country which raided our frontiers and indulged in slavery';[47] Sellassie should expect little help from these quarters.

But here, as we know, the government miscalculated. Britain's lack of leadership in Geneva – and, still more, its attempt to extract territorial concessions for Italy from the Abyssinians – caused a major political scandal, forcing the resignation of the new Foreign Secretary, Sir Samuel Hoare, and catalysing the first major Commons rebellion against the policy of appeasement. And while parliamentary critics may have been more concerned about the League's authority than about Abyssinia's sovereignty, they understood that the two went hand in hand. They thus saw Mussolini's promise to bring 'order and progress' to a state that was 'a blot on civilisation'[48] as the cynical ploy it was, and a few actually argued that Britain, as a progressive imperial power, had a special obligation to come to Abyssinia's defence. If Britain betrayed Abyssinia, Rathbone warned in the Commons at the height of the war, 'we shall have lost the respect of all the coloured peoples of the world' – and, 'after all, this Empire is the greatest Empire of coloured peoples in the world'.[49] Here we see the concept of trusteeship transformed into something very different, with the empire reimagined as a multiracial common-wealth pledged to defend the right to self-government and equal citizenship across racial lines.

This was Winifred Holtby's ideal as well, although – as *Mandoa, Mandoa!* makes clear – she did not expect many liberals or humanitarians to share it. They were, she thought, too easily seduced by the language of benevolent rule, too prone to invent a 'barbarism' that they could then 'civilize', and too unconscious of the ways in which their interventions could mask more virulent political or economic aims. But while Holtby accurately pinpointed the many ways in which these progressive elites were – by their very idealism – helping to accommodate imperialism to a democratic age, she underestimated just how awkward and sometimes destabilizing these new ideological formulations could prove. For while colonial secretaries might, under pressure, adopt the rhetoric of 'trusteeship', stressing their commitment to the development and 'uplift' of Britain's colonial territories or even – as Cunliffe Lister did in 1932 – condemning the existence of racial prejudice within Britain itself,[50] their promises came up against not only

Treasury parsimony and a Home Office determined to restrict non-white entry into Britain[51] but also the incomprehension and anger of the 'men on the ground'. Sir Arnold Hodson, Governor of Sierra Leone, for example, responded to Cunliffe Lister's gentle proddings toward racial tolerance with dismay, admitting that he viewed the prospect of equal social intercourse and intermarriage between Africans and Europeans with 'abhorrence'. Nor did Hodson agree that the empire would survive such a transformation. Britain was able to hold and rule Africa with a handful of Europeans, he quite typically argued, because of their 'superiority complex'; he himself treated Africans not 'equally' but like 'a benevolent despot', with 'firmness, kindness and tact'. 'Once we admit we are *all equal* what is going to happen?!' This question might still be avoidable today, he warned; but it would have to be faced in the future.[52]

And on this point Hodson was certainly right. The doctrine of trusteeship could hold things together for a time, providing a humanitarian justification for an intensification of rule, and shielding its adherents from that quintessentially modern understanding – beautifully captured by Holtby – of the inevitably interested and 'impure' nature of relations of power. But even in the 1930s, at the height of its ascendency, 'trusteeship' was vulnerable, albeit less to the ridicule of intellectuals like Waugh and Holtby than because its own promises raised expectations – whether of a power purged of self-interest or of a multicultural empire spanning the globe – that it could not possibly fulfil.

Notes

1 For a good account of Waugh's travels and writings, see Martin Stannard, *Evelyn Waugh: The Early Years, 1903–1939* (New York: W. W. Norton, 1986); information on Holtby's life is drawn primarily from Vera Brittain's biography of her friend, *Testament of Friendship: The Story of Winifred Holtby* (London: Macmillan and Co., 1940).

2 Evelyn Waugh, *Black Mischief* (1932; reprint, Boston: Little, Brown, 1977), p. 22.

3 Ibid., pp. 54, 194.

4 Evelyn Waugh, 'Converted to Rome', *Daily Express*, 20 October 1930, in *The Essays, Articles and Reviews of Evelyn Waugh*, ed. Donat Gallagher (Boston: Little, Brown, 1984), p. 104.

5 *Black Mischief*, pp. 54, 35.

6 Winifred Holtby, *Mandoa, Mandoa!: A Comedy of Irrelevance* (1933; reprint London: Virago, 1982), p. 24.

7 Ibid., p. 220.

8 Ibid., p. 277.

9 Evelyn Waugh, 'An Open Letter to His Eminence the Cardinal Archbishop of Westminster', May 1933, in *The Letters of Evelyn Waugh*, ed. Mark Amory (New Haven, CT and New York: Ticknor & Fields, 1980), p. 77.

10 *Black Mischief*, pp. 284–5.

11 *Mandoa, Mandoa!*, pp. 317–18.

12 Evelyn Waugh, *Remote People* (1931; London: Duckworth, 1934), p. 53.

13 Evelyn Waugh, *The Diaries of Evelyn Waugh*, ed. Michael Davie, (Boston: Little, Brown and Company, 1976), p. 332.

14 Ibid.

15 This is a point made by Martin Stannard, *Evelyn Waugh: The Early Years, 1903–1939*, pp. 238 -9; Robert R. Garnett, *From Grimes to Brideshead: The Early Novels of Evelyn Waugh* (Lewisburg, PA: Bucknell University Press, 1990), p. 94; Calvin W. Lane, *Evelyn Waugh* (Boston: Twayne Publishers, 1981), p. 67; Jeffrey Heath, *The Picturesque Prison: Evelyn Waugh and His Writing* (Kingston and Montreal: McGill-Queen's University Press, 1982), p. 95. By contrast, William Myers, rightly in my view, argues that while Waugh 'makes Europe look as foolish as Africa', he also insists that barbarism is never the better state. See William Myers, *Evelyn Waugh and the Problem of Evil* (London: Faber and Faber, 1991), pp. 33–6.

16 Seamus Deane, 'Imperialism/Nationalism', in Frank Lentricchia and Thomas McLaughlin (eds), *Critical Terms for Literary Study*, 2nd edn (Chicago: University of Chicago Press, 1995), p. 359.

17 *Remote People*, pp. 166–7.

18 Ibid., pp. 182 -3.

19 Ibid., p. 191.

20 *Mandoa, Mandoa!*, p. 312.

21 Holtby, 'Better and Brighter Natives', *The Nation and Athenaeum*, 23 November 1929, in Paul Berry and Alan Bishop (eds), *Testament of a Generation: The Journalism of Vera Brittain and Winifred Holtby* (London: Virago, 1985), p. 181.

22 *Mandoa, Mandoa*, p. 375.

23 For Holtby's involvements in Africa, see Brittain, *Testament of Friendship*, pp. 234 –57.

24 F. D. Lugard, *The Dual Mandate in British Tropical Africa* (1922; reprint Hamden, CT: Archon Books, 1965), p. 617.

25 The best account of the evolution of the doctrine of trusteeship, and of its tensions, remains Kenneth Robinson, *The Dilemmas of Trusteeship: Aspects of British Colonial Policy between the Wars* (London: Oxford University Press, 1965); also Andrew Roberts, 'The Imperial Mind,' in A. Roberts (ed.), *The Colonial Moment in Africa* (Cambridge: Cambridge University Press, 1990), pp. 24–76.

26 For which see, e.g., Cameron's brilliant response to Sidney Webb's request for information on women's health and welfare in Tanganyika territory, 22 May 1930, in Colonial Office [hereafter CO] 323/1067/2, Public Record Office, London [hereafter PRO].

27 Stephen Howe, *Anticolonialism in British Politics: The Left and the End of Empire, 1918–1964* (Oxford: Clarendon Press, 1993).

28 For which see, in addition to Howe, *Anticolonialism*, Penelope Hetherington, *British Paternalism and Africa, 1920–1940* (London: Frank Cass, 1978); and John Cell (ed.), *By Kenya Possessed: The Correspondence of Norman Leys and J. H. Oldham* (Chicago: University of Chicago Press, 1976).

29 For this debate, see 233 *H. C. Debs.*, 5th ser., 11 December 1929, cols. 581–616.

30 Antoinette Burton, *Burdens of History: British Feminists, Indian Women and Imperial Culture, 1865–1915* (Chicago: University of Chicago Press, 1995).

31 Susan Pedersen, 'The Maternalist Moment in British Colonial Policy: The Campaign Against "Child Slavery" in Hong Kong, 1917-1941', *Past and Present*, forthcoming; also, Norman Miners, *Hong Kong under Imperial Rule, 1912–1941* (Hong Kong: Oxford University Press, 1987), pp. 153–91.

32 The minutes of the Committee for the Protection of Coloured Women, which was active in 1929–30, are held in the Rathbone Papers, University of Liverpool Library; for an account of the controversy over clitoridectomy in 1929–30, see Susan Pedersen, 'National Bodies, Unspeakable Acts: The Sexual Politics of Colonial Policymaking', *Journal of Modern History*, 63 (4) (1991): 647–80.

33 This Council seems to have been only sporadically active; for one deputation to Sidney Webb to urge vigorous action to combat female slavery, see, 'Notes of a Meeting held in the Secretary of State's Room . . . 8 April, 1930,' CO 323/1071/8, PRO.

34 British Commonwealth League reports are held at the Fawcett Library.

35 Officials of the Government of India and the India Office corresponded anxiously about how to handle Mayo after the *Mother India* debacle; in the end, the Government of India simply prohibited entry to a further Mayo book on India on the grounds that it would be offensive to Hindus; see file L/I/1/1456, India Office Library, London.

36 In 1928, Boyle acccused the Anti-Slavery Society of 'slackness' for their unwillingness to take up the question of bride price; see Anti-Slavery Society Minutes Books, 7 June 1928, item 4244, p. 137, MSS Brit. Emp. S20, E2/16, Rhodes House Library, Oxford. The Colonial Office also found itself answering Boyle's charges; see CO 323/1027/6, PRO, for correspondence in 1929 and CO 323/1320/4, PRO, for correspondence and meetings in 1935.

37 Note by G. Grindle, 4 April 1930, CO 323/1071/8, PRO.

38 For one set of governors' responses, sent in answer to Sidney Webb's request for information on the prevalence of female circumcision, see CO 323/1067/1-6, PRO.

39 This comment is from a memo of 29 July 1930, in a file making clear the office's reservations about the Permanent Slavery Commission, CO 323/1071/9, PRO; see also the correspondence with Cecil in CO 323/1071/8, PRO.

40 Colonial Office papers are littered with disparaging remarks about Maxwell. See, e.g.: Gent of the Colonial Office to Stevenson of the Foreign Office, 5 June 1934, CO 323/1257/13, PRO; Note by H. R. Cowell, 22 Nov. 1935, CO 323/1320/6, PRO.

41 Speech by Sir Philip Cunliffe Lister to a dinner of the African Society, 31 May 1931; printed extract in CO 323/1199/6, PRO.

42 As she told the Commons in December of 1929, '[t]here can be no equal citizenship between coloured men and white men till there is equal citizenship between coloured men and coloured women': 233 *H. C. Debs.*, 5th ser., 11 December 1929, col. 608.

43 Holtby's Frau von Schelden in particular reminds one of Rathbone. See Holtby, *Mandoa, Mandoa!*, pp. 235, 251, 253.

44 247 *H. C. Debs.*, 26 Jan. 1931, col. 713.

45 260 *H. C. Debs.*, 2 Dec. 1931, col. 1190; also, 296 *H. C. Debs.*, 11 Dec. 1934, cols. 315–22.

46 247 *H. C. Debs.*, 26 Jan. 1931, col. 714.

47 Sir Sidney Barton to Sir John Simon, 16 April 1934, in *British Documents on Foreign Affairs: Reports and Papers from the Foreign Office Confidential Print*, Vol. 28, *Abyssinia, July 1931–May 1935* (University Publications of America, 1997), p. 227.

48 Sir Eric Drummond to Sir John Simon, 21 May 1935, in *British Documents on Foreign Affairs: Reports and Papers from the Foreign Office Confidential Print*, Vol. 29, *Abyssinia, May 1935-February 1939* (University Publications of America, 1997), pp. 5–6.

49 307 *H. C. Debs.*, 5th ser., 10 December 1935, col. 849.

50 Speech by Sir Philip Cunliffe Lister [Note 41 above].

51 For disagreements between the Home Office and the Colonial Office about treatment of colonial subjects within Britain, see Laura Tabili, *'We Ask for British Justice': Workers and Racial Difference in Late Imperial Britain* (Ithaca, NY: Cornell University Press, 1994).

52 PRO, CO 323/1199/6, Hodson to Sir Samuel Wilson, 5 Sept. 1932. For a fine examination of the paternalistic ethos Hodson expressed, see Kathryn Tidrick, *Empire and the English Character* (London: I.B. Tauris, 1992).

–11–

From Somebodies to Nobodies: Britons Returning Home from India

Elizabeth Buettner

In 1912, Alice Perrin published *The Anglo-Indians*, one of her many fictional accounts of the British community in India. Like countless other Britons who described colonial society, she wrote on the basis of long-term personal experience there, her father having been a general in the Bengal Cavalry and her husband an officer in the Public Works Department.[1] In *The Anglo-Indians*, however, she focused on aspects largely neglected by most other novelists who explored British life as it was lived in India, and instead devoted most of her book to the experience of families returning 'home' once men had retired.[2] Through her portrayal of John Fleetwood, 'a mightily senior civilian' in the Indian Civil Service, his wife Emily, and their three daughters, Perrin highlighted the sharp contrasts between years in India and their aftermath in Britain.[3] At their large bungalow, encircled by verandas, an orange grove, and 'a small village of stables and servants' quarters' for the thirty Indian domestics they employed, Emily indulged her penchant for hosting large parties, while John enjoyed hunting, fishing, and riding, along with the prestige and responsibility his high-ranking occupation brought.[4] All was soon to change when he reached the compulsory retirement age of fifty-five:

> A difficult time lay ahead for the Fleetwood family when they should find themselves in England, pensioned, unimportant . . . with nothing considerable in the way of savings, and no realization of the cost of living at home. . . . Here in India it was quite another matter, where the Fleetwoods were people of consequence and could live luxuriously and entertain with lavish generosity.[5]

Perrin's account of the Fleetwoods' ignorance of what awaited them when they returned to Britain and the unpleasant discoveries they made there shares much in common with other renditions of resettlement in the metropole, both during periods of leave and on retirement. Widely-expressed dissatisfaction with British life centred on the loss of status in relation to British society at large in combination with a sense of cultural alienation, sentiments that came to the surface when Anglo-Indians encountered and evaluated aspects of metropolitan modernity. The following pages will expand upon these issues, considering how the Fleetwoods' experiences just before the First World War compare with similar stories recorded throughout the period of British Crown Rule in India, which dated from the end of the 1857–58 'Mutiny' and lasted until independence in 1947. Narratives of colonizers' returns home showed much continuity over this ninety-year period, although conditions during the interwar era caused their problematic relationship to metropolitan society to be discussed in increasingly strident terms. Furthermore, although men and women reacted similarly to certain aspects of their new lives, in other key respects their experiences were gender-specific. Finally, this chapter concludes by considering a range of solutions that Anglo-Indians envisioned and sometimes attempted to overcome what they perceived to be the pitfalls of modern British life.

Together, these accounts help us to arrive at new perspectives on the nation's modernity, as well as to situate the ways in which this was fully dependent upon Britain's dominant role within an imperial system that problematized many long-established conceptions of the nation itself. Indeed, the vantage point of returned colonizers provides unique insight into these issues. To draw upon Paul Gilroy's analysis of how national cultures and ideas of belonging in them have been falsely delineated to incorporate some ethnicities and cultures while excluding others, Anglo-Indians can be positioned as simultaneously 'insiders' and 'outsiders' in Britain – 'coming home', but also estranged from British society by virtue of long absences and distinct mentalities developed while in India.[6] In a manner resembling the Australian women visiting Britain Angela Woollacott has studied, Anglo-Indians were imperial insiders by virtue of their white racial status and British ancestry, but nonetheless remained outsiders in the metropole because of their colonial identity.[7]

* * *

Many descriptions of how returned colonials reacted to their homeland following lengthy absences focus on impressions developed immediately upon return. As such, these centre on experiences in London, the first place most went to after their ships docked and in which many stayed for a considerable part of their leaves, or inhabited either permanently or temporarily in retirement. In the capital city of both the nation and the empire, variants of modernity were instantly apparent and became themes upon which numerous writers dwelt. If 'modernity' is defined as 'the consciousness of living in a new age', characterized by a process of continual and chaotic change in which all innovation becomes ephemeral, and in which – as was noted by Karl Marx, in a phrase re-invoked by Marshall Berman – 'all that is solid melts into air', then it is unsurprising that Britons who had been away for extended periods expressed shock and unease upon their return.[8] Their sense of alienation in the place they called 'home' derived in part from realizing how out of touch they had become with metropolitan lifestyles during their absence. One response was the attempt to become reintegrated as quickly as possible, perhaps most symbolically through buying new clothes.

Fashion, as the researches of Elizabeth Wilson have shown, is among modernity's most emblematic aspects, encompassing not merely dress but its rapidly transforming styles, revealing society's dynamism and craving for change.[9] Many renditions of returning to Britain from India note fears of appearing out of date, with shopping excursions hurriedly undertaken in the effort to erase outward signs that might distinguish the Anglo-Indian from mainstream British society. In his memoir of childhood in India, George Roche described his family's visit to London in 1918 after having been in India for five years, when a visit to Harrods assumed great importance for his mother. While trying on hats, her delight in consumption was tempered by the concern that she might choose one that labelled her as being out of step with contemporary English tastes. She is recalled as saying, 'everyone will be looking at us, you know, and I don't want them to think I've got old-fashioned since I've been in India'.[10] Alice Perrin's novel echoes this sentiment, noting of the Fleetwoods' first day in London, 'of course the question of new clothes must be considered at once. The whole party were very shabby – people always looked shabby when they first arrived from India, even if they saved up perfectly new clothes to land in, or even got them from home on purpose.'[11] As in George Roche's memoir, women were depicted as those most concerned about maintaining a fashionable appearance, with Emily Fleetwood and her daughters beginning to shop on their first morning in London, while John preferred to visit his gentlemen's club. Just as London contained numerous shops specializing in men's tropical outfits for the outward-bound, however, others also attempted to attract those coming back, indicating that men might also be concerned about the latest styles. A 1930 advertisement for Austin Reed's on Regent Street promised to renew men's outdated attire and overall appearance in short order:

> Is it possible, in London, to get really good clothes quickly? To the man, just home on leave, sadly aware of the anachronisms in his wardrobe, this is always a burning problem.
>
> Let a man take a taxi straight from Victoria. Within two hours he can leave Austin Reed's possessed of all the kit he will need while he is in England. Before he leaves the shop he can have a bath, a shave, a haircut, a manicure: he can hire a car . . .[12]

Austin Reed's thus portrayed itself as enabling men to emerge re-equipped with all the necessary accoutrements for tackling modern life afresh: reclothed, regroomed, and in temporary possession of a car, the quintessential modern vehicle of the era, which allowed them to reacquaint themselves with their homeland independently of more public forms of transport.

While these accounts emphasize a common desire to blend in with metropolitan circles through fashion, in other respects the idea of completely merging into the cultural, social, and economic mainstream could be equally distasteful, if not more so. Edward Waring's 1866 book *The Tropical Resident at Home* discussed multiple causes for returned colonials' dissatisfaction, which writers in later decades reiterated, stressing the loss of special status as a prime grievance:

> Another source of disappointment arises from a feeling, which is more or less experienced by all, but especially by those who have held high and important positions in India and other portions of our colonial empire, of their comparative insignificance as individuals in the busy world of England, and of London in particular. For years, perhaps, in their distant homes, they have been held in high and deserved respect, have exercised a wide and powerful influence, have been leaders in the society in which their lot has been cast . . . They come to London and find that they are nobodies . . . they are speedily lost in the crowd.[13]

Words such as 'insignificance', 'nobodies', and 'lost in the crowd' illustrate some of the many ways that those returning from India might perceive themselves to have fallen behind in British society, seemingly pushed aside 'in the busy world of England'. The sense of being overwhelmed by the fast-paced tempo of London life coupled with unease at the prospect of becoming indistinguishable from others in the crowd reappears in *The Anglo-Indians*, when Perrin describes John Fleetwood's response to walking the city streets:

> Since last he was at home the traffic seemed to have increased a thousandfold; the noise was bewildering; the crowd irritated him – hurrying, heedless people who jostled and pushed . . . [and] who blocked the pavements without consideration . . . an omnibus passed him packed with people . . . He recognized the profile of a fellow-civilian, rather senior to himself, who had retired two or three years ago after holding a very high appointment. Grimly Mr Fleetwood smiled. Logan was on a state elephant last time he saw him, going to open some show or other – now here he was in a 'bus, squeezed up in a row of very ordinary people, looking very ordinary himself; paying a penny for his fare![14]

Expressions of displeasure at the prospect of being merely 'ordinary' and 'insignificant' in Britain touch upon two interrelated ways that those returning from India saw their status decline once they came home. The first pertains to their white racial status and its differential value in Britain and India. While residing in a part of the overseas empire where white Britons were a small minority amidst a large population, whiteness was one of the most symbolic attributes that identified them as rulers rather than ruled. Britons in India, even those situated below the higher echelons of European society, enjoyed greatly enhanced prestige and opportunities because of their racial status and national affiliation to the colonial power. Upon returning to the metropole, however, this privileged status lacked a comparable ability to set them apart and above most of 'native' British society. George Roche's recollections of childhood, for example, repeatedly emphasized the country's racial composition when describing its unfamiliarity: 'everyone was white' in the crowds on Oxford Street; at Harrods, his family were attended by 'white assistants', while in India the women working in the department stores they knew were typically Eurasian; and, at his grandfather's house, 'it seemed strange that . . . the servants were white. I had never seen white ladies in that role before.'[15] Those coming back from India returned with enhanced understandings of the prestige that whiteness might carry with it overseas, which could make it disconcerting when it lost its power to distinguish them from crowds in the street or those who worked as shop assistants and domestic servants.

Losing the privileged distinctiveness that whiteness allowed in colonial India merged with a second factor that caused returned colonials to perceive themselves to have declined to the level of the 'ordinary' at home. Aside from the military rank and file, many Britons who were supported by Indian careers, despite their wide range of occupations and incomes, were middle-class in socio-economic terms. In India, however, race combined with class to enable them to constitute what Francis Hutchins described as a 'middle-class aristocracy', living 'in a manner well above the station from which they had sprung in England'.[16] For those belonging to Britain's 'second eleven' and falling below the highest levels of metropolitan society, time in India could provide career opportunities and salaries far more difficult to obtain at home, along with other trappings of power, including numerous servants, honour, and prestige.[17] In his collection of essays *At Home on Furlough* published in 1875, Charles Lawson summarized the different status men who chose Indian careers might have expected if they had remained in Britain:

There is no small temptation for a man who has discovered that he is somebody in India, to think that had he remained at home, he would have been recognised as a somebody in England, and been rewarded in proportion to his present estimate of his merits. But it is pretty certain that a very small proportion even of the highest officials in India could, had they remained at home, have found the means of earning a comfortable livelihood . . . Had the average Anglo-Indian for example, never gone abroad, he might have become Lord Chancellor, Prime Minister, Field Marshal, Admiral of the Fleet, Speaker, or something of that sort; but . . . the chances were in favour of his lapsing into lifelong genteel poverty . . . Without capital, influential friends, or genius, he must be a rarely fortunate man who succeeds in making head way . . . in England . . .[18]

Incomes that enabled exalted lifestyles in a colonial arena, however, were not sufficient to make their earners part of the upper classes – or 'a somebody', as it is described here – when they returned to the metropole on leave, nor were the reduced pensions that replaced full salaries upon retirement. In the 1860s Waring believed that at least £500 a year was essential, for 'no married man, who in the tropics has held the position of "an officer and a gentleman", can secure the comforts of home life . . . with an income of less amount than this'; by the 1930s, 'Mauser' – the author of *How to Live in England on a Pension* - assumed he was writing for civil and military officers who would have an average of £800 a year.[19] Many retiring from India certainly had far less at their disposal, however, including those who had been employed in less prestigious professions, those invalided out of service early, and many widows. Clearly, the annual sum men and their families had varied greatly and also depended upon the existence of private incomes that may have supplemented pensions; but in most cases returning Anglo-Indians fell into a broadly-defined middle class. While their standard of living therefore was high when contrasted with that of most Britons, frequent reference was made to their 'comparative poverty at home', Waring for instance noting that '"old Indians" of the present day, in comparison with the upper ten thousand of English society, are a poor class'.[20] In the eyes of many back from India, 'poverty' thus meant riding on crowded buses – as Alice Perrin described – as opposed to the more exclusive forms of private transport enjoyed by the more affluent. Advertising for Austin Reed's men's shop such as that cited above might assume that cars would be a part of everyday life in Britain for those on leave during the interwar era; but other commentators considered them far beyond the means of many retired colonials. 'Mauser', for example, estimated that the costs of owning a car made it likely that 'the sahib goes afoot', or acquired a 'second-hand push bike' for short journeys.[21]

As the attitudes expressed by the authors discussed here suggest, the conditions of life in Britain described by many returned Anglo-Indians in the mid-nineteenth century and in the 1930s shared many common features.[22] Accounts written about the interwar era, however, indicate that the increased costs of living and taxes in Britain, which reduced the real value of pensions, made the transition from colonial working life to metropolitan retirement more difficult than before. A letter to the editor of the Indian newspaper *The Pioneer* from a newly-retired Indian Army Colonel in 1919 described how higher prices for clothing, food, rents, and houses made it 'a safe estimate to add at least a third to the general cost of living in England compared with pre-war costs'. He advised others about to retire to bring back as many household goods and clothes as possible in order to decrease the costs of resettlement. There was a limit to the comforts enjoyed in India that might be imported, however: 'be prepared to pay high wages for servants', he stressed, 'they are very difficult to get. My wife and I find it absolutely necessary to do most of the housework ourselves. We have a small house and are lucky to get one servant.'[23]

The 'servant problem' in Britain provides one of the best illustrations both of the continuities of Anglo-Indian lifestyles and discontents across the ninety-year period in question, and also of the changed circumstances of the 1920s and 1930s. Prior to the First World War, complaints about British domestic servants were common, exemplified by Perrin's rendition of the Fleetwoods' dissatisfaction with both the number and quality of those they employed. After having had thirty servants in India, the four they could afford at home seemed insufficient. Furthermore, 'when servants stayed they were usually incompetent; when they knew their work and did it they either had illnesses, or did not like something connected with the situation and gave notice. They came and went, principally went.' Emily Fleetwood summed up her attitude towards her English maids and cooks by sighing, 'no one knows what I suffer with these people!'[24] In later decades, however, those back from India would have considered a 'servant problem' of this degree to be minor compared with their own in the interwar years, which witnessed the sharp decline of domestic service as an institution as more and more working-class women took advantage of other forms of employment.[25] Like the officer writing to *The Pioneer* cited above, many middle-class families could only afford one maid, who was increasingly likely to work as a 'daily help' as opposed to 'living in'.

Accounts of the relationships between retired colonial families and their 'maids of all work' in the 1920s and 1930s offer some of the most detailed depictions of their attitude towards their reduced circumstances after leaving India. In his book, first published in 1930 and reissued in new editions throughout the decade, 'Mauser' – also a retired Indian Army officer – repeatedly linked problems associated with 'the modern maid' to the more general social and economic conditions affecting persons like himself. While discussing ways to reduce fuel bills, he portrayed those employing servants but needing to economize as at the mercy of inherently wasteful members of the 'lower orders':

> A gas-cooker is very good, and if you use it yourself it will be effectual and economical; but if a domestic uses it you are helpless to control it. The extravagance of a burning jet never seems to strike the lower orders unless they are paying for it themselves . . . The modern maid will leave a gas fire burning in one room while she sits in another, without batting an eyelash. She doesn't have to pay.[26]

The lack of consideration 'Mauser' attributed to servants symbolized how he perceived wealthier groups to have 'lost out' more generally to the working classes since the war, with the former paying higher taxes for the benefit of the latter.[27] Moreover, he listed the higher working-class incomes that resulted from wartime prosperity as a prime cause of the servant shortage. The alternative employments that women found more attractive derived from other aspects of interwar British modernity he disparaged because they were evidence of an expanding mass consumer culture:

The raising of the working-class income has brought little wisdom with it. Light come, light go. The lower classes are living up to every pound note of their incomes, while we are living down to every penny of ours. The result has been the multiplication of tearooms, restaurants, picture palaces, milliners' shops, and the cheaper forms of motor traffic. In these, the money is spent; and bar the last-named, are practically entirely staffed by young women.[28]

Given these 'counter-attractions', finding and retaining capable maids necessitated sacrifices by their employers, for 'in these days one must bow before the domestic help'.[29] The contrast between servant-keeping in India and Britain could not have been stronger, for along with being far more numerous, 'Indian menials' were 'maddening but biddable' – a succinct illustration of how drastically the ability to hire servants as well as to dictate their conditions of work was thought to have declined once Anglo-Indians came home.[30]

These changed domestic conditions, although described here by male writers, affected women's lives far more directly than their husbands'. In several crucial respects, the loss of status discussed thus far had very different manifestations for men and women. When a man's working life in India ended, his wife's responsibilities typically became more of a burden once they resettled in Britain. Women bore the brunt of the household economies that British domesticity entailed when compared with their years overseas. In the 1860s, Waring alluded to the predicaments faced by 'tropical lady housekeepers' in Britain, who during their time in India had grown accustomed to spending 'with a lavish hand, and taking little or no forethought for to-morrow'. After several decades of an affluent colonial lifestyle, 'they have to return to England to live on comparatively small means, with less knowledge of household affairs than is possessed by nine out of ten women of the same age and position in life at home'.[31] With the more limited availability of domestic servants after the First World War, women were forced to play a more active role in undertaking the physical aspects of housework than before, when their primary responsibilities included managing servants and housekeeping expenses. M. M. Kaye's memoir recounting her family's return to England after her father retired in the mid-1920s devoted much attention to how her mother had to do many household chores herself for the first time, since they were unable to employ a cook or a daily servant. One anecdote described the day her mother 'answered the doorbell wearing a duster tied round her head, a vast and rather grubby cooking apron over her dress, and with her hands blackened and her face liberally adorned by the dark smudges that an amateur at the job is apt to acquire when first trying her hand at cleaning either silver or brass' – to find neighbours paying a welcoming visit:

Confronted by two elderly, grey-haired ladies dressed in their best . . . armed with calling cards and inquiring in impeccable upper-class accents if her mistress was at home, Mother said baldly: 'Yes.' And, having ushered them into the drawing-room, fled upstairs . . . and returned after a few minutes looking as serene as any lady of leisure, apologizing for keeping them waiting. Believe it or not, they never realized that the 'maid' and the 'mistress' were one and the same.[32]

Kaye's representation of her mother's transition from privileged 'memsahib' in India to a woman of indeterminate status somewhere between domestic servant and 'lady of leisure' in Britain suggests how women might find their domestic role reversed once they left colonial life behind. As Ella Leakey wrote in the journal *Overseas* in 1931, 'many a wife whose husband is due for retirement looks forward only with dread to the tussle she knows awaits her' while living on a pension that amounted to half their former income. Necessary economies included drastically reducing the scale of entertaining and largely curtailing other leisure activities; but the biggest savings, she felt, came when 'all but the minimum of paid services [were] dispensed with'. The cheaper alternative in the long run to hiring a servant was recourse to other integral features of British modern life of this period, namely new electrical household technologies: 'If health permits, it is always the wisest plan to spend every possible penny on labour-saving devices: electric cookers, irons, kettles, ideal boilers, vacuum cleaners, and to have simple furnishings and few ornaments, so that where possible the work of the house can be done by the lady of the house herself.'[33] 'Mauser' wrote in the same vein, indicating that while many aspects of modernity in the metropole might be disparaged, others partly compensated for the drawbacks and compared favourably with the 'archaic' conditions they had known in India. He extolled the benefits of newer houses built on 'labour-saving' lines that ensured up-to-date electricity and water supplies, since those 'leaving India, wish also to be quit for ever of the three archaic miseries, kerosene oil, bathroom arrangements, and the surface well'.[34] Modern houses enabled 'all the cleverly-designed electric labour-savers' to be 'a boon to the housewife in these days of servant difficulty', and he also suggested foregoing servants altogether as a result.[35] Despite the advantages of new household appliances to those able to afford them, however, it is debatable whether they were truly labour-saving if used by women who had formerly had most of their housework done by others. As Ruth Schwartz Cowan has noted of developments in household technology, 'the labor saved by labor-saving devices was not that of the housewife but of her helpers'.[36] With domestic service in decline, middle-class women spent more time doing housework regardless of how many appliances they might own.[37]

Men's experiences after leaving India often stood in complete contrast to those of their wives. While 'memsahibs' were portrayed as having far greater domestic responsibilities once their husbands retired, men were repeatedly said to find themselves at a loss to fill the empty hours. Alongside her description of a woman's new domestic burdens, Ella Leakey depicted the typical husband as 'a busy man suddenly turned idle. He has a good chance of at least twenty years of life before him. What is he going to do?'[38] Because the retirement age in Indian state services was about fifty-five, many men faced the dilemma of what Charles Lawson summarized as 'compulsory idleness' when they were still energetic.[39] Writers suggested a number of ways to combat forced inactivity, boredom, and a general lack of purpose once 'the guillotine of completed service' had been reached.[40] Waring elaborated upon the mental stimulation men could find by taking up new hobbies including 'entomology, conchology, and geology', while 'Mauser' suggested gardening, hiking, carpentry, or becoming a boy scout master.[41] The common factor recommending these new amusements was their low cost, since many forms of sport men had enjoyed in India proved unaffordable in Britain on a pension. In *The Anglo-Indians*, for example, John Fleetwood's riding, shooting, and fishing became 'a dream of the past' in England, and the only recreational expense he allowed himself was his club membership, where he 'talked with men he had known in India, smoked and read the papers, and found he looked forward to seeing *The Pioneer Mail*'.[42] Furthermore, should men wish to supplement their pensions or fill their time by finding a paying occupation, they were warned that employers were unlikely to consider them for the few available positions, because they were middle-aged and lacked experience that was marketable outside colonial settings.[43] Opportunities to play a more active role in modern life through a new career and enjoy the expanded range of consumer goods and leisure activities that additional income would allow were thus said to be largely foreclosed to ageing returned Anglo-Indians. According to 'Mauser', it was only possible to earn substantial additional income by working independently, and he recommended starting a small fruit farm by purchasing a house with additional acres adjacent to it. In this way, men might earn several hundred extra pounds annually for the ten years they remained physically active after retiring, as well as reducing living expenses by residing outside urban areas.[44]

Thus, although men's difficulties readjusting to British life were distinct from women's in many ways, both sexes underwent a substantial transition from one working role to another less empowered one. Women often undertook more domestic work formerly done by servants after their husbands retired, while men searched for new occupations once their years as salaried professionals ended; but reduced financial circumstances underlay their experiences irrespective of gender. Of course, these conditions also characterized the later part of the modern life cycle of many middle-class retired men and their wives who had no overseas connections; but the manner in which returned Anglo-Indians might respond to them reflected their specific colonial background. Their new socio-economic status worked in tandem with shared cultural understandings developed during their years in India to influence how many returned colonials sought ways to ease the transition between their old and new lives.

* * *

Many men and women returning from overseas attempted to mitigate their feelings of alienation at home by maintaining their colonial social network. John Fleetwood's frequent visits to his London club to meet other men who had worked in India provide one illustration of this phenomenon; another was the place of residence he chose. After living temporarily in South Kensington, one of London's most affluent neighbourhoods, the Fleetwood family were forced to economize and moved into a house appropriately named 'Combe Down' in 'Norbleton', a less expensive suburb of London made attractive because of its large community of fellow Anglo-Indians.[45] This fictional enclave of returned colonials had many counterparts in reality. Waring described the tendency of 'old Indians' to 'fix their tents in close proximity to each other' in the 1860s, attributing this phenomenon to cultural as well as economic reasons. 'When brought into immediate contact with the richer classes, they feel their poverty, and this leads them to enter into a common cause, and they form these small communities, colonies you may almost call them, where something like an equality of means exists amongst the members', he wrote. Furthermore, they came together because of shared experiences:

> Though they may never have met before, they have topics of conversation which have special interest to each; they have resided, perhaps at different periods, in the same localities; they have hosts of mutual acquaintances; . . . and they understand each other's language; they require no aid from a dictionary to understand the meaning of *'Durzee'* or *Ghorawallah*, and they do not want an explanation if you should happen to speak of a *pucka* house! In fact, their past lives and present ideas cannot do otherwise than form a strong bond of union.[46]

In London, the neighbourhood said to have the strongest colonial connections was Bayswater, causing it to become known as 'Asia Minor' because of its many residents who had been in India.[47] From the mid-nineteenth century until the interwar era, this middle-class area of west London attracted not only colonial retirees but also those home on leave, along with wives and children of men still in India. Evidence of its population's ties with India appeared in many guises, with local merchants of the 1880s providing 'an Indian outfit complete at a day's notice' along with fruits and vegetables commonly eaten in the subcontinent; the neighbourhood was also home to 'zenana missions', the London headquarters of the Theosophical Society, and many 'crammers' tutoring men for entrance exams for the Indian services.[48] Stories regularly reprinted from Indian newspapers in the weekly *Paddington, Kensington, and Bayswater Chronicle* during this period also attest to a substantial community interested in political and military events occurring in the empire.[49] Bayswater's proximity to Hyde Park, Kensington, and the West End made it appealing for those who could not afford more exclusive districts but wanted to live centrally and respectably. The neighbourhood was particularly well equipped to cater to those in London only temporarily while on leave, for along with houses for rent it had one of the city's largest concentrations of hotels and boarding houses.[50]

The facility with which Bayswater met transients' needs added another dimension to its 'Asia Minor' status, since Indians as well as Anglo-Indians often stayed there while in London. As the author of a London guidebook wrote in 1902, 'here live the rich and cultured Orientals, those who have come over for pleasure, business, trade, or education'.[51] Lala Baijnath, a judge who visited London in the 1890s, similarly noted how Indians typically found lodgings in Bayswater, adding that a number of students rented rooms in the homes of retired Anglo-Indian families.[52] While they may have sought lodgers to provide additional income, what is more striking is the apparent enthusiasm with which some sought contact with Indians once they returned to Britain. Baijnath, for instance, described being frequently approached in the street by 'those who had been in India [and] seemed to take a pleasure in speaking to me in broken or half-forgotten Hindustani'. Their friendliness and interest in 'keeping up their knowledge of India' also appeared ironic, however:

> Another thing which I often noticed about many of them, was the extraordinary fondness for India and its people which their retirement had created in their minds. To some of them, the country and its inhabitants seemed to possess attributes which they would probably never have given them credit for in India. Others seemed to pine for it more keenly than they did for England when in India. The value of water is felt when the well is dry![53]

T. N. Mukharji, another Indian who wrote of his encounters in late Victorian London, noted how despite meeting a few who 'pompously displayed their acquaintance with the Hindi language, however slight it might be, and their power and superiority over us', that 'a fellow-feeling existed between the Anglo-Indians and ourselves as if they were our countrymen in that strange land'.[54] Interacting with those over whom they had once held power in the empire served as a comforting reminder of their former elevated status once this declined upon reaching the metropole. Living in neighbourhoods like Bayswater and joining groups that patronized Indians like the Northbrook Indian Society or the National Indian Association were two interrelated ways that Anglo-Indians formed 'colonies' that helped them perpetuate a form of colonial culture in the 'strange land' that Britain had become.[55]

Other localities in the metropole were also well known for their high concentrations of Anglo-Indians. Cheltenham Spa and Bedford both hosted many families with Indian military and civil service connections between the Victorian era and the mid-twentieth century. Like Bayswater, these towns allowed those who had been overseas to continue to enjoy the company of others sharing their background, which for men might help alleviate the boredom many suffered once their working lives ended. A former tea planter writing in a 1913 Bedford promotional pamphlet recommended its social opportunities, contrasting it to places where 'the unfortunate retired officer finds himself with no companionship to his taste during the greater part of the day; the men go off to their business . . . and only return in the evening. This is not the case in Bedford, where birds of this feather have flocked together.'[56] Cheltenham, a spa town with a long-established reputation for curing tropical ailments, offered similar attractions. Perhaps more importantly, both places catered to the needs of 'past, present, and future Anglo-Indians' – as Lawson affirmed of Cheltenham in the 1870s – in that they not only provided entertainment and some degree of continuity for adults but also served as channels via which many sons and daughters of Anglo-Indians later returned overseas.[57] Bedford Grammar School and Cheltenham College were both known for their success in directing boys into colonial careers, and were important reasons why parents chose to settle in their vicinity; similarly, daughters often married Anglo-Indian men on leave met through their parents' circle of colonial acquaintances. For offspring of both sexes, Bedford and Cheltenham illustrate the extent to which colonial work and residence easily became a multigenerational family tradition, encouraged by a combination of school and community influences along with the many dissatisfactions with British life that caused so many Anglo-Indians to live largely among themselves in the metropole.[58]

While settling in communities heavily populated with other returned colonials appeared to mitigate the perceived drawbacks of life at home for some, others expressed their discontent by choosing not to return to Britain at all once they retired from India. One alternative to going home was to 'stay on' in India, typically at one of the British-built towns in the Himalayan or Nilgiri foothills. A 1926 account described Ootacamund's appeal for 'those who fly from the taxes, rents, servants, and labour troubles of England', where they 'passed contentedly the evening of their days in the sweet half-English Nilgiri air'.[59] Nonetheless, writers who focused on Britain's drawbacks more commonly advocated other retirement venues. Some praised towns on the French Riviera or other Mediterranean resorts, such as Majorca, Alassio, and Rapallo, that offered a pleasant climate and the company of other retired Britons, many of whom had also worked in the empire.[60] The places recommended most frequently, however, were other parts of the British empire, ranging from Cyprus, Kenya, and Rhodesia to the dominions, especially Canada.

Discussions about retiring from India to other imperial settings became far more widespread during the interwar era. In part, this stemmed from the economic and social conditions examined above, which caused many pensioners to feel that middle-class standards of living in Britain had declined since the war, particularly for those on a fixed income. Cyprus, for instance, was praised in the Overseas League's journal because it offered an escape from inflation and higher taxes, allowing a family to 'live well' on £300 a year.[61] Other parts of the empire were more heavily targeted, however, as part of interlocking campaigns to promote imperial settlement in the dominions and white settler colonies in Africa and to defuse the social tensions Britain experienced during a period of mass demobilization and high unemployment after the war. Soldier settlement and other schemes that facilitated emigration throughout the 1920s and 1930s focused on ex-officers as well as rank-and-file servicemen, attracting men forced to retire early along with those leaving work at more standard ages.[62]

Those retiring from India or other colonial arenas, whether from the military, the civil service, or the non-official professions, appear to have been among the most likely to contemplate settling overseas, because living outside Britain had become normal for them, and, as has been argued here, had come to be seen as increasingly desirable. Alongside the prospect of being able to live 'comfortably' on £400 a year and to be considered rich with an income of £1,000, Nova Scotia and British Columbia promised the comforts of 'modern civilization', ample sporting opportunities at little cost, cheap education for children, and, like the 'colonies' of Anglo-Indians in Britain, the companionship of others who had also worked in India.[63] These advantages led one retired engineer to describe Nova Scotia as a 'real white man's country', for it enabled a lifestyle that returning to the metropole largely foreclosed for middle-class pensioners.[64] Again, the ways in which a white racial identity became defined as inseparable from a privileged socio-economic status in Anglo-Indian eyes could make the higher standards of living obtainable in the 'white' dominions far more attractive than returning to the 'old country'. For some, this same conception of racial privilege led them to prefer Kenya, where (as in India) they would remain a small and empowered community, settled among a predominantly African population, over a dominion where, despite its socio-economic advantages, they merged with the majority of its inhabitants in racial terms just as they did in Britain.[65]

* * *

This chapter has examined how Britons who understood themselves racially and culturally in ways that derived from experiences in India, at home, and sometimes in other colonies and dominions as well, provide an important example of the inseparability of Britain's modernity from its historical status as an imperial power. Studies by Arjun Appadurai, Edward Said, Paul Gilroy, C. A. Bayly, and Antoinette Burton – to name a few – provide a useful framework through which to examine modernity as an inherently global phenomenon, allowing us to examine alternative geographical and cultural entities as units of analysis in combination with – or even in place of – the nation state.[66] Appadurai's exploration of late twentieth-century global migration and transnational media forms, Gilroy's delineation of the 'Black Atlantic', and Burton's study of Indians in Victorian Britain all suggest the extent to which Britain's domestic and imperial pasts need to be united to form one conceptual arena of debate. Although Anglo-Indians often disparaged aspects of the nation's modernity at home, their travels, status, and work in India along with the perspectives that emerged from these experiences were only possible because of Britain's imperial presence and projects that were equally emblematic of the modern. Indicatively, however, these narratives of return say little about the ceaseless political, economic, and cultural changes the Indian subcontinent experienced under colonialism's modernity. Instead, they variously extol or criticize the India they knew as 'archaic' and less fast-paced than the metropole. Time spent in India in turn caused them to feel 'old-fashioned', out of step, and underprivileged once they came home – or a 'nobody' rather than a 'somebody' – and became the lens through which they evaluated Britain's modernity. As individuals whose identities were formed by repeatedly crossing the borders between the nation and its overseas territories, Anglo-Indians thus provide a clear warning against examining metropolitan and colonial variants of modernity in isolation, for each played a role in determining how the other was defined and perceived.

Notes

1 On Perrin's writing and life, see Benita Parry, *Delusions and Discoveries: India in the British Imagination, 1880–1930* (Berkeley, CA: University of California Press, 1972; London and New York: Verso, 1998), pp. 78–102, 266.

2 Prior to the early twentieth century, the term 'Anglo-Indian' referred mainly to Britons in India who were exclusively of European ancestry, but afterwards it was also used to describe persons of mixed European and Indian descent (who were also widely known as 'Eurasians') – thereby shifting from a marker of spatial to racial hybridity. In this chapter the sources analysed use it in its earlier sense.

3 Alice Perrin, *The Anglo-Indians* (London: Methuen, 1912), p. 15.

4 Ibid., pp. 53, 62.

5 Ibid., pp. 18–19.

6 Paul Gilroy, *The Black Atlantic: Modernity and Double Consciousness* (Cambridge, MA: Harvard University Press, 1993).

7 Angela Woollacott, '"All This Is the Empire, I Told Myself": Australian Women's Voyages "Home" and the Articulation of Colonial Whiteness', *American Historical Review* 102 (no. 4) (1997): 1003–29.

8 Jose Harris, *Private Lives, Public Spirit: Britain, 1870–1914* (Harmondsworth: Penguin, 1994), p. 32; Rita Felski, *The Gender of Modernity* (Cambridge, MA:

Harvard University Press, 1995), p. 40; and Marshall Berman, *All That is Solid Melts Into Air: The Experience of Modernity* (London: Verso, 1983), pp. 16, 18–19, 23, 95, 98, 288.

9 Elizabeth Wilson, *Adorned in Dreams: Fashion and Modernity* (London: Virago, 1985), pp. 10, 60, 115.

10 George Roche, *Childhood in India: Tales from Sholapur*, comp. and ed. Richard Terrell (London and New York: Radcliffe Press, 1994), p. 14.

11 Perrin, *Anglo-Indians*, p. 146.

12 Advertisement for Austin Reed's, in *Overseas: The Monthly Journal of the Over-Seas League* XV, no. 168 (January 1930): v.

13 Edward J. Waring, *The Tropical Resident at Home. Letters Addressed to Europeans Returning from India and the Colonies on Subjects Connected with their Health and General Welfare* (London: John Churchill & Sons, 1866), pp. 14–15.

14 Perrin, *Anglo-Indians*, p. 148–9. See also Parry, *Delusions and Discoveries*, p. 95–6.

15 Roche, *Childhood in India*, p. 10–13, 20–1. A number of recent studies have stressed the importance of 'whiteness' as a critical category in the construction of European identities both at home and in the overseas empires. Along with Woollacott's '"All This is the Empire"', see Ann Laura Stoler, *Race and the Education of Desire: Foucault's History of Sexuality and the Colonial Order of Things* (Durham, NC: Duke University Press, 1995); Vron Ware, *Beyond the Pale: White Women, Racism, and History* (London: Verso, 1992); Catherine Hall, *White, Male, and Middle Class: Explorations in Feminism and History* (New York: Routledge, 1992), pp. 21, 206; and Richard Dyer, *White* (London: Routledge, 1997).

16 Francis G. Hutchins, *The Illusion of Permanence: British Imperialism in India* (Princeton, NJ: Princeton University Press, 1967), pp. 107–8.

17 On India-connected Britons being part of the 'second eleven' at home, see J. M. Bourne, *Patronage and Society in Nineteenth-Century England* (London: Edward Arnold, 1986), p. 181; see also P. J. Marshall's discussion of their social origins in 'British Immigration into India in the Nineteenth Century', in *European Expansion and Migration: Essays on the Intercontinental Migration from Africa, Asia, and Europe*, ed. P. C. Emmer and M. Moerner (New York and Oxford: Berg, 1992), pp. 188–90.

18 Charles A. Lawson, *At Home on Furlough*, 2nd ser. (Madras: The 'Madras Mail' Press, 1875), pp. 465–6.

19 Waring, *Tropical Resident*, p. 233; 'Mauser' (pseud.), *How to Live in England on a Pension: A Guide for Public Servants Abroad and at Home* (London: W. Thacker & Co.; Calcutta and Simla: Thacker, Spink & Co., 1930).

20 Lawson, *At Home*, p. 465; 'Mauser', *How to Live*, p. x; Waring, *Tropical Resident*, p. 62.

21 'Mauser', *How to Live*, pp. 92–3.

22 B. J. Moore-Gilbert briefly alludes to a number of Anglo-Indian texts dating from the 1840s to the 1880s that detail difficulties adjusting to British life and the sense of 'deprivation' upon return in *Kipling and 'Orientalism'* (London and Sydney: Croom Helm, 1986), pp. 42–7; see also Parry, *Delusions and Disocoveries*, pp. 50–3.

23 'Indian Army Colonel', 'Living in England: To The Editor', *The Pioneer*, 9 June 1919.

24 Perrin, *Anglo-Indians*, pp. 165, 193, 211.

25 Miriam Glucksmann, *Women Assemble: Women Workers and the New Industries in Inter-War Britain* (London and New York: Routledge, 1990), pp. 37–8, 50–4, 244–52; Judy Giles, *Women, Identity and Private Life in Britain, 1900–1950* (London: Macmillan, 1995), pp. 84, 133–8.

26 'Mauser', *How to Live*, p. 18.

27 Ibid., pp. 102–5.

28 Ibid., p. 182.

29 Ibid., p. 58.

30 'Mauser' (pseud), *How to Live in England on a Pension: A Guide to Public Servants Abroad and At Home*, new and enlarged edn (London: 'Mauser', 1934), p. 152.

31 Waring, *Tropical Resident*, pp. 235–6.

32 M. M. Kaye, *The Sun in the Morning: My Early Years in India and England* (New York: St Martin's Press, 1990), pp. 411–12.

33 Ella F. M. Leakey, 'On Retiring', *Overseas* XVI, no. 190 (November 1931): 59–60.

34 'Mauser', *How to Live* (1930 edn), pp. 7, 14, 17–23.

35 'Mauser' (pseud), *How to Live in England on a Pension*, 3d edn (London: Oxford University Press, 1938), p. 41; 'Mauser', *How to Live* (1934 edn), p. 155.

36 Ruth Schwartz Cowan, *More Work for Mother: The Ironies of Household Technology from the Open Hearth to the Microwave* (New York: Basic Books, 1983), p. 178.

37 Adrian Forty, *Objects of Desire: Design and Society Since 1750* (Moffat, Dumfriesshire: Cameron, 1986; London: Thames and Hudson, 1995), p. 210; Sue Bowden and Avner Offer, 'The Technological Revolution That Never Was: Gender, Class, and the Diffusion of Household Appliances in Interwar England', in *The Sex of Things: Gender and Consumption in Historical Perspective*, ed. Victoria de Grazia with Ellen Furlough (Berkeley, CA: University of California Press, 1996), p. 268.

38 Leakey, *On Retiring*, p. 58.

39 Lawson, *At Home*, p. 464.

40 Perrin, *Anglo-Indians*, pp. 204–5.

41 Waring, *Tropical Resident*, pp. 23–39; 'Mauser', *How to Live* (1930 edn), 167–77.

42 Perrin, *Anglo-Indians*, pp. 187, 164; see also 179, 218, 225, 227.

43 Lawson, *At Home*, pp. 462–4; Perrin, *Anglo-Indians*, pp. 183–4; 'Mauser', *How to Live* (1930 edn), pp. 113–16, 145–55.

44 'Mauser', *How to Live* (1930 edn), pp. 114–44, 154; (1934 edn), p. 113.

45 Perrin, *Anglo-Indians*, pp. 184–92. 'Norbleton' is most likely a thinly-disguised depiction of Norbiton, a town in Surrey bordering on Kingston-on-Thames, about ten miles from central London.

46 Waring, *Tropical Resident*, pp. 59, 62–3. *Durzee* translates as 'tailor', *Ghora-wallah* as 'white man', and *pucka* as 'genuine', or 'proper'.

47 Ibid., p. 59.

48 City of Westminster Archives Centre, London, 'Bayswater: The "Asia Minor" of Anglo-Indians', *The Bayswater Annual* (London, 1885): 5.

49 See for example 'A Tiger Hunt in Calcutta' and 'Indian News', *The Paddington, Kensington, and Bayswater Chronicle*, 22 February 1879.

50 D. A. Reeder, 'A Theatre of Suburbs: Some Patterns of Development in West London, 1801–1911', in *The Study of Urban History*, ed. H. J. Dyos (London: Edward Arnold, 1968), pp. 255–6, 263–4.

51 Mrs E. T. Cook, *Highways and Byways in London* (London: Macmillan, 1902), p. 295.

52 Lala Baijnath, *England and India: Being Impressions of Persons and Things, English and Indian, and Brief Notes of Visits to France, Switzerland, Italy, and Ceylon* (Bombay: Jehangir B. Karani, 1893), pp. 29, 159.

53 Ibid., pp. 38–9.

54 T. N. Mukharji, *A Visit to Europe* (Calcutta: W. Newman; London: Edward Stanford, 1889), p. 106. See also Antoinette Burton, *At the Heart of the Empire: Indians and the Colonial Encounter in Late-Victorian London* (Berkeley, CA: University of California Press, 1998), pp. 176–7, on Mukharji's and Baijnath's discussion of Bayswater.

55 On the Northbrook Society and the National Indian Association, see Baijnath, *England and India*, pp. 96, 159–60; Mukharji, *A Visit to Europe*, p. 193; Rozina Visram, *Ayahs, Lascars and Princes: The Story of Indians in Britain, 1700–1947* (London: Pluto, 1986), p. 180; Burton, *Heart of the Empire*, pp. 55–62, 120–2.

56 C. J. Maltby, 'Bedford as seen by the Anglo-Indian', in the Bedford Trade Protection Society's *Bedford Town and Bedford Schools* (Bedford: The Beds. Times Publishing Co. Ltd., 1913), p. 13.

57 Lawson, *At Home*, p. 203.

58 For a far more extended treatment of Bedford and Cheltenham's schools and Anglo-Indian communities, see Elizabeth Ann Buettner, 'Families, Children, and Memories: Britons in India, 1857–1947' (Ph.D. dissertation, University of Michigan, Ann Arbor, 1998), pp. 239–64, 295–322.

59 J. Chartres Molony, *A Book of South India* (London: Methuen, 1926), p. 47.

60 Leakey, 'On Retiring', p. 60; Mauser, *How to Live* (1930 edn), p. 156; C. du Pré Thornton, 'The Advantage of Retiring to the Riviera for Anglo-Indians', *The Cooper's Hill Magazine* XII (no. 5) (1925): 70–2.

61 S. H. C. Hawtrey, 'Orange Growing in Cyprus', *Overseas* XVII, no. 200 (September 1932): 33–5.

62 On the promotion of empire settlement during the interwar era, see Kent Fedorowich, *Unfit for Heroes: Reconstruction and Soldier Settlement in the Empire Between the Wars* (Manchester: Manchester University Press, 1995); and Stephen Constantine (ed.), *Emigrants and Empire: British Settlement in the Dominions Between the Wars* (Manchester: Manchester University Press, 1990).

63 'The Over-Seas League Migration Committee', *Overseas* XII, no. 137 (June 1927): 31–2; 'British Columbia from the Interior, by a Member in B. C.', *Overseas* XIII, no. 144 (January 1928): 53–4; Lt.-Col. D. G. Robinson, 'A Suggestion for Would-be Emigrants of the Middle Classes', *Overseas* XIII, no. 153 (October 1928): 47–8; and 'The O.-S. League Migration Bureau: The Charm of British Columbia', *Overseas* XV, no. 169 (February 1930): 41–2.

64 'Mente Manuque', 'Nova Scotia for Proportional Pensioners', *The Cooper's Hill Magazine* XII, no. 5 (1925): 70.

65 After the First World War, Kenya attracted a number of Indian Army officers under its soldier settlement scheme for this reason. See C. J. Duder, '"Men of the Officer Class": The Participants in the 1919 Soldier Settlement Scheme in Kenya', *African Affairs* 92, no. 366 (1993): 69–87, and 'The Settler Response to the Indian Crisis of 1922 in Kenya: Brigadier General Philip Wheatley and "Direct Action"', *Journal of Imperial and Commonwealth History* XVII, no. 3 (May 1989): 349–73.

66 Arjun Appadurai, *Modernity at Large: Cultural Dimensions of Globalization* (Minneapolis, MN: University of Minnesota Press, 1996), p. 19; Edward W. Said, *Culture and Imperialism* (New York: Alfred A. Knopf, 1993); Gilroy, *Black Atlantic*; C. A. Bayly, *Imperial Meridian: The British Empire and the World, 1780–1830* (London: Longman, 1989); and Burton, *Heart of the Empire*. See also Antoinette Burton, 'Who Needs the Nation?: Interrogating "British" History', *Journal of Historical Sociology* 10, no. 3 (1997): 227–48; Ann Laura Stoler and Frederick Cooper, 'Between Metropole and Colony: Rethinking a Research Agenda', in *Tensions of Empire: Colonial Cultures in*

a Bourgeois World, ed. Frederick Cooper and Ann Laura Stoler (Berkeley, CA: University of California Press, 1997), pp. 1–56; Shula Marks, 'History, the Nation, and Empire: Sniping from the Periphery', *History Workshop Journal* 29 (1990): 111–19; and Julia Bush, 'Moving On – and Looking Back', *History Workshop Journal* 36 (1993): 183–94.

Index

Index